Grounding God

SUNY series on Religion and the Environment

Harold Coward, editor

Grounding God
Religious Responses to the Anthropocene

Arianne Conty

SUNY
PRESS

Cover: Su Boe de Otzana (Sardinian bull mask). Photograph © Carlo Marras / carlomarrasphotography.com

Published by State University of New York Press, Albany

© 2023 State University of New York

All rights reserved

Printed in the United States of America

No part of this book may be used or reproduced in any manner whatsoever without written permission. No part of this book may be stored in a retrieval system or transmitted in any form or by any means including electronic, electrostatic, magnetic tape, mechanical, photocopying, recording, or otherwise without the prior permission in writing of the publisher.

For information, contact State University of New York Press, Albany, NY www.sunypress.edu

Library of Congress Cataloging-in-Publication Data

Name: Conty, Arianne, author.
Title: Grounding God : religious responses to the Anthropocene / Arianne Conty.
Description: Albany : State University of New York Press, [2023] | Series:
    SUNY series on Religion and the Environment | Includes bibliographical
    references and index.
Identifiers: ISBN 9781438495750 (hardcover : alk. paper) | ISBN 9781438495767
    (ebook) | ISBN 9781438495743 (pbk. : alk. paper)
Further information is available at the Library of Congress.

10 9 8 7 6 5 4 3 2 1

This book is dedicated to the earth beings inhabiting the multiple worlds on our single earth.

Contents

Acknowledgments	ix
Introduction: One Earth, Many Worlds	1
Chapter 1 The Ends of the Anthropocene: Eschatology in Uncertain Times	17

Part I. Religious Responses to the Anthropocene

Chapter 2 Christian Responses to the Anthropocene	41
Chapter 3 A Buddhist Response to the Anthropocene: *Fudo*	55
Chapter 4 Neopaganism and the Grounding of the Sacred	75
Chapter 5 Animism in the Anthropocene	99

Part II. Philosophical Responses to the Anthropocene

Chapter 6 Panpsychism: A Metaphysics for the Anthropocene Age	121
Chapter 7 Ecosophy: New Values for the Anthropocene Age	143
Notes	169
Bibliography	181
Index	213

Acknowledgments

An earlier version of chapter 2, entitled "Religion in the Anthropocene," was originally published in *Environmental Values* 30, no. 2 (January 4, 2021): 215–34.

An earlier version of chapter 5, entitled "Animism in the Anthropocene," was originally published in *Theory, Culture & Society* 39, no. 5 (September 30, 2021): 1–27.

An earlier version of chapter 6, entitled "Panpsychism: A Response to the Anthropocene Age," was originally published in the *Journal of Speculative Philosophy* 35, no. 1 (2021): 27–49.

Introduction

One Earth, Many Worlds

A Klee painting named *Angelus Novus* shows an angel looking as though he is about to move away from something he is fixedly contemplating. His eyes are staring, his mouth is open, his wings are spread. This is how one pictures the angel of history. His face is turned toward the past. Where we perceive a chain of events, he sees one single catastrophe which keeps piling wreckage upon wreckage and hurls it in front of his feet. The angel would like to stay, awaken the dead, and make whole what has been smashed. But a storm is blowing from Paradise; it has got caught in his wings with such violence that the angel can no longer close them. This storm irresistibly propels him into the future to which his back is turned, while the pile of debris before him grows skyward. This storm is what we call progress.

—Benjamin (1968): 257–58

Today, in what has come to be called the Anthropocene Age, we feel a bit like Walter Benjamin's angel, moving ever forward while contemplating the ever-accumulating wreckage we leave behind us on the planet, in a multitude of signs that the Anthropos (the human species) has indeed left his mark on the entire ecosphere. Like Benjamin's angel, our future seems always to be shrinking, becoming ever-more apocalyptic. And if blame for the climate catastrophe is so difficult to adjudicate, it is for the reason Benjamin mentions: because such a catastrophe was created in the name of a certain conception of progress.

In his *Theses on History,* where Walter Benjamin mentions this angel, he also mentions that if the future appears apocalyptic, the messiah is always

2 | Grounding God

behind us, ready to appear to the angel who has turned back to seek him out. In this way, Benjamin, who was also living an end-time, that of Nazi fascism, tells his readers to look to the past to find the possibility of an open future. Because his present life under National Socialism was intolerable, he knew that such a present could only determine an equally oppressive future. Hope, if hope there could be, could only be found in the possibilities of the past that had been buried from view by the hegemonic forces of the present. Excavating these pasts could allow for future potentials, lost from view in a hopeless present, to once again become possible.

Though we have known for hundreds of years that we are polluting our planet and destroying its ecosystems, and that the detritus of carbon isotopes and radionuclides as well as artificial molecules (due to plastics) are a health hazard, we continue to go about our affairs as though infinite capitalist growth by means of extracting and appropriating resources could continue forever. In addition to rising C02 levels and thus world temperatures, the sixth great mass extinction of animal species, sediment shifts, sea-level rise, and nitrogen and phosphorus fluxes due to fertilizers, the consequences on humans and the ecosphere have been made abundantly clear by scientists, again and again and again. Yet we are doing very, very little. It seems that thinking of alternatives to a capitalist ideology of infinite growth and private gain at the expense of ecosystems, communal solidarity, and indigenous peoples is something we don't want, or have become unable, to consider. The best future we can hope such a present will create is that of enhanced geoengineering and a managerial "stewardship" of the entire planet that often takes the form of requiring all humans to live in cities, and all nonhuman environments to be transformed into mass-industrial globalized food production units. Welcome to the Anthropocene!

If hegemonic powers bury other potentials in the name of the one norm that becomes a univocal present, perhaps we should follow Walter Benjamin's lead in turning to other ontologies that have been buried from view, and digging them up to see if they might provide messianic potential for envisioning a different and open future. Digging deep into the layers of the past to uncover these ontologies can allow for a future different from the one the hegemonic present has made inevitable.

Today, these pasts are not entirely buried from view. They struggle on, they continue to resist the unicity of one hegemonic world, and allow other potentials to be seen. But they are well-nigh invisible, never mentioned when policymakers consider solutions, and usually considered remnants of a past that "progress" has superseded and made redundant. By positing such pasts as hopelessly outdated, inferior, and primitive, we have deprived ourselves of the human plasticity intrinsic to our nature, and of the possibility of becoming other, and thinking otherwise.

This book will reveal the ways that the modern ontology has become untenable today in the Anthropocene Age, and will need to be replaced with a relational ontology. There were many relational ontologies prior to the development of modernity, and many struggle to persevere in and against the globalization that threatens their existence. In looking at some of these other ontologies, we will notice that they are better suited to life on planet earth as opposed to the modern ontology, which has aptly been called a thanatology. Such a thanatocene (Bonneuil and Fressoz 2013), bent on destruction and ecocide, cannot ensure a future for life on planet earth. Philosopher and anthropologist Peter Skafish is one among many scholars who are seeking such alternatives in "nonmodern variations of thought" in the hope that these might "render humans cohesive among themselves and with other beings, rather than working at all of their expense." [1]

This book will develop the anthropological thesis that the climate crisis is part of a larger crisis enabled by certain ontological presuppositions, those associated with Western modernity. This thesis was advanced in the work of anthropologist Philippe Descola when he formulated the fourfold ontological presuppositions intrinsic to different cultures. Descola's world ontologies are those of naturalism, the ontology of Western modernity; animism, adhered to by indigenous hunting peoples of South and North America as well as Siberia; totemism, adhered to by aboriginal cultures of Australia; and analogism, as represented in the cosmologies of China, parts of inner and southern Asia, Polynesia, West Africa, Mesoamerica, the Andes, and Europe during the Renaissance, as well as in Western esotericism and New Age traditions. In naturalism, each animal self is dissimilar, whereas bodies are the same. This contrasts with totemism, where both selves and bodies are similar; animism, where selves are similar but bodies are different; and analogism, where both selves and bodies are dissimilar. Only the naturalist ontology ascribes value only to human selves, understood as somehow not coevolved as part of nature and having value to the extent that they are somehow bodiless souls, constituted by culture as opposed to nature. Only naturalism has pitted culture against nature and humans against the natural world that created them and continues to sustain them. In this book we will privilege analogical and animistic ontologies, but the same could and has been done elsewhere with totemism.[2] It is therefore time to replace the dualisms of naturalism with a fluid and relational understanding of life on

4 | Grounding God

planet earth, one that is based in plural ontologies, capable of liberating different human potentials in order to avoid an apocalyptic future.

In his article "Towards a Fifth Ontology for the Anthropocene," Clive Hamilton has claimed that instead of gaining inspiration from these non-modern ontologies, we should invent a new, fifth ontology, since for him the Anthropocene is without ontological precedent. He writes:

> I'm suggesting that the conditions of life will be transformed in a way that renders all existing ontological understandings anach-ronistic, and we will be groping towards the elements of a fifth ontology beyond the four described by Descola, one rooted in the radically new dispensation brought by the Anthropocene rupture, a dispensation that destabilises all previous understandings of the human, of nature and of the relationship between the two. And I will suggest that by entering a state never before experienced in its 4.5-billion-year history, the Earth is now something without ontological precedent. (112)

Hamilton maintains that ontological pluralism is a mistake, and thus that we need one single (Western) solution. For him such a solution involves retaining the dualisms of naturalism; he repeats that nature has become an "untamed beast" that must be "confronted" and "calmed" by means of "technology and management practices."

Hamilton's fifth ontology is problematic in three very Western ways. First, it is not at all new; it is simply more of the same naturalist Western ontology. Second, he takes for granted the temporality of Western progress, implying that the earth moves from one hegemonic ontology to the next, and thus that the multiple ontologies of different nonhegemonic cultures cannot survive and should not be revived. But the earth is inhabited by multiple ontologies, and reducing such ontologies to one was the goal of universalizing modernity and its colonial conquest, and thus one of the things Westerners should be seeking to redress. The thousands of societies practicing the other three ontologies described by Descola cannot be rele-gated to the past, no matter the extent that their populations and cultures have been desecrated by Western colonialism.

Lastly, Hamilton seems to take for granted the modernist presupposi-tions of the ecomodernist movement,[3] namely, that technological innovations are necessarily progressive and that they are somehow objectively neutral rather than embedded in neoliberal political ideologies. Tied as it is to belief in modern progress as universally beneficial, the signatories of the *Ecomodernist Manifesto* call for what they call a "good Anthropocene," the result of decoupling human beings from the natural world when humans are "liberated" from the land and forced to live in cities. Because it squarely places responsibility in the hands of humans, the Anthropocene is taken by these scholars to represent the potential for total human mastery of the earth and of their own destiny in what these scholars understand as a future where market growth, when tied to ecological sustainability, can lead to the end of hunger and want and the beginning of a utopian synthetic human future decoupled from nature. This is what biologist Donna Haraway calls "cosmofaith in technofixes" (2016b:3) and economist Joan Martinez-Alier calls "the Gospel of eco-efficiency," which seeks to create a happy marriage between capitalism and ecology and thus is rendered immune to any critique of infinite growth and industrial overproduction.

Relying upon capitalist techno-fixes is counterintuitive, however, since as Einstein once pointed out, you cannot solve a problem with the faulty premises that created the problem. Mary-Jane Rubenstein explains this point well: "After all, such technologies—which reliably promise to deliver profit as well as a habitably hacked planet—are the product of the colonially and genocidally fueled white-industrial capitalism that created the disaster they now endeavor to fix" (2018:129). Such a vision of infinite growth requires separating economics from both politics and ecology, both of which replace the concept of infinite growth with contingent limits. In calling for a continuation of the modern capitalist paradigm, these authors ignore the role played by power, politics, and inequality, preferring to replace actual human beings and their systems of meaning with abstract economic calculation and algorithms. Yet, as Sundberg, Dempsey, and Collard make clear in their response to the manifesto, "any indicators of human flourishing, even those mentioned in the manifesto (life expectancy, resilience to infectious disease, disasters), are distributed in deeply uneven ways, not only between nations but also along class, race, and gender lines" (2015:228). Ignoring such uneven semantic lines allows the manifesto to recommend the abstract mapping of nature as an external resource grid, a tactic that has indeed proved to be an excellent means of capital accumulation. And it is such abstraction that leads both Hamilton and the authors of the manifesto to claim that the earth can continue to feed an ever-increasing human population that has now exceeded 7.8 billion (January 2021). As sociologist Eileen Crist's response

6 | Grounding God

to the manifesto makes clear, the premise of the manifesto is correct, but only if one takes for granted that the entire nonhuman world has no value and can be pushed to extinction. She writes:

> What makes it true that there exist no limits to human growth is that one percent of the temperate zone remains as temperate grassland ecologies, half or more of Earth's life-rich wetlands are gone, and the rainforests are falling. What makes it true that no limits to growth exist is that glyphosate is everywhere and almost one billion monarch butterflies are missing; that freshwater biodiversity has suffered massive losses and there seems so little hope for what remains. What makes no-limits to human growth true is that the zoomass of wild vertebrates has become "vanishingly small" in comparison to the combined weight of humans and domestic animals, while the once enormous abundance of living beings in the ocean is gone—and who remembers? What makes it true is that the great animal migrations are disappearing, wild animal populations are plummeting, and so many beings (wild and domestic) are deprived of the freedom to move, enjoy life, or even exist. We live in a time of extinctions and of mass extinction exactly because there are "no limits" to human growth. (2015:250–51)

Since Hamilton ignores the particular historical and cultural specificities of such a capitalist ideology, he and the authors of the manifesto speak in the name of all of "humanity," of general "human progress," and of undefined "better" or "worse" strategies, the "best" strategies always entailing "more" of something, never "less": more urbanization, more aquaculture, more agricultural intensification, and more nuclear power.[4] Andreas Malm has clearly indicated the problems involved in such a generalization: "If humanity as a whole drives the locomotive, there is no one to depose. A revolt against business-as-usual becomes inconceivable" (Malm 2016:389).

Many responses to the *Ecomodernist Manifesto* have pointed to its contradictions, dangerous elisions, and unfounded premises, and have proposed alternatives, from degrowth solutions to anarchist reconstructions of the commons (Crist 2015).[5] In his address to the ecomodernists entitled "Fifty Shades of Green," presented at the Breakthrough Institute in 2015, philosopher Bruno Latour focuses on the danger of their seemingly apolitical stance and on the way the ecomodernists reinforce the modern dichotomy between archaic past and future progress and thereby elide the very real dangers and risks that inhere in the Anthropocene.

For Latour, "ecomodernism" "sounds much like the news that an electronic cigarette is going to save a chain smoker from addiction" (2015b:220). Looking at the key concept of modernism, Latour problematizes the connotations of this word, which has come to mean an emancipation from the past, often understood as a dependence on nature that stunted human growth. But as Latour emphasizes in his address to the ecomodernists, such an emancipation never occurred, and we have continuously "entangled ourselves in the fabric of nature" (221). And now that the Anthropocene has given us a name for this entanglement, being modern in the sense of a separation from these interdependencies constitutes what Latour calls "inauthenticity" or "an imposture" (221). By beating those who remain backward "into submission" the ecomodernists use terms such as *modern* and *ecological* for political ends, while at the same time ignoring all explicit politics. This is the major insight of Latour's address to the ecomodernists. If politics can occur only when there is "no referee, no arbiter, no providence, no court of appeal" (224), the ecomodernists will need to sacrifice what Latour calls their "uchronist" stance, "as if they were living at a time when they alone were in command" (223). If Hamilton and the ecomodernists claim they have no enemies and are only tracing "the inevitable path of progress and reason," then, according to Latour, they are following religious ideology and avoiding all politics. If, on the other hand, they want to do politics, then they will need to define their friends and their enemies, and explain how their manifesto can chart a path toward political consensus building that includes all of the nonhuman agencies that are entangled with human agency. Latour asks: "How do you invent the political constitution that is able to absorb the Anthropocene, namely the reaction of the earth system to our action, in a way that renders politics again comprehensible to those who are simultaneously actor, victim, accomplices and responsible for such a situation?" (224). But for such a political attitude to grow, ecomodernists must face the facts of the Anthropocene and cease their New Age "positive thinking" attitude that scorns the devastating scientific predictions, and by which "they seriously believe that nothing will happen to them and that they may continue forever, just as before" (224).

Not only will human animals continue to die, but they will probably begin to do so at an alarming rate if no political solutions to the Anthropocene are found. By ignoring politics and universalizing their position as "modern" as opposed to archaic environmentalists and indigenous pastoralists, Latour

8 | Grounding God

thinks the ecomodernists have let Frankenstein loose and "abandoned their creature" rather than taking responsibility for the monster they have created.

This book believes that "good Anthropocenes" can ensue from rejecting modern ontologies of progress founded in economic growth linked to the expropriation of natural resources, and seeking multiple ontological alternatives. Following the work of Arturo Escobar, we will seek alternatives *to* modernity, rather than the more common alternative modernities proposed by Hamilton and other ecomodernists (2016:17). In order for such alternatives to exist, we must exit the ideology of there being one world and seek to promote a decolonial ideology of multiple worlds. I write *decolonial* and not *postcolonial* because there are many peoples, and thus many worlds, that have not been directly colonized and that therefore provide valid alternative worlds to that of Western modernity. It may be difficult for many Westerners to accept an ontology of many worlds, trained as they are in centuries of scientific and philosophic justifications of one universal world, reachable by means of transcendent reason. Yet this is what this book will advocate as absolutely necessary if we are to seek solutions to our current climate crisis. There is one earth, inhabited by multiple worlds, only some of them human.

If we study the solutions to our climate crisis proposed by Western scholars, we can see that the unitary world that is presupposed leads to solutions that have been contested for their inability to leave behind the dichotomies that are held to be the causes of the current crisis. Carolyn Merchant (1990:66–67) argues that what she calls "egocentric ethics" is rooted in the seventeenth-century philosopher Thomas Hobbes's notion of nature as a common resource for which everyone competes. As anthropologist Bruce Albert has pointed out, both exploitation and preservation presuppose a reified and objectified nature cut off from human culture and subjected to its anthropocentric will.[6]

When Lynn White Jr. published his article "The Historical Roots of Our Ecological Crisis" in 1967, he famously traced the techno-scientific regime of Western modernity back to innovations in the Middle Ages, and sought the ideological causes for such a regime in the anthropocentrism of the Christian worldview. For White, a change in the West would require the transformation of this ideology and the replacement of anthropocentrism with a relational ecology.

Central to his critique was the anthropocentrism intrinsic to the Christian worldview. By stating that man is made in God's image, the Hebrew Bible gave man dominance over all other animals to exploit and control them. Such anthropocentrism led Westerners to think of their identity as somehow transcendent (like God) and hence, rather than empathizing with other animals, to think of themselves as ineffable souls rather than mortal animal bodies. Made in God's image, humans could not only contemplate God's creation but imitate God in seeking to understand it, and to control the natural world with God-like powers developed by techno-scientific means. White writes: "Hence we shall continue to have a worsening ecologic crisis until we reject the Christian axiom that nature has no reason for existence save to serve man" (1967:505).

According to White, more techno-science will not resolve our ecological crisis. Rather, he contends, we need an ideology that involves more than pure reason. For White such a change would require the assistance of religions, since religions typically involve the human in a cosmology that involves the whole person. Though he respected Buddhism and the Zen tradition that have become so popular in the Western world, he thought that the West could not adopt a foreign tradition but rather had to develop its own traditions in ecological ways by eschewing anthropocentrism and the objectification of nature for human ends. "Since the roots of our trouble are so largely religious, the remedy must also be essentially religious, whether we call it that or not. We must rethink and refeel our nature and destiny. The profoundly religious, but heretical, sense of the primitive Franciscans for the spiritual autonomy of all parts of nature may point a direction. I propose Francis as a patron saint for ecologists" (1967:506).

Though White maintained that the transformation had to come from within, and therefore from a transformation within Christianity itself, both paganism and animism are also traditions that are autochthonous to the Western world, albeit from earlier periods. And just as becoming Christian entailed adopting and transforming a religion from without, that of a Jewish carpenter from Palestine, so have peoples ever since borrowed, adopted, and transformed religious traditions from across the globe. This book therefore agrees with White that religions have the power to transform cultural ideologies and that such a change is necessary, but will look at traditions both within the West and outside it for inspiration.

White is not alone in blaming anthropocentrism for our current predicament. Arne Johan Vetlesen has similarly shown the causal relationship between anthropocentrism and the Anthropocene:

> If the Anthropocene is the historical product of anthropocentrism, it is also what forces us to abandon it and search for

10 | Grounding God

> alternatives—alternatives whose first assignment is to be less destructive to the natural world that humanity depends upon: to help us learn, finally, to appreciate that world for what it is in itself. . . . Indeed, in keeping with the urgency of the situation, to be worth its salt a philosophy for tomorrow's world needs to rethink the relationship between humans and the rest of nature in a way that helps us recognize the manifold of agents and agencies in beings other than humans. This undertaking is no less normative than the one it seeks to replace. Only its normativity is explicit not implicit, and—what matters most—it's of a substantially different kind in acknowledging value as well as agency in so many different beings and forms of life in nature. In rejecting the thesis of human exceptionalism on which anthropocentrism is premised, humans are a part of nature, not apart from nature. Not only have we been wrong about all those "others," taking them to be what we are not, and vice versa, but we have been wrong about ourselves as well. (2019:9)

Though such an ideological change is the work of philosophy proper, the difficulty of abstract reasoning among the general public points to the limitations of philosophical arguments in enacting change. For this reason I will focus here on religion, which, contrary to the theories of the great sociologists of the twentieth century, has shown no sign of ceding its place to secularism, and instead has begotten many new movements as well as reviving many that had been deemed moribund. Because academic responses to climate change have proved so inadequate in the transformation of minds and actions, we will turn to religious approaches that have successfully deconstructed the nature–culture divide and provided ecological alternatives to replace it. If dogmatic monotheistic responses have been considered inadequate by many scholars and practitioners, many alternatives have been developed in order to find a healthier religious relationship to the nonhuman world. Indeed, the authors of an article entitled "Climate Change and Religion as Global Phenomena" claim that religions will indeed play an essential role in the global response to climate change for the following four reasons:

1. Religions influence the worldviews or cosmologies of believers, motivating them to climate activism or to quietism or denial.

2. Many people respond to the moral authority wielded by religions.

3. Religious institutions have institutional and economic resources, which can be channeled into or against sustainability.

4. Potential to provide social connectivity and collective action. Religions create social cohesion and overlap civil society in many ways. (Veldman, Szasz, and Haluza-DeLay 2014a:309)

We will therefore look at the ways different religious traditions have been transformed by the Anthropocene and have sought to understand what it means to be human, not over and against the natural world but as a codependent and relational part of it. By focusing on how worlds can be made rather than destroyed, we will study how different religious traditions provide an ethos in harmony with the nonhuman world. Studying Christian, pagan, animist, and Buddhist approaches to environmental collapse will show how these traditions reveal potential lifeworlds that replace modern dichotomies with symbiotic survival strategies that could provide the necessary resistance to the end-times enabled by techno-industrial capitalist growth.

The last two chapters of the book develop the philosophical foundations of the many conclusions drawn from these different religious traditions. With a chapter exploring panpsychism as a metaphysics to ground the different religious beliefs within systematic philosophical truth claims, and a final chapter that sets forth new values for an interdisciplinary ecosophy, the book seeks to demonstrate that the different worlds portrayed in its different chapters all fit together, like pieces of a puzzle, on a single earth.

Chapter Contents

The first chapter will elucidate the growing apocalypticism toward a future life on the planet earth, looking at media responses to the devastating scientific reports by the Intergovernmental Panel on Climate Change (IPCC) that chart the repercussions on planet earth of anthropogenic destruction of ecosystems. As we transform the earth into a "no-go zone for human beings" by placing industrial profit above ecosystem flourishing, many people are feeling so disempowered that they are privileging narratives of escape over narratives of transformation of the status quo. Thus chapter 1 will chart the movements of escape to live in vivariums on Mars, in underground bunkers, or off-grid in the wilderness, as different responses to apocalyptic fears. Depicting the strategies of indigenous peoples who have already survived the end-time when colonial powers destroyed their lives, cultures, and

12 | Grounding God

environments, chapter 1 will propose "preemptively apocalyptic thinking" in order to seek out the surviving interspecies and lichen cyborgs proliferating in the ruins. Using the work of biologist and consciousness-studies scholar Donna Haraway, this chapter will seek alternative ontological presuppositions for the Anthropocene Age that can overcome the ontological foundations responsible for the climate crisis, and celebrate the many worlds, both human and nonhuman, that co-inhabit our earthly home and allow for pluralism to reinforce ecosystem interdependence and solidarity.

After elucidating White's (1967) ecological critique of Christianity in terms of anthropocentrism and the exploitation of the natural world for human purposes, chapter 2 considers different responses to this critique that have attempted to make Christianity more ecological. The chapter first looks at apologetic responses, focusing on those of Pope Francis and the Orthodox tradition, both of which retain the transcendental as superior to the immanent. We then look at more audacious sacramental responses that have attempted to render immanence itself sacred, such as those of Fox and of Wallace, as well as feminist approaches (of Peterson and of Primavesi) that decry the "violence of God traditions" and seek to replace them with an embodied theology focused on life on earth rather than the afterlife. Finally, the chapter considers ways of transforming Christian foundations in line with science and ecology, focusing on the work of scientists Kaufman and Abrams.

The third chapter turns to Buddhism, an example of an analogical ontology, which has the advantage of being founded in dogma that is inherently in harmony with both science and the environment. Though Lynn White Jr. acknowledged that Buddhism was more ecological than Western approaches, he nonetheless claimed that the West could not borrow ecological solutions from foreign traditions. Yet many scholars disagree with him, asserting that if it is the very presuppositions of Western ideology that are to blame, a solution cannot be founded on these premises. Because Buddhism does not adhere to the Cartesian separation of the body from the soul, and of the material world from the truth discovered by reason, it can be of assistance in developing an ecocentric, rather than anthropocentric, understanding. The first section of this chapter thus details some of the fundamentals of Buddhist dogma that are deemed essential for ecocentrism, namely interdependence, the Buddhahood of all beings, interspecies kinship intrinsic to the idea of reincarnation, and the lack of inherent existence (*śūnyatā*) necessary for interdependence. Yet how are we to borrow these tenets without appropriating Buddhism and disembedding it from the context in which it has meaning? To avoid these pitfalls, this chapter will focus on the Japanese theory of *fudo* developed by philosopher Tetsuro Watsuji in the mid-twentieth century. In this theory, Watsuji maintains that we become human by means of acclimatization, influenced by the physical forces of nature that constitute weather as milieu (*fudo*). The human being, then, cannot be separated or abstracted from this milieu. We cannot universalize human nature nor focus on intrinsic essences at the expense of relationality, as Western culture tends to do. These changes are enough to radically shift the way we understand and relate to the environment and to ourselves, and could help us to take to heart the symbiotic relations between self and milieu (*fudo*).

Chapter 4 traces several of the growing pagan forms of spirituality that have rejected many of the claims of monotheism in order to provide spiritual sustenance that is earthly rather than heavenly, feminine rather than male, and material rather than transcendent. Neopaganism is a diverse and pluralistic tradition that belies definition, since it requires neither scripture nor deities, creed nor hierarchical authority. Yet neopagans all share veneration for and celebration of the living earth, a belief in the immanence of the divine, and the conviction that they can communicate with the energies of the universe. Tracing these characteristics back to goddess worship, Druid traditions, and northern shamanism, neopagans seek to retrieve and revalorize these traditions that were destroyed and oppressed by Christianity. Providing structure to organize religious rituals focused on veneration of nature, neopaganism has developed into many different traditions that practice this devotion to nature in different ways. Chapter 4 focuses on two of these traditions, that of Wicca (involving the worship of a mother goddess and a horned god during Sabbat ceremonies marking equinox and lunar events) and the tradition of religious naturalism as expressed in the Gaia tradition (in which the earth is considered a living organism, regulating the conditions for the thriving of life on earth).

The fifth chapter turns to indigenous animism, focusing particularly on the animist ontology of tribes living in the Amazon basin of South America. If philosopher Bruno Latour has famously claimed that "we have never been modern," religious-studies scholar Graham Harvey has recently added that "perhaps we have always been animists." If we have repressed and unlearned how to share our world with nonhuman others, today it is our Cartesian dualisms that cause us shame, and we are seeking as best we can to decolonize our thought and reclaim animism in order to develop a more sustainable ontology. This chapter elucidates animism by focusing on the characteristics of personhood, relationality, location, and ontological

14 | Grounding God

boundary crossing. If all living beings are persons with souls, then our communication must expand to include the indexical and the iconic, allowing us to develop a cosmopolitics for the Anthropocene Age. After clarifying indigenous animism, this chapter uses the thought of philosopher and psychoanalyst Félix Guattari to develop what he called a "machinic animism." Guattari thought that we should "pass through animist thought" so as to develop the solidarity and kinship that is so sorely lacking in modern culture. Ontological boundary crossing is already available to us in literature when we imagine ourselves as women and men, beggars and emperors, Maggie Tulliver and the Princess de Clève. But it is also required in order to do politics, since it is essential to developing the moral judgments necessary for democratic governance. It should thus not be too difficult to develop an animist cosmopolitics that includes other animals and ecosystems.

Chapter 6 will develop the philosophy of panpsychism, which provides an organic monism in line with the ecological religious traditions to be studied. In this chapter we will propose a philosophy that respects contemporary science and the relational ontologies set forth in the previous chapters, while providing a necessary metaphysical framework to overcome the mind–body divide and give to matter the respect that it deserves. Rather than insensate matter driven by mechanical forces, panpsychism claims that matter itself possesses subjective mental properties and is capable of experience, self-regulation, and relationality. Using the research of anthropologists Tim Ingold and Eduardo Kohn, and the philosophy of Alfred North Whitehead, this chapter will differentiate between different forms of matter so as to avoid the conflations between animate and inanimate matter that have become widespread in the work of philosophers like Mathews and Bennett. Such a conflation leaves us unable to make ethical assessments that adjudicate between a rock and an indigenous Yanomami person, between a washing machine and an endangered jaguar. As Kohn makes clear, life is semiotic and semiosis exists only for selves. Such a Peircean semiotic definition allows Kohn to include ecosystems as living forms, but it is Whitehead who assigned material forms into six separate categories allowing us to differentiate between aggregative and nonaggregative forms of matter. A panpsychist understanding of the earth can have important ethical consequences, since sharing mind with the earth can overturn human exceptionalism and replace it with empathy for other configurations of matter. Panpsychism could go far in replacing dualism with an organic monism capable of reintegrating mind into matter, culture into nature, and value into the nonhuman world. If matter is enminded, then sentience, awareness, and relationality can be extended to the nonhuman world and with them, the values and rights attributed to the human person.

Finally, chapter 7 will make use of the ontological presuppositions from the preceding chapters to develop an ecosophy (an ecological philosophy) capable of correcting some of the central errors of modernity and replacing the modern dualistic ontology with a relational one. Borrowing the term *ecosophy* from Guattari, we will place together the spheres of subjectivity, sociology, politics, ecology, and religion, thereby showing that thinking these disciplines transversally is the only way to understand the relational nature of the living world of which we are a part. This last chapter will formulate several new values for the Anthropocene Age, thus replacing the dualisms of modern naturalism with ecological values. We will propose moral egalitarianism instead of perfectionism, relational instead of autonomous selves, individuation instead of individuals, a pluriverse instead of a universe, and finally, we will replace the dogma of truth with ethical consequences, because although truth matters, it cannot give value to mountains, rivers, and polar bears. Only the consequences of their annihilation can allow them to be defended and can reveal the poverty of human existence without them.

Chapter One

The Ends of the Anthropocene
Eschatology in Uncertain Times

It was once religion which told us that we are all sinners, because of original sin. It is now the ecology of our planet which pronounces us all to be sinners because of the excessive exploits of human inventiveness. It was once religion which threatened us with a last judgment at the end of days. It is now our tortured planet which predicts the arrival of such a day without any heavenly intervention. The latest revelation—from no Mount Sinai, from no Mount of the Sermon, from no Bo (tree of Buddha)—is the outcry of mute things themselves that we must heed by curbing our powers over creation, lest we perish together on a wasteland of what was creation.

—Jonas (1996:201–2)

Après moi le déluge

From the Greek *anthropos,* human, and *kainos,* new, the term Anthropocene was coined by atmospheric chemist Paul Crutzen in 2000 (Crutzen and Stoermer 2000:17–18) in light of the research on the ozone layer that earned him a Nobel Prize. Following upon the Holocene, the Anthropocene is the name given to a new geological era to indicate the fact that the strata of the earth have been indelibly marked by the presence of the Anthropos, the human species. "The Anthropocene represents a new phase in the history of the Earth, when natural forces and human forces became intertwined,

18 | Grounding God

so that the fate of one determines the fate of the other. Geologically, this is a remarkable episode in the history of the planet" (Zalasiewicz et al. 2010:2231).[1] The term has now been adopted by many geologists and environmental scientists, and the International Commission on Stratigraphy has organized an Anthropocene Working Group to decide upon the geological relevance of the human-wrought changes to the ecosphere, as well as the best date for the end of the Holocene and the beginning of this new geological era. Some scientists point to the atomic bomb at mid-century as marking this shift, since it left significant levels of plutonium in the earth's strata, or the period of accelerationism after World War II, but others point to industrialization in the eighteenth century, or the birth of capitalism in the sixteenth century as the start date for the Anthropocene, since it sets in place a strategy of "cheap nature" that is implemented by techno-industrial means. Though most scientists today seem to favor accelerationism because of the exponential growth linked to ecosystem changes, Crutzen himself has favored the Industrial Revolution as the major shifting point, focusing his research on the hole in the ozone layer humans have created over Antarctica, the level of methane in the atmosphere, and the 30 percent rise in carbon dioxide emissions. Indeed, since the mid-twentieth century, the detritus of carbon isotopes and radionuclides from burning fossil fuels as well as artificial molecules (due to plastics) have become a major health hazard. And that is not all. Rising $CO2$ levels and thus world temperatures, the sixth great mass extinction of animal species, sediment shifts, sea-level rise, nitrogen and phosphorus fluxes due to excessive fertilizers, the loss of Arctic ice, the acidification of the oceans, and the ensuing droughts, wildfires, flooding, heat waves, tornadoes, and melting glaciers are on the front page of newspapers every day.

Though developed as a geological term in the arcane offices of climatology, the Anthropocene has been taken up by scholars of all disciplines and has come to mark both a paradigm shift and an eschatology for Western modernity. This climate crisis is the consequence of what we call human progress, if we are to attribute this word to the techno-industrial revolution and capitalist resource extraction that are today the global forces of the status quo of modernity. Thus what moderns called progress, in other words techno-industrial development to give people cars and washing machines and air conditioning, has suddenly become culpable, because it represents "the conversion of everything that exists in the mangrove-world into 'nature' and 'nature' into 'resources'; the effacing of the life-enabling materiality of the entire domains of the inorganic and the non-human, and its treatment as 'objects' to be had, destroyed, or extracted; and linking the forest worlds so transformed to 'world markets' for profit" (Escobar 2016:19).

It is this progress that is now being repudiated as the cause of the climate crisis. Because the changes to the earth's ecosystem are human-wrought, we are left wondering who we are, and how some of us could have so wrongly interpreted the relationship between nature and culture to cause such disruption. If what we were told was good has suddenly become bad, how are we to think about ourselves and our values? If we are destroying the earth that sustains us and all of sentient life, what does it even mean to be good? The shock to our self-understanding is momentous. If a logical solution might have been to force the ideology of modernity into extinction for having brought about the conditions of environmental collapse, many people prefer ecosystem extinctions so long as they can still believe in capitalist growth and the notion of urban "progress" it entails. Because of this moral wasteland, instead of the Renaissance values of human dignity through freedom to choose our own destiny, or Enlightenment notions of moral autonomy through the use of reason, we are now being told that the human being has become "a cancer," "a virus," a deadly "bacteria" infecting and killing its host, the earth. If we are neither particularly reasonable nor a deadly virus, then what are we, and "how did we get caught up in this mess" (Malm 2016:3)? For many, the Anthropocene has come to represent the eschatology of life on planet earth because anthropogenic climate change has reached such alarming proportions and the political responses are so inadequate that apocalyptic proclamations have become common.

The results of the sixth scientific report on climate change (September 2022), published by the Intergovernmental Panel on Climate Change (IPCC), are indeed devastating. In addition to the sixth great extinction of biodiversity already underway and ocean acidification killing the coral reefs and the ocean life they feed, the scientists from 198 countries who wrote the IPCC study warn of rising heat waves, droughts, floods, storms, hurricanes and tornadoes, sea levels rising between two and four feet, freshwater sources decreasing, the Atlantic thermohaline currents weakening, crop yields dropping, and infectious diseases spreading.[2] We are now being told that even a rise of 1.5 degrees of CO2 pollution, estimated to occur within eleven years, will result in submerging many tropical islands and flooding many coastal regions. And the study predicts a rise to 2 degrees soon thereafter unless drastic measures are immediately taken: cutting fossil-fuel use in half in less than fifteen years and entirely within thirty years, and adding ten million square kilometers of forests by 2050.

20 | Grounding God

These results have been confirmed by the thirteen US federal agencies (including the Energy Department and the National Oceanic and Atmospheric Administration [NOAA]) mandated by the US Congress under the auspices of the Global Change Research Program to study the effects of climate change on the US economy. The report (published on November 23, 2018) explains in clear and blunt language that if CO2 emissions continue to rise at their current rates, the end of the century will bring losses estimated at $141 billion per year for labor-related losses due to extreme heat, $118 billion per year due to sea-level rises, storms, and flooding, and $32 billion per year for infrastructure damage. Because much of American industry is overseas in regions that will be even harder-hit by flooding, droughts, and other extreme weather conditions, the report predicts that the entire American supply chain will incur enormous losses and price spikes. Such events are "virtually certain to increasingly affect U.S. trade and economy, including import and export prices and businesses with overseas operations and supply chains," the report states. Regarding agricultural losses, the report warns that crop yields and quality could regress by 2050 to levels not seen since the 1980s, and livestock health could be seriously threatened. "Rising temperatures, extreme heat, drought, wildfire on rangelands and heavy downpours are expected to increasingly disrupt agricultural productivity in the U.S."[3] With fossil-fuel companies and banks pulling out of renewable-energy investments and lobbying against cuts and taxes, and heads of government in countries such as Australia and Brazil denying climate change and/or pulling out of the Paris Agreement, it is highly unlikely that the needed measures will be implemented. COP 27 (the United Nations Climate Change Conference) in Cairo in 2022 has given a bit more reason for hope, since nations with zero carbon footprints are demanding that wealthy polluting nations compensate them for the environmental devastation they are facing, but according to Harald Welzer's analysis in his *Climate Wars: What People Will Be Killed For in the 21ˢᵗ Century*, such changes are insufficient and come far too late. Welcome to the Anthropocene.

Anthropomorphizing ecosystem reactions is one of the most striking recent responses to the many environmental disasters we have been witnessing; such reactions are described as the "revenge" or "anger" of what used to be thought of as generous Mother Nature. Many journals have been characterizing the climate crisis as "Nature Strikes Back!," reinforcing a growing fear that "Mother Nature" has metamorphized into what philosopher Clive Hamilton has called an "ornery beast" taking her revenge. This is indeed

The Ends of the Anthropocene | 21

what UN Secretary-General António Gutteres corroborated at the 2019 Climate Action Summit when he warned:

> Nature is angry. And we fool ourselves if we think we can fool nature. Because nature always strikes back. And around the world, nature is striking back with fury. . . . I have seen it with my own eyes, from Dominica to the Sahel to the South Pacific. In May, I went to the island nation of Tuvalu, where I witnessed an entire country fighting for its very existence against the rising seas. Two months ago, I visited Mozambique, which was pummelled by unprecedented back-to-back cyclones. A few days ago, I was in the Bahamas, where Hurricane Dorian pounded the country for two unrelenting days. The destruction was not simply appalling. It was apocalyptic.[4]

Such transformations of planet earth have led youths like Greta Thunberg to tell us that "we have stolen their futures," bearing testimony to the "unbearable destiny" (Malm 2016:10) that awaits us now that the Holocene conditions for life have been destabilized. In November 2022, UN Secretary-General Guterres told the COP 27 attendees in Cairo that "we are on a highway to climate hell with our foot still on the accelerator."[5] Newspaper headlines such as "Final call to save the world from climate catastrophe" (BBC), "World close to irreversible climate breakdown" (*The Guardian*), "UN Says Climate Genocide Is Coming" (*Intelligencer*), and "The climate apocalypse is coming" (Franzen, *New Yorker*, 2019) have become commonplace. Many new books are also taking up this apocalyptic surge. Titles such as *Geoengineering the Apocalypse, Ocean Acidification and the Apocalypse, Conversations on the Edge of the Apocalypse, The End of the World as We Know It, The Ends of the World, The Mushroom at the End of the World,* and journalist David Wallace-Wells's terrifying bestseller *The Uninhabitable Earth* show the central place apocalypticism has assumed in our understanding of the climate crisis.

As historians Christophe Bonneuil and Jean-Baptiste Fressoz have shown in their book *L'Événement anthropocène*, scholarly research pointing to the signs of environmental decline and seeking alternatives was widespread at least since 1750, but then as now such warnings were not heeded. After a long list of avoidable climate catastrophes, from decreasing butterfly populations, tipping points in Arctic ecosystems, the browning of rain forests, and

22 | Grounding God

the possibility of wiping out the entire crop of maize, soybeans, wheat, and rice by the end of the century, human ecologist Andreas Malm observes:

> Whether one chooses to ignore, suppress, deny or agonise over the knowledge of what is happening, it is there, in the air, heavier by the year. And yet the descendants of the Lancashire manufacturers, whose dominion now span the globe, are taking decisions on a daily basis to invest in new oil wells, new coal-fired power plants, new airports, new highways, new liquefied natural gas facilities, new machines to replace human workers, so that emissions are not only continuing to grow but doing so at a higher speed. In the 1990's, the annual increase in global CO2 emissions stood at an average 1 percent; since 2000, the figure has been 3.1 percent—tripled growth rate, exceeding the worst-case scenarios developed by the IPCCC and expressing a trend that still does not show any sign of reversal: the more knowledge there is of the consequences, the more fossil fuels are burnt. How did we get caught up in this mess? (2016:3)

So difficult has it become today to address the social causes of global warming in the current neoliberal ideology, which has led to what Malm calls "carbon lock-in" (2016:7), that many people prefer to accept the destruction of the earth as a fait accompli and either seek to escape from the earth to live in a vivarium on Mars or wallow in a nihilistic indifference. Others have become so cynical about corporate and government irresponsibility that they have opted out, moving off-grid or joining anarchist, ZAD (Zone à défendre), or other communitarian groups that abide by ecological guidelines making them better equipped than governments to prepare for collapse.

Indeed, collapsology has become a popular movement in its own right, founded by entomologist Pablo Servigne and environmental manager and holistic scientist Raphaël Stevens. As philosopher Pierre Charbonnier notes:

> A string of environmental crises and unprecedented pressure on natural resources, the consequences of the way we choose to live our lives, will sooner or later trigger a breakdown in our food and energy supply systems and bring down the (relatively) stable and peaceful political structures we know today. The compilation of scientific data that "collapsologists" claim to interpret forces industrial civilization to look its imminent demise in the face,

The Ends of the Anthropocene | 23

with no legacy but a ravaged natural environment and a traumatized population. (Charbonnier 2019:89)[6]

If apocalyptic discourses are common whenever natural or social disasters destabilize the present and call for taking stock of what has been accomplished and what has been left undone, it is only in the twentieth century that the end of the world, the apocalypse, has left the world of metaphysics to become a historical possibility. This is the well-known view of philosopher Günther Anders, who has stated: "It is today that these terms (apocalypse, end of the world) take on a serious and no longer metaphysical meaning: since the year 0 (1945), they designate for the first time an end that is truly possible" (2007:103). A telltale example of how the current generation is providing for future generations can be seen in the radioactive-waste facility built in the New Mexican desert. Burying nuclear waste with a life span of twenty-four thousand years, while at the same time admitting the possibility of climate and human catastrophes, has led the nuclear semioticians to imagine a doomsday scenario where the nuclear waste may be found by future survivors who are unaware of its toxicity. They plan on writing a warning on the entrance to the storage room in all official UN languages and also in Navaho, the language of the indigenous community that lives nearby. Though the site will not be sealed until 2038, the message has already been devised: "This site was known as the WIPP (Waste Isolation Pilot Plant Site) when it was closed in 2038 AD. . . . Do not expose this room unless the information centre messages are lost. Leave the room buried for future generations." In a 2016 *Guardian* article, Robert Macfarlane rightly sees in this message to the future an archetype of the Anthropocene Age, as we destroy the Holocene conditions of the earth, ignore both the scientific consensus warning of coming catastrophe and the window still available to take immediate action to slow the harm, and leave a plundered earth "for future generations" to deal with. He writes: "I think of that configuration of berm, chamber, shaft, disc and hot cell—all set atop the casks of pulsing radioactive molecules entombed deep in the Permian strata—as perhaps our purest Anthropocene architecture. And I think of those multiply repeated incantations—pitched somewhere between confession, caution and black mass; leave the room buried for future generations, leave the room buried for future generations . . .—as perhaps our most perfected Anthropocene text" (Macfarlane 2016).

If nuclear energy poses a very real historical threat to life on planet earth, one that would come in a sudden explosion, the Anthropocene poses

24 | Grounding God

a threat that has been creeping up on us imperceptibly since the Industrial Revolution, with its harvesting of coal and oil and destruction of forests. What might be the reaction of "future generations" to such an inheritance of toxic waste and climate destruction? Hopelessness is one reaction, as many youth accuse the adults around them of robbing them of a future. To cite just one example, these are the words published on a blog by Florian, a fifteen-year-old French teenager: "You really take no account of what happens to us. When I talk to young people of my generation, who are about two or three years older or younger than me, they all say the same: we no longer have the dream to found a family, to have children, or a profession, or ideals, like you did when you were teenagers. That's all over, because we are sure that we will be the last generation, or one of the last, before the end."[7]

Similarly, sixteen-year-old Greta Thunberg of Sweden told world leaders that they had stolen her dreams and her childhood. "We are in the beginning of a mass extinction and all you can talk about is the money and fairy tales of eternal economic growth. How dare you. . . . But the young people are starting to understand your betrayal. The eyes of all future generations are upon you. And if you choose to fail us I say we will never forgive you."[8] Though we might simply explain Florian and Greta's apocalypticism as the exaggerated fears of adolescents, Frank Fenner, emeritus professor of microbiology at the Australian National University, similarly maintains that along with most other species, the human species will become extinct within a century because of the population explosion and "unbridled consumption." Similarly, sociologist Steve Fuller asserts that the earth may very soon become "a no-go zone for human beings." Such a vision of the earth as a "no-go zone," and such perceptions by teenagers who think of themselves as one of the last generations before the end, have become common amid the lack of concerted effort to leave a future worth wanting to the next generation. Treating the earth as a free resource for industrial profit and thereby a storage room for toxic waste has led to what sociologist Jason Moore calls the "theft of planetary life and our—and our children's—futures" (Macfarlane 2016:11).

Armageddon

"How did we get caught up in this mess?" Christian eschatology and capitalism share a blind belief in the future as bringing redemption, and hence in the utilitarian need to sacrifice the present (be it workers' rights or the fate of humankind) for a Second Coming that is always to come. This belief in historical progress is intrinsic to modernity and fuels the confident belief that things can only get better, even if this future good entails surviving an apocalypse or moving to the dead planet Mars.

In the last book of the Christian Bible, the book of Revelation, also called the Apocalypse of John, the author John makes a prophecy that Jesus Christ will return again. This epistolary prophecy was probably included in the canon because the Second Coming was thought to be crucial to belief in Jesus as a supernatural God. Since the Hebrew tradition had developed a messianic theme that involved power and glory (the messiah was meant to set the Jewish people free from the Romans), the putting to death of Jesus as a petty criminal by the Romans had undermined his credentials as a messiah. It was thus necessary for his believers that he return in glory, and hence a Second Coming became dogma thanks to the inclusion of John's Revelation in Scripture. John's vision proclaimed that when the Seven Seals were opened, peace would be taken from the earth, and a quarter of the earth would be given over to death. A great earthquake was predicted, and "the stars of heaven fall to the earth and the sky recedes like a scroll being rolled up" (6:13–14). Mountains and islands are dislodged, and human beings retreat to live in mountain caves. Hail and fire ravage the earth and burn up a third of the trees. A third of the sea creatures are killed and the rivers and springs are poisoned. Locusts appear and the Four Angels use plague, fire, smoke, and brimstone to kill a third of humankind. After many more horrors, including strange beasts and speaking dragons, the sun scorches the earth with intense heat (16:8–9) and the final battle at Armageddon is waged between the forces of good and evil (16:12–13). The wicked are cast into the Lake of Fire, and a "new heaven and new earth" replace the old ones (21:1–8). God dwells with humanity in the New Jerusalem, sin is no more, and the River and Tree of Life heal the nations and their peoples.

Such a renewal coming after devastation has led many religious moderns imbued with Christian culture to welcome the Anthropocene crisis, and to welcome a climate apocalypse so as to hasten the redemption of the Second Coming. In a secularized form, capitalist ideology repeats this story, sacrificing social goods and communitarian traditions to ensure the New Jerusalem of generalized market wealth, understood as the only salvation worth seeking. Indeed, for many, the market has assumed the role of a transcendent god, the only correct attitude being faith in the omnipotent and omniscient market to find a solution and foster greater wealth and greater technological

26 | Grounding God

comfort, at any cost. Whether consciously or not, such a narrative reinforces the ideology of utilitarianism, in which a greater future goal justifies present ethical sacrifices and accepts devastation as a prelude to a greater good. In his *The Protestant Ethic and the Spirit of Capitalism,* Max Weber had of course shown that such capitalist utilitarianism and Christian eschatology are intrinsically connected. In a secular framework, this confident laissez-faire attitude has been equated with a disregard for future generations, since this belief in future redemption, whether capitalist or Christian, does not consider the hardships of living on the earth once the Holocene conditions have been destabilized, once human solidarity and cooperation have been sacrificed for the greed of individuals to gain wealth at the expense of the social good, with the Second Coming continually postponed.

Escape to Mars

Those who are unwilling to address the socioeconomic causes of global warming and prefer willed ignorance and commonplace thoughtlessness to flexing the muscle of solidarity will continue to accept the destruction of the earth as a fait accompli. Disengaged from community and uprooted from place, such nihilistic indifference is now being taken to its logical extreme: to escape from the earth we are destroying and live in a vivarium on Mars. Rather than addressing the intractable problems of limiting consumption, forbidding corporate lobbying, preventing ecosystem depletion amid population growth, and finding global diplomatic solutions that different nations and peoples could agree upon, a growing number of people prefer to give up on the earth altogether and plan a future on the planet Mars. As Elon Musk, the founder of SpaceX, which is planning a space station on Mars, put it in an interview to *National Geographic*: "Either we're going to become a multiplanet species and a spacefaring civilization, or we're going be stuck on one planet until an extinction event." Project Persephone (note the irony that Persephone is the Greek queen of the dead), the British equivalent of SpaceX, is building a "living spaceship" or "exovivaria"—closed ecosystems inside satellites—to be launched within a century and carry human survivors away from a dying earth (*The Times*, April 28, 2014). NASA and DARPA (the Pentagon's Defense Advanced Research Projects Agency) are also developing a "worldship" designed to take a multigenerational community of humans away from a no-longer-habitable earth beyond the solar system. And finally, the Egyptian government as well is investing in a city on Mars, which, to quote from space-agency official Ahmed Abreel, will create "a better future for all of us"; one, he adds, "that is hopefully free of politics and instead focused on our future."[9] According to Abreel, not only will politics be unable to produce the changes needed to save the earth, but a world without politics would be altogether better and would enable us to focus on a future on Mars—which, let us be quite clear, does not support life and is without oxygen. Because the Egyptian population has increased by one million in the last six months to reach 109 million, and because limiting population growth is apparently inconceivable, he adds that such a new frontier is a necessary response to the population explosion. Progress indeed!

Such Mars enthusiasts repeat that human civilization must be preserved at all costs, without ever asking what the value of human civilization is. Is the value of human civilization preserved by imprisoning humans in space suits in an artificial environment, on a planet that does not support life? Has progress come to mean mere survival, at the expense of moral responsibility and intellectual engagement? As Robert Macfarlane asked in the abovementioned *Guardian* article: "What is a civilisation worth if it cannot protect the natural conditions that gave birth to it? Those who fly off leaving behind a ruined Earth would carry into space a fallen civilisation. As the Earth receded into the all-consuming blackness those who looked back on it would be the beings that had shirked their most primordial responsibility, beings corroded by nostalgia and survivor guilt." Is the value of the human being linked, as McFarlane notes, to the flourishing of the earth, or does being human have a value that can be freed from the habitus[10] or Dasein of dwelling on and caring for the earth? By separating human value from the natural world, moderns have become unmoored from the habitus of the earth, the *oikos* or dwelling in relationality in an interdependent multispecies world. By recognizing ourselves as relational interdependent earthlings and cultivating ourselves by cultivating the soil in ways that benefit life, we can avoid transforming our earth into a lifeless planet like Mars.

Doomsday Bunkers

In light of the cost and risks of a one-way ticket to Mars (there can be no round-trip voyage), many millionaires have been investing in doomsday bunkers as another option to survive the destruction of the earth's biosphere. As one prepper put it, "We can't build a celestial ark like Elon Musk, we can't leave the Earth, so we're going to go into the earth. I'm building a

28 | Grounding God

spaceship in the Earth."[11] Sales have skyrocketed 700 percent for these bunkers in the last few years, indicating that for many, "the future is down."[12] Indeed, even without climate destruction, the present and future pandemics, growing inequality, the crisis of democracy, and fears of globalization and violent populism mean for some people that "the future of humanity is not in the stars after all—but deep under the surface of the Earth."[13] These bunkers are guaranteed to repel nuclear blast, airline crashes, military strikes, earthquakes, tsunamis, and floods. Journal titles about these facilities bear such apt titles as "Billionaire Bunkers That Could Shelter the Superrich during an Apocalypse,"[14] "The Bunker Builders Preparing for Doomsday,"[15] "Affordable Bunkers to Survive the Apocalypse,"[16] "World Ending? Elite Apocalypse-Proof Underground Homes,"[17] "How the 1% Are Preparing for the Apocalypse,"[18] and "Inside the Post-Apocalyptic Underground Future."[19]

One such bunker complex is Europe One, which has transformed an ex–Soviet hangar built underneath a mountain in Rothenstein, which was then in East Germany. Buying a bunker in this complex includes twenty-four-hour surveillance and security. Each bunker has 760 square meters of space and includes pool tables and a movie theater. Common venues include a pub, a chapel, and a pool. Europe One has only thirty-four units, so for those unable to invest there, a similar option exists in South Dakota, called xPoint. Built by military engineers, xPoint has its own electricity and water system, so inhabitants can survive a full year without going outside. There are 575 bunkers here, each one 670 square meters in size. Co-owned, the bunkers begin at $35,000 per person but also cost $1,000 in rent per year. The company Vivos, which sells these bunkers, has said that "interest has skyrocketed" in the last few years. Another American project, the Survival Condo, was transformed from a former missile silo and can hold only twelve families, for a total of seventy-five people. The complex is fifteen stories high, each unit with 550 square meters and advertised at $3 million. This complex includes a gym, a dog park, and a climbing wall, and promises five years of survival without surfacing, though there are SWAT trucks waiting outside should anyone have the courage to visit the surface of the earth.[20] Larry Hall, the owner of Survival Condo, wanted to sell his buyers a "normal life—even if the world is burning outside."[21] Journalist Claire Reilly points to what she calls the "grim irony" of such "apocalypse proof" bunkers:

> I guess there's a grim irony in the idea that even when the nukes
> drop and the very fabric of society has disintegrated beyond rec-

ognition, the rich and powerful will still have it better off than the rest of us. We'll still be a society of haves and have-nots. Except in this case, the haves will be watching Armageddon from the comfort of their air-conditioned, underground cinema. And the have-nots will be out in the wilderness, freezing through nuclear winter and picking over the bones of our loved ones, trying to survive the real thing.[22]

Surviving the Apocalypse

If the end of the world may very well be on its way for industrialized moderns, for indigenous peoples the end of the world is old news; it has already happened. Five centuries ago, "viruses . . . iron, gunpowder and paper" massacred 95 percent of the peoples of the Americas, along with most of their living environments (Danowski and Viveiros de Castro 2017: 104). Eva Horn and Hannes Bergthaller write:

> The calamities to which the moderns still look forward in fearful expectation have long been a reality for indigenous peoples: "the hardships many non-Indigenous people dread most of the climate crisis are ones that Indigenous peoples have endured already due to different forms of colonialism: ecosystem collapse, species loss, economic crash, drastic relocation, and cultural disintegration" (Whyte 2018, p. 226). If there is one thing to be learned from indigenous people today, it is not primarily a new humility before nature, but rather the search for social practices which allow a collective to bind itself to a particular territory even in the face of disaster. (2019:22)

As Danowski and de Castro point out in their book *The Ends of the World*, indigenous peoples who have already survived the end "have something to teach us when it comes to apocalypses, losses of world, demographic catastrophes, and ends of History" (2017:104). Perhaps they could teach moderns the correct approach to dealing with the end-times, such that, "diminished yet defiant," they may yet find ways to resist.

Such resistance is what Michael Taussig calls "preemptively apocalyptic thinking" (2009:14). Nils Bubandt finds such preemptive thinking in contemporary attempts to think the Anthropocene beyond "the temporality and

30 | Grounding God

politics of progress and hope" (in Latour et al. 2018:587), that is, beyond the modern utopias of capitalist techno-scientific progress that require moving to Mars in order to achieve their dream of total growth. Such an alternative politics would seek out a good apocalypse, the subtle signs of interspecies dwelling in rubble, the lichen proliferations that will grow even in concrete dead zones, the surviving earthlings engaging in kin reciprocities.

A good example of such a modern *Adivasa* or earthling can be found in the biologist and interspecies philosopher Donna Haraway. Haraway is famous for her work celebrating the nature–culture cyborgs that are constitutive of modernity, and has more recently been defending more dirty cyborgs as constitutive of the Anthropocene, as when she claims that "we are all lichen now" (2015:8). As lichen cyborgs, we belong to what Haraway has called the Chthulucene to honor the beings that dwell on and in the earth, a better-suited term than the Anthropocene to describe our current paradigm. In a presentation entitled "Chthulucene, Capitalocene, Anthropocene" (2014),[23] Haraway focuses on the chthonic beings of the earth who "cultivate response-ability" in the here and now, by bringing together interspecies nongenealogical kin.[24] By replacing procreated kin with interspecies kin relations, interspecies communities are formed while at the same time addressing the overpopulation of the planet. Rather than adopting the point of view of the scientists (though she has a PhD in biology) or of calling for democratic reform (though it is certainly needed), Haraway speaks for all of those forces that are not part of the problem, not responsible for the Anthropocene, and whom she believes already constitute the solution. She speaks for indigenous cultures that have already developed reciprocal relations with nonhuman actors, but also for all those Westerners who do not feed into the capitalist machine and its ideology of growth. Invoking all of the earthly, embodied forces that do not deplete the earth so as to transform shared resources into individual profit, she celebrates the myriad gestures of solidarity that work in jungle and city to heal the damaged earth.

Such a repoliticization of nature does not wait for governments to act or for multinational corporations to be sued, for the Chthulucene is a repoliticization of the daily activities of each worldling, participating in a web of interrelations that affect us all. Worlds are places where we live together, eat together, work together, profit together, and suffer together on a damaged earth. And because the Chthulucene names the earthly creatures that we are, it also names the only struggle that will matter for us, a cosmopolitics that Haraway calls "a kind of timeplace for learning to stay with the trouble of living and dying in response-ability on a damaged earth" (2016a:20).

In her latest book *Staying with the Trouble: Making Kin in the Chthulucene* (2016b), Haraway makes use of Hannah Arendt's famous analysis of the banality of evil to explain what she calls the "commonplace thoughtlessness" intrinsic to the separation of the human animal from the political and ethical sphere of earthly relations. For Haraway, the Anthropocene is the result of allowing our governments and scientific academies, our industries and banks, to delegate labor and profit, commodities and pollution, to those who do not participate directly in the local environments where politics and ethics, and also life, happen. For Haraway, surrender to such thoughtlessness is the result of separating individuals from the interspecies communities and environments that constitute what she calls *worlding*: "The world does not matter in ordinary thoughtlessness. The hollowed-out spaces are all filled with assessing information, determining friends and enemies, and doing busy jobs; negativity, the hollowing out of such positivity, is missed, an astonishing abandonment of thinking. This quality was not an emotional lack, a lack of compassion, although surely that was true of Eichmann, but a deeper surrender to what I would call immateriality, inconsequentiality, or, in Arendt's and also my idiom, thoughtlessness" (2016b:69).

In a world that has been reduced to material forces and algorithms, to statistics, calculation, and profit margins, we have indeed become thoughtless. To counter the "sublime despair and its politics of sublime indifference" (2016b:23), so common in our contemporary world, Haraway asks us to get curious about actual on-the-ground situations, to re-become embedded in particular places, and to get involved with all of the actors that make such places complex and interesting, the "corporations, farms, clinics, labs, homes, sciences, technologies, and multispecies lives entangled in multi-scalar, multitemporal, multimaterial worlding." It is only in the details of such involvement that we flex "a muscle critical for caring about flourishing" (180) and are able to relate to each other and to make collective decisions that benefit all involved.

Haraway is not alone. She is part of a growing community of men and especially women who are reclaiming their identity as lichen cyborgs. Adivasi such as Vandana Shiva, Joanna Macy, Jane Goodall, Wangari Maathai, Marina Silva, Berta Isabel Caceres Flores, Winona LaDuke, Sheila Watt-Cloutier, and the new generation such as Greta Thunberg and Vanessa Nakate are recognizing all other earthly animals as kin, and founding a world ecology to heal our metaphysics and with it our actions on the planet. Such a new world ecology could replace Cartesian substance dualism and provide the shared values that we need to find solutions to the climate crisis.

32 | Grounding God

With the collapse of modern ideology, do we see solutions to the climate crisis budding from the contaminated soil? Indeed, thanks to thousands of social and natural science papers, we actually know what needs to be done. Here is Ian Angus's list of material transformations we must make in order to address our current crisis:

1. Phase out fossil fuels and biofuels, replacing them with clean energy.

2. Support farmers to convert to ecological agriculture, defend local food production and distribution and restore soil fertility, while eliminating factory farms and polluting agribusinesses.

3. Introduce free and efficient public transport networks and urban planning that reduce the need for private trucks and cars.

4. Restructure distribution systems to eliminate waste, planned obsolescence, pollution, and manipulative advertising, placing industries under public control.

5. Retrofitting home and buildings for energy efficiency and establishing strict guidelines for green architecture.

6. Ceasing all military operations at home and elsewhere, transforming armies into volunteer teams to restore ecosystems and assist victims of environmental disasters.

7. Ensure universal health care.

8. Launch reforestation, carbon farming and biodiversity programs. (2016:199–200)

Why have we not adopted these changes? According to anthropologist Arturo Escobar, we will only be able to do so once we have demonstrated the harm intrinsic to the naturalist ontology and have replaced it with a "New Story" about who we are, a story that might reembed us within the earth:

Given that we cannot be intimate with the Earth within a mechanistic paradigm, we are in dire need of a New Story that might enable us to reunite the sacred and the universe, the human and the non-human. The wisdom traditions, including

The Ends of the Anthropocene | 33

those of indigenous peoples, are a partial guide towards this goal of re-embedding ourselves within the Earth. Within these traditions, humans are embedded within the earth, are part of its consciousness, not an individual consciousness existing in an inert world. Every living being exists because all others exist. (2016:27)

Such a new story could help us adopt what he calls "transition discourses" from the North and the South, in order to prepare the way for the changes listed above. Many such discourses exist and are gaining traction. In the North, in addition to the efforts of the United Nations, we can witness degrowth and reclaiming-the-commons initiatives as well as interreligious dialogue. We can read about Rob Hopkins's Transition Town Initiative (TTI, UK), the Great Transition Initiative (GTI, Tellus Institute, US), Joanna Macy's Great Turning, Thomas Berry's "Great Work or transition to an Ecozoic era," and Tony Fry's "transition from The Enlightenment to an age of Sustainment." In the South, we can find various postdevelopment and alternatives-to-development movements, "communal logics and autonomía," efforts toward food sovereignty, transitions to postextractivism, and the Buen Vivir movement. That movement is explained as follows by indigenist Bolivian activist Gustavo Soto Santiesteban, for whom *buen vivir* is aimed

at making visible and expressible aspects of reality that are ignored by the dominant paradigm. It is a proposal from a radical and spiritual perspective of ecology, and is logically incompatible with development and industrialization. . . . It is a community practice that finds organizational expression in the . . . rural agricultural space where reciprocity predominates. It is evident that these enunciations are made from the commons, from the community, from the first-person plural, and not from "me," from the individual. Strictly speaking, the "individual" without community is bereft, orphaned, incomplete. (cited in A. Weber 2019:118–19)

All of these movements testify to a growing awareness of the plight of the ecosphere, and of the consequences of industrial farming on the well-being of all the multiple species living in and on the soil. The "resistance to the present" that is growing among terrans can be witnessed in their understanding of culture as the cultivation of the earth (*cultivars*). The first

34 | Grounding God

successful lawsuit against the carcinogenic properties of Monsanto pesticides and fertilizers in October 2018 has raised public awareness about the health hazards involved. Nine thousand more lawsuits are now in progress. Just as soil erosion due to pesticides, herbicides, and soil fertilizers is reaching monumental proportions, we seem to be coming to terms with what we are losing and learning a new appreciation for the living earth and the essential role played by frogs and bees, by worms, nematodes, and microbes.

Such a new awareness can be witnessed in many new publications about what philosopher Maria Puig della Bellacasa has called the "foodwebs" and "multispecies world" (2017:172) of the earth. Books intended for the general public are being published about ecological problems linked to the extinction of frog species (Souder 2000; Stuart et al. 2008) and of many migrating bird species (Van Dooren 2014) about the webs of fungus that allow tree roots to communicate and share resources (Wohlleben 2016), about journeying into the subterranean world of water bears, microscopic bacteria, mole rats, and burrowing owls (Wolfe 2002), and so much more. The world beneath our feet is suddenly coming alive, and we are becoming aware of "the work that plants do" (Ernwein, Gin, and Palmer 2021), and that "treating the soil like dirt" might be a "fatal mistake" (Monbiot 2014).

If Westerners attribute personhood to their domestic animals, they must learn to attribute personhood to other living organisms as well. Because many moderns lack phenomenological evidence of consciousness and agency in other animals because of their isolation from natural ecosystems, they may require scientific confirmation of the animist recognition of other animals as intentional, purposive agents. Such evidence is now readily available. Developments in ethology, cognitive science, and behavioral psychology demonstrate the intelligence, tool use, consciousness, and self-consciousness of many other animals (de Waal; Bekoff; Korsgaard; Oliver; Corbey; Godfrey-Smith; Coppens; Narby). Studies have been published showing consciousness (Edelman, Baars, and Seth 2005) and "core emotions" (Panksepp 2005) to be intrinsic to all mammals equipped with a thalamo-cortico complex; and recognizing amniotes and octopi as capable of simulation and expecting consequences has enlarged the scope of conscious beings from mammals to all amniotes (Cabanac, Cabanac, and Parent 2009) and cephalopods (Merker 2005; Edelman, Baars, and Seth 2005; Edelman and Seth 2009).

Similarly, a plethora of books on plant intelligence are now widely available (Marder, Coccia, de Kroon, Dudley, Bais, Wohlleben, Biedrzycki, Hall, Karban, Halle), in books with titles such as *Plants as Persons, Plant Thinking, The Revolutionary Genius of Plants, The Language of Plants, The*

Imagination of Plants, The Hidden Life of Trees, How Forests Think, all of which point to the 'repression of the living' typical of Western philosophy and science (Coccia, 2018:24). This moral inclusion of plants was confirmed by the Federal Ethics Committee on Non-Human Biotechnology (ECNH), when it published a scientific study in 2008 ascertaining that humans do not have 'unrestricted power over plants. We may not use them just as we please' not only because 'we may influence or even destroy other players of the natural world, and so alter their relationships' but also because 'individual plants have an inherent worth.'[25]

Though Western culture is still locked inside an identity myth founded in intrinsic essential qualities, much science has gone into undermining such a view and showing, whether in physics (Einstein, Prigogine, Bohm, McDaniel, Jeans, Sherrington, Wright, Rensch, Walker, Cochran, Bohm, Dyson, Rohm, Hameroff), biology (Margulis, Midgley, Clarke, Kauffman, Agar, de Quincey), or politics (Sandel, Walzer, MacIntyre, Taylor), that humans and all other life-forms are relational, their identities dependent upon the many agencies external and internal to them. If most Westerners live in metropolises, and virtual worlds that alienate them from the ecosystems that sustain them, the importance of locality is the subject of a good deal of recent research, and many local movements are organizing themselves to defend the habitus and local solidarity over and against international corporations and states that seek shareholder or national profits over democratic cooperation and ecological renewal. Indeed, indigenous sustainability methods for biodiversity preservation have been introduced and discussed by the Intergovernmental Panel on Climate Change (IPCC) as well as Assessment Reports and the Convention on Biological Diversity (CBD) (see Mazzochi 2020:3). Many scholars have also been seeking to include Traditional Ecological Knowledge (TEK) in their academic research and promote indigenous sustainable practices such as traditional burning techniques, rotation of hunting areas, shifting cultivation, and terrace farming (see, for instance, Pierotti and Wildcat 2000; Mazzochi 2020; McGregor 2004; E. Salmon 2000; Haila 2000; Sundberg 2014; Cajete 2000; Waters 2018).

Books on agroecology and permaculture are selling out, organic food has gone mainstream, Slow Food has spread from Italy to the rest of the world, and some young people in the industrialized world are leaving "bullshit jobs" (Graeber 2018) in the cities to return to the land (D'Allens and Leclerc 2016). Many peasant movements have been forming and gaining support, from the Indian People's Movement, the Alliance for Tribal Self-Rule, and the Navadaniya Seed Movement in the Adivasi region of India

36 | Grounding God

to the PRATEC in the Andes and the Zapatista Army of National Liberation (EZLN) in Chiapas. Seeking to protect their lands from toxification and state-driven export expropriation, these movements follow EZLN in calling for common landholdings, control over the means of production, and self-governing councils (Parajuli 2001:575–76). Authors such as Paul Hawken have gone so far as to define these many movements as the "largest social movement in history" (2007). Often such practices are perceived as backward by moderns because they invoke and integrate pre-technoscientific farming practices from indigenous communities. Yet, as noted by soil scientist Desiraju Rao: "The ancient wisdom and indigenous technical knowledge about benefits of manuring, reduced tillage, conservation farming and other practices abandoned somewhere on the way, need to be relearnt" (cited in Bellacasa 2017:116).

Such relearning is indeed becoming mainstream in engineering and design departments where biomimicry is all the rage, and even the USDA has recommended indigenous techniques (Bellacasa 2017:212). According to Bellacasa, such borrowings should not be interpreted as idealistic nostalgia but rather as "innovative in the present situation" (212), a situation that "requires humans to reconfigure themselves, from soil consumers into soil community members" (213). If climate change and resource depletion are forcing Western culture to see what it has ignored for several hundred years, the West will need to relearn reciprocal relations with soil communities and to understand the earth as what chemist James Lovelock has called Gaia, and indigenous communities Pachamama, a living and interdependent planet. Only such a return to the soil can allow us all, indigenists and moderns alike, to live well.

Indeed, now that the climate crisis has brought ecological concerns to center stage, the extraordinary ecoliteracy of indigenous communities has led ethnologist Thomas Karl Alberts to speak of an "indigenist-environmentalist alliance" (2015:131).[26] If "land is synonymous with the very life of indigenous populations," according to the 1,500-page UN study of indigenous peoples from thirty-five different communities compiled by José Martinez Cobo (UNCHR 1983b: paras. 50, 56, 73, 196–97, cited in Alberts 2015:102–3, 205), the destruction of their homelands by mining and logging corporations has led them to organize to protect their own lands, but also to fight more generally against climate change and environmental destruction. In speaking at the First Congress of South American Indian Movements in Cuzco in 1980, Julio Carduño, a Mexican Indian leader, made this struggle quite clear: "Perhaps what most unites us is the defense of our land. The land has never been merchandise for us, as it is with capitalism, but it is the support for our cultural universe. . . . There can be no economic interest superior to the necessity of preserving the ecosystem; we do not want a bonanza today at the cost of a desolate future" (cited in Bodley 2014:192). Similarly, Yanomami Shaman Davi Kopenawa, known as "the Dalaï Lama of the rainforest," was asked to address the UN in 1992, where he told moderns:

> Stop the destruction, stop taking minerals from under the ground, and stop building roads through forests. Our word is to protect nature, the wind, the mountains, the forest, the animals, and this is what we want to teach you. The leaders of the rich, industrialized world think that they are the owners of the world. But the shaboris (Shamans) are the ones that have true knowledge. They are the real First World. And if their knowledge is destroyed, then the white people too will die. It will be the end of the world. This is what we want to avoid. (cited in Alberts, 2015:154)

Such indigenous struggles for ecological sustainability led to fourteen indigenous organizations and twenty-four NGOs signing the Indigenous and Environmentalist Alliance for an Amazon for Humanity in 1980, and subsequently forming the Alliance for the Environment, a network of organizations struggling to protect all the living beings of the Amazon basin (Alberts 2015:151–52). More recently, the Tebtebba Organisation in the Philippines, as well as Indigenous Partnership on Climate Change and Forests, and Indigenous Peoples Global Network on Climate Change and Sustainable Development (IPCCSD), are among the largest ecological organizations in the world, operating in sixteen countries.

As the modern system continues to collapse, these local movements will gain strength, these Adivasis' voices will be heard, and we will need to reconfigure a "we" instead of a "me." As Mary-Jane Rubenstein puts it, "It must be possible, in other words, to find ways of world-making in an unworlded world" (2018:133). Perhaps we will learn from the indigenous how to survive the apocalypse, and how to reconfigure history without progress. Perhaps we may learn from the survivors how to create the conditions for a good apocalypse after all.

Part I

Religious Responses to the Anthropocene

Chapter Two

Christian Responses to the Anthropocene

Because Genesis 1:28 does indeed tell human beings to "subdue the earth" and "have dominion" over "every living thing that moveth upon the earth," monotheistic religions have often been understood as complicit in the human exceptionalism that is thought to have created the conditions for the Anthropocene. Such a view was most clearly exposed in Lynn White Jr.'s infamous 1967 article "The Historical Roots of our Ecologic Crisis." In this article, White highlighted the anthropocentrism intrinsic to the biblical justification for the spoliation of nature. Though other species, such as the coral polyp, also profoundly modify their habitat, our present combustion of fossil fuels, population explosion, planless urbanism, and problems of sewage and garbage led White to claim that "surely no creature other than man has ever managed to foul its nest in such short order" (1967:497). Looking at the ideological presuppositions of our modern techno-scientific world, White sought to show that the technological dominance of the Western world could be traced back to medieval Catholic dogma that had justified the actions of these early moderns. As he put it: "No item in the physical creation had any purpose save to serve man's purposes. And, although man's body is made of clay, he is not simply part of nature: he is made in God's image" (502). Sharing God's transcendence of nature, the human being exploits nature for his proper ends. Whereas the pagan world was animistic, which meant that trees and streams had guardian spirits that had to be consulted before chopping a tree or poisoning a river, "by destroying pagan animism, Christianity made it possible to exploit nature in a mood of indifference to the feelings of natural objects. . . . Despite Darwin, we are not, in our hearts, part of the natural process. We are superior to nature, contemptuous

41

42 | Grounding God

of it, willing to use it for our slightest whim. . . . Hence we shall continue to have worsening ecologic crisis until we reject the Christian axiom that nature has no reason for existence save to serve man" (1967:502–5).

Though in White's view Christianity bears "a huge burden of guilt" (1967:504), he firmly believed that science and technology are not enough to solve the ecological crisis, and that religion is necessary. Though he notes that other religions are more ecological, such as Buddhism, he seemed to think that the West needed to build upon its own foundation, calling for us to "rethink our old one" (506). Calling for humility instead of hubris, he turned to Saint Francis of Assisi as the patron saint for ecologists. Celebrating a form of panpsychism wherein all animals are equally God's creatures, Professor White advocated a revolution from within Christianity in the hope that Saint Francis's example could overcome Christianity's anthropocentrism and provide an adequate ecological response.

Though he never directly references Lynn White's article, Pope Francis's 2015 *Laudato si'* encyclical can be read as a response to White's influential essay in that he seeks to enact just such an internal revolution in order to rehabilitate the ecological contribution of the Christian tradition. Though Pope Francis admits that Christians have sometimes erred in their scriptural interpretations, the sanctioned interpretation of Scripture should focus not on dominion over nature but on stewardship of it (Gen. 2:15), where "to steward" should be reinterpreted not as control but rather "to protect, care for, preserve, conserve, watch over. This implies a relationship of reciprocal responsibility between human beings and nature" (2015:77). And Pope Francis follows White in turning to his namesake Saint Francis for inspiration and direction. Though many of Francis's followers were burned at the stake by the Church as heretics, and Francis himself escaped heresy only because of his immense popularity, Pope Francis firmly places the contemporary Church behind his eponym, focusing particularly on the fact that for Saint Francis, the care for nature, justice for the poor, social effort, and inner peace were all inseparable (34).[1] In this sense, ecological decline and human and ethical decline are, he claims, "intimately connected" (68). Pope Francis reminds us that the austerity and poverty of Saint Francis were a means of rejecting a worldview that transforms reality into an object of use and domination (35). He asks us to be wary of allowing technology, tied to financial gain, to provide the unique solution to the ecological disaster, because such a response is not capable of "seeing the mystery of the multiple relations that exist between all things, and thus, in trying to resolve one problem, creates others" (43).[2] Instead of one-sided approaches that ignore

Christian Responses to the Anthropocene | 43

the interconnectedness of reality, Pope Francis asks us to seek a productive dialogue between science and religion, in order to pursue a solution that is both scientific and moral, material and at the same time spiritual (73).

Though there is much to praise in Pope Francis's encyclical, and one may hope that it will have a profound influence on reforming the Catholic tradition, he nonetheless retains the human exceptionalism inherent in humanism and warns against pantheisms that divinize the earth, which he claims lead to an "asphyxiating closure within immanence" (2015:117).[3] He thus remains clearly apologetic. According to this apologetic approach, the Christian tradition has always provided an adequate response to the environmental crisis, and there is thus no need for radical revision and transformation.

The Orthodox tradition as well remains apologetic, though there are leaders who have gone far in placing the environment at the center of Orthodox faith. Metropolitan John of Pergamon has attempted to develop a religious ethos that might existentially affect humans more deeply than fear and utility. He writes: "We must be ready to propose not simply an ethic but an ethos, and to root our ethical demands deep in human existence and not simply in human behaviour. . . . What kind of existential reasons suggest or necessitate an environmental ethic?"[4] And Ecumenical Patriarch Bartholomew has also dedicated much effort to aligning the Orthodox Church with ecological renewal. He has organized many environmental journeys to raise awareness, highlighted the sacramental and hence material nature of the creator's relationship to the created, and has explicitly defined environmental degradation as a sin. For example, in his homily in Saint Barbara's Church in Santa Barbara, California, in November 1997, he stated:

> It follows that to commit a crime against the natural world is a sin. For human beings to cause species to become extinct and to destroy the biological diversity of God's creation; for human beings to degrade the integrity of the earth by causing changes in its climate, by stripping the earth of its natural forests, or by destroying its wetlands; for human beings to injure other human beings with disease; for human beings to contaminate the earth's waters, its land, its air, and its life, with poisonous substances—all of these are sins.[5]

But theologian John F. Haught is not alone in thinking that boasting of Saint Francis or making ecological degradation a sin is not enough to

44 | Grounding God

make Christianity ecologically attractive. For Haught, such an approach does not go far enough "in opening Christian faith to the radical renewal the ecological crisis seems to demand" (2004:235).[6] Asserting that Christianity "has been at best ambiguous" (233), he cites Saints Martin and John of Ephesus, who called for and abetted deforestation, and points to the widespread Christian desire to escape from nature so as to reach the transcendent realm of God. When we read, for example, the common Declaration that Pope John Paul II and Ecumenical Patriarch Bartholomew wrote together, we can clearly discern both a strict human exceptionalism: "At the center of the whole of creation, he placed us human beings, with our inalienable human dignity," as well as an antiscientific statement that "the original harmony of creation" was destroyed at the creation of the world because of human sin. But perhaps most worrisome for many scholars is God's mandate to human beings "to be stewards called to collaborate with God in watching over creation."[7] Though many scholars of all disciplines continue to defend this anthropocentric line, calling for humans to be better stewards over the natural world, Haught is not alone in taking issue not only with human domination over nature but also with the biblical call for stewardship reiterated by the Pope and the Ecumenical Patriarch. Haught writes:

> Stewardship, even when it is exegetically purged of the distortions to which the notion has been subjected, is still too managerial a concept to support the kind of ecological ethic we need today. Most ecologists would argue that the earth's life systems were a lot better off before we humans came along to manage them. . . . So even if we nuance the notions of stewardship and dominion in the light of recent scholarship, the biblical tradition is still too anthropocentric. (239)

Environmental scientist James Lovelock concurs with this view, emphasizing the hubris involved in such a Christian conception: "Our religions have not yet given us the rules and guidance for our relationship with Gaia. The humanist concept of sustainable development and the Christian concept of stewardship are flawed by unconscious hubris. We have neither the knowledge nor the capacity to achieve them. We are no more qualified to be the stewards or developers of the Earth than are goats to be gardeners" (2006:137). Religious-studies scholar Anna Peterson also points to the dangers of the vertical relationship between the human being and God in making it difficult to recognize the embodied nature of our interbeing on the earth with other species. When tied to our exclusive ownership of a soul as opposed to other animals, she holds that such doctrines are not in harmony with ecological concerns:

> In any of these interpretations of Genesis 1, it is clear that the assertion of humanity's uniqueness—its creation in the image of God—is inextricably tied to human power over the earth and other animals. The soul that all other animals lack both defines humans and gives them transcendent value. . . . This means, crucially, that humanity's real home does not lie among the rest of creation but rather with God in heaven. It also means that humans' most important relationship is the vertical stretch to the divine rather than—or at least before—horizontal ties to other people or creatures. Thus humanity is defined first and foremost not by relations among persons, by physical embodiedness, or by embeddedness in the natural world, but by an invisible tie to an invisible God. (2000:240)

Similarly, theologian Anne Primavesi points to the patriarchal and violent traits intrinsic to the Christian tradition that make it difficult to reach an understanding of the interdependent ecosystem from its premises:

> Both implicitly and explicitly it has ignored and even promoted the violent character of our interactions with the more-than-human community and their effects on our shared environment. When made aware of it, all too often it has sanctioned an increase of that violence: in the name of an omnipotent, punitive God invoked on behalf of our self-interest alone. Exploitation of land and animal resources for financial gain has been formally and consistently blessed by Christian ministers throughout western Christendom and in its colonialist expansion across the world. (2010:87–88)[8]

Because awareness of what she calls "violence-of-God traditions" is a prerequisite for any attempt to remedy such negative religious impact on the planet, such traditions must be acknowledged by all Christians in order to reenvision "our religious narratives within the larger context of earth's history. Discarding our theological partiality (in every sense) means giving up a view of ourselves as specially created and blessed by God, with its implication

46 | Grounding God

that we are outside general evolutionary processes and the constraints of ecological principles. Furthermore, we must learn to discard the idea that we are destined to enjoy a life with God in some distant heavenly world rather than the earthly one we now inhabit" (Primavesi 2009:34).

Because it retains anthropocentrism, which is considered one of the chief causes of our environmental crisis, and treats the management of the natural world as a God-given human responsibility, much apologetic Christian theology has been replaced by what Haught calls the sacramental approach, which places the emphasis on the sacred quality of the universe rather than on religious textuality and stewardship. The sacramental approach interprets the natural world as the primary symbolic disclosure of God, and of the continuity of humans with the rest of the natural world (2004:235). Overcoming sin means overcoming our alienation from the cosmos. The mystery of God is revealed in the evolution of matter. According to such a view, the natural world is itself the expression of divinity, and is thus godly, in and of itself, and has no need for human stewardship.

Defrocked Dominican priest Matthew Fox takes this sacramental approach in his attempt to provide a "liberation theology" for first-world peoples. In his book *Creation Spirituality: Liberating Gifts for the Peoples of the Earth*, he claims that his liberation theology provides a necessary bridge between science and religion (1991:15) by adding a sense of awe to the scientific creation story. Such a sense of awe is intended to enact a metanoia, a conversion to responding differently to creation and overcoming the alienation that accompanies a human-centered world. Fox thus goes beyond the bounds of Catholic dogma in order to overcome the anthropocentrism intrinsic to its placing of the human being in an exclusive relationship with God, to the exclusion of other beings. A panentheist, Fox agrees with German mystic Mechtild of Magdeburg that "all things (are) in God and God in all things" (41). Such an interpretation allows for an interpretation of Christianity that focuses on mutuality and interdependence rather than a scale of values with the human being at the top. In Fox's own words: "Panentheism is not only democratic, it is also ecological. Theism, on the other hand, reinforces anthropocentrism because it puts the human at the top of the ladder in an exclusive relationship with divinity. . . . Panentheism renders our relationships with other species more mutual, reminding us that we are all beautiful, all interdependent, all necessary in a single web of life" (105).

In a similar sacramental move, religious-studies scholar Mark Wallace has defended Christian animism in his recent book *When God Was a Bird:*

Christianity, Animism, and the Re-Enchantment of the World. Attempting to defend Christianity from Lynn White's attack, Wallace maintains that White's critique is "inattentive to historical complexity and contemporary nuance." Though the Christian triumph over animism did involve the desacralization of nature, and the "axe-wielding saint" is part of Christian history, for Wallace "this trope only tells one side of the story" (2018:42). Telling the other side of the story would entail drawing attention to the immanence of Jesus Christ as man and the Holy Spirit as a bird, what Wallace calls "living enfleshments of divinity in the world" (3). If the Holy Spirit was a Bird-God in early Christianity, such an incarnation "opens up the possibility that all things today are filled with God and thereby deserving of our reverence and care" (32). Such "enfleshments" are what he calls "sublations" of animism, which preserve "animism's reverence for sacred nature within the horizon of its own incarnational belief system" (42).[9] Though responses such as that of Fox and Wallace could go far toward adapting Christianity to the Anthropocene Age by transforming the nature–culture divide into a symbiotic and interdependent relationality, to the extent that Fox and other panentheists have been defrocked and Wallace pushed to the periphery of his own religious tradition, their work may lack the moral authority, institutional resources, and collective action that religious traditions wield (Veldman, Szasz, and Haluza-DeLay 2014a:309) and thus limit the reach of such transformations.

Christianity and Twenty-First-Century Science

In his book *Reinventing the Sacred*, Stuart Kauffman, professor of biocomplexity and informatics specialized in emergence theory, agrees with Matthew Fox's Catholic celebration of scientific creation, but claims that scientific reductionism is unable to correctly interpret evolutionary emergence and must thus be abandoned. By "breaking the Galilean spell" (2010:xi) that everything can be explained by unchanging natural laws, Kauffman sets out to show that the biosphere as well as human history cannot be fully described by means of such laws. If reductionism holds that all of reality, from organisms to couples in love, are nothing but particles in motion, such a theory cannot explain evolution, precisely because evolution emerges. This means that you cannot get the biosphere from physics. Nor can particle physics explain the ontological relevance of things like hearts, trees, or possums, human culture, consciousness, or agency, since these entities are all emergent.

48 | Grounding God

What replaces such unchanging laws for Kauffman is "partial lawlessness," a radical creativity that can neither be predicted nor controlled. In Kauffman's view, the nonergodic structure of life reveals the infinite creative potential of evolution as an emergent phenomenon.

The reductionist worldview that remains normative in science claims that everything can be reduced to particles in motion, and thus that human agency, meaning, and values are all illusions since they are not part of the natural world. A religious worldview that finds this troublesome can claim that these values and meaning exist in a supernatural or metaphysical world, which is thus separated from the natural world of science. Rather than accepting such a science–religion divide, Kauffman seeks to show that human agency can be traced back to what he calls "minimal molecular autonomous agency" at the origin of life itself, in order to demonstrate that action, meaning, and value are emergent realities in the universe and can be explained without recourse to a transcendent reality. Not only are we clearly not the only animals with agency, but agency goes all the way down for Kauffman, for he attributes it to bacteria as well. Values enter life, he claims, when bacteria swim up the glucose gradient, since their lives depend upon them choosing to do so. Meaning, purpose, and agency thus extend at least as far down as bacteria. "With agency, with the bacterium swimming up the glucose gradient, values enter. . . . Values, meaning, doing, action, and 'ought' are real parts of the furniture of the universe" (2010:87).

Once he has explained how agency and thus values are intrinsic to all of life, the very unpredictability of emergence highlights the creative process at work in cosmic evolution. And it is here, in this intrinsic creativity, that Kauffman locates the sacred. Rather than negating past religions, he chooses to usurp and transform them in accordance with an understanding of the creative universe. Because life arises naturally from nonlife according to molecular self-reproduction in collective autocatalytic sets that arise spontaneously in complex chemical-reaction networks, Kaufman claims that "a transcendent creator God loses its force" (2010:45). He writes: "Life has emerged in the universe without requiring special intervention from a Creator God. Should that fact lessen our wonder at the emergence and evolution of life and the evolution of the biosphere? No. Since we hold life to be sacred, we are stepping towards the reinvention of the sacred as the creativity in nature" (2010). And thus he uses the "God" word in order "to honorably steal its aura to authorize the sacredness of the creativity in nature" (44–45). Though he holds that God and the gods are human inventions, such inventions are no less miraculous for Kauffman and no less sacred.[10] "Our view of God is that God is our chosen name for the ceaseless creativity in the natural universe, biosphere, and human cultures" (xi). By reinventing religion in this way, Kauffman seeks to overcome four "injuries" that harm the modern world:

- the artificial division between science and the humanities. (7)

- the reductionistic scientific worldview.

- agnostic and secular humanists have been quietly taught that spirituality is foolish, or, at best, questionable.

- all of us, whether we are secular or of faith, lack a global ethic. (8)

The global ethic that inheres in Kauffman's understanding of the creative universe does not depend upon faith or belief, for it is grounded in the actual unfolding of evolution. And thus, as he puts it, "this God is real. The split between reason and faith is healed. The split between reason and the rest of our humanity is healed" (288).

Though she does not mention Kauffman's work, Nancy Ellen Abrams develops a very similar theory in her book *A God That Could Be Real: Spirituality, Science, and the Future of Our Planet.* She agrees with Kauffman that God is a human invention, and she follows Kauffman in identifying such a God with creativity, in her case with our ability to have aspirations that drive history and human potential forward. Just as we saw in Kauffman's theory, for Abrams as well human beings and God are emergent phenomena and thus bring unpredictable new realities into being. Such a God is important for Abrams precisely because it allows us to cultivate meaningful motivations in order to work together to create an ecologically sustainable and shared world.

To abet such a sustainable world, Abrams believes that Christianity must evolve in light of scientific advancements. The "where" of a transcendent God makes no sense in light of an expanding universe, and yet religious leaders regularly ignore the scientific understanding of our cosmos in order to retain theological beliefs that contradict such understanding. "We have no believable big picture of how we and our God fit into the cosmos. The unconscious need to compensate for this loss of meaning may be what propels so many people today into dogma, denial, or distractions. But it doesn't have to be this way. For the first time we know enough that we can

50 | Grounding God

rediscover the sense of integrity and coherence with our universe and our God—if we have the courage to think in a new way" (2015:3–4). Because religious ideas evolve and are transformed over time, it is crucial that we seek alternatives in line with our scientific understanding, instead of living in denial or with two contradictory worldviews. Abrams claims that the problems arise when we move from an inevitable unconscious evolution to conscious evolution, with many religions punishing those who seek consciously to transform their traditions. "So it seems that the *unconscious* evolution of ideas about God is inevitable, but to evolve god *consciously* is frightening and unacceptable. This has to change. There is nothing to fear" (19). Science has already proved untrue many dogmatic religious beliefs, and these beliefs must be relinquished in order to live in a comprehensive world with a God that could be scientifically real. "Since all major religions were developed in prescientific times, their origin stories and pictures of physical, biological, and social reality reflect the thinking of those earlier times. The modern scientific picture can be to these religions as Einstein has been to Newton—that is, a later and better-supported theory that helps define the walls of the religion's truth box" (123).

The ideas that cannot be supported by science and must be rejected are the following five: the idea that God existed before the universe; that God created the universe; that God knows everything; that God plans what happens; and that God can violate the laws of nature (2015:23). Because complexity evolves from simple states, it is scientifically impossible that an intelligence such as that imputed to God could have existed to design the world before evolution began (24). And such a God could not have set the universe in motion using evolution, since evolution does not function by means of intentions at all. Evolution is unpredictable because it depends on random mutations interacting with a constantly changing environment (27). For this reason, we cannot use intentionality to understand the planet. Random mutation and adaptation have no plan and no destiny (122). Furthermore, attributing to God an omniscient and perfect mind, similar to our own, is to "embalm God like a mummy in the tight wrappings of our own self-image" (28). And such a God cannot exist outside the universe, because there is no outside the universe. Within the universe, all existence must obey the laws of nature, God included, and it is thus false to believe that God can change such laws.

Once we take science seriously, Abrams believes that we can finally address the ecological needs of the planet both scientifically and religiously. The "planetary moral principles" that could ensue "should not tell us what

Christian Responses to the Anthropocene | 51

to do but suggest *how to envision and what to cultivate*" (2015:141). Rather than clinging to a God that "forces us to think in primitive ways" (149), we are asked to "let God be real," an intrinsic part of the real universe. For Abrams such an evolved religiosity could help us to "experience, cherish and protect our special place on this planet" (147) and develop an understanding of God worthy of our hopes and dreams for a sustainable future. "God emerges from our aspirations, so embrace aspirations worthy of the kind of God you want" (142).

Toward a Second Axial Age

These attempts to transform monotheistic foundations into twenty-first-century religions in line with science and ecology are one means to give religion a central place in the ecological struggle to improve the human environmental footprint. Yet for many scholars and religious activists fighting for ecological awareness, adopting an evolutionary, scientific, and ecological perspective can come only at the price of sacrificing transcendental monotheistic beliefs altogether. Instead of transcendent deities and life after death, such activists tend toward pantheism and panentheism, asking that we infuse nature with the sacred instead of isolating the sacred in a distant transcendent realm, often opposed to the sinful world of material nature below. Morris Berman, for instance, calls for the "reenchantment of the world" by rendering science more holistic and asserts that such a task is the "great project, and the great drama of the twentieth century" (1989:186). Bron Taylor has called for a "sensory post-Darwinian religion" (2010:222), one that is both rational and socially powerful, capable of developing innovative responses to Darwinian evolution that include what he calls "dark green religion" (x). Such a "dark green religion" often takes the form of Gaian and indigenous spiritualities that tend to be nonsupernatural and nontheistic, in order to celebrate what Dave Foreman calls the blind and nonteleological "flow of life."[11]

Even an understanding of contemporary biology requires leaving behind fundamental aspects of monotheism, since according to Philip Clayton and Elizabeth Singleton, defining the human animal as a "unique soul-substance," a *res cogitans* with an independent identity created in God's image, is an impediment to understanding how the planet functions and must be abandoned if one hopes "to take on board the lessons that contemporary biology is teaching" (2017:148). This is because such views impede an understanding of evolution as a system of processual interbeing, reciprocity, and

52 | Grounding God

interdependency: "Non-Western cultures are millennia ahead of us in this regard: indigenous cultures and lifeways, India's *Advaita Vedanta*, the Jain call to do no harm (*ahimsa*) to any living being, and the wealth of cultures nourished on the Buddhist teachings of Dependent Arising and interbeing. Indeed, the whole dispute between Gaia advocates and their opponents could be reread as a battle between the world view or 'metaphysic' of interbeing and that of independent or substantial being" (149).

Therefore, notwithstanding the apologetic and sacramental attempts to the contrary, for many scholars monotheisms remain mired in anthropocentrism and individualism when compared with other traditions. The sacred evolution that such scholars propound is thus understood as replacing anthropocentrism with biocentrism, a new or transformed religion that is capable of moving beyond the monotheistic idea of stewardship in order to take into consideration the agency and well-being of all of nature. Having adopted such a biocentric approach, environmentalist Paul Watson calls for the development of a philosophy in which "a redwood tree is more sacred than a human-made religious icon, where a species of bird or butterfly is of more value and deserving of more respect than the crown jewels of a nation, and where the survival of a species of cacti or flower is more important than the survival of a monument to human conceit like the pyramids" (2005:178). For John B. Cobb Jr., to cite another example, because monotheisms are focused on the salvation of individuals, they are disconnected from changes in the physical world. For Cobb, if we truly hope to find ecological religiosity, it is to indigenous traditions that we should turn. "A truly ecological consciousness was far more clearly and effectively present in hunting and gathering societies than in our traditions. When we look for religious versions of deep ecology, it is to them that we should turn" (2004a:248).

In light of the ideological setbacks linked to monotheistic religiosity, many ecotheological responses to the Anthropocene Age have been growing among neopagans, pantheists, and animists, and a renewed interest in indigenous ecology and religiosity has brought to the fore non-Western ontologies that are ecocentric instead of anthropocentric. Indeed, if it was indigenous anthropology that allowed us to see that the nature–culture divide was a particular Western invention, we might learn something from indigenous peoples who, instead of separating the world into active subjects and passive objects, attribute subjectivity universally to all entities. Indeed, perhaps such indigenous cultures can help us to develop a new myth or metanarrative to replace what Bronislaw Szerszynski calls the "amythia" that plagues the secular

West. In line with science and with ecology, such a new myth would need to provide a holistic vision of the earth capable of inspiring what he calls a "second axial age" (2017:42). Can nonmonotheistic religious traditions help to inspire such a holistic vision? The next three chapters elucidate the religious traditions of neopaganism, indigenous animism, and Buddhism in order to better understand the contributions they can make toward inspiring such a second axial age.

Chapter Three

A Buddhist Response to the Anthropocene

Fudo

In his article "The Historical Roots of Our Ecologic Crisis," historian Lynn White Jr. (1967) noted that non-Western traditions such as Buddhism were more ecological than Western ones, but he maintained that the West could not simply borrow foreign traditions, and thus proposed choosing ecological leaders like Saint Francis from within the Western Christian tradition itself in order to reform Christianity from within. But if the Western mindset responsible for ecological destruction is itself thought to be to blame, then Western solutions may themselves be tainted by the ideological presuppositions that it is the task of environmental philosophy to question. If metaphysical assumptions intrinsic to the Western paradigm are part of the problem, they cannot be used to find a solution.

For many ecologists and environmental philosophers, the dualisms intrinsic to modernity that separate body from spirit, and nature from culture, must be deconstructed in order to reach an understanding of nature in line with science and an inclusive morality. For many of these scholars, solutions to the environmental crisis depend upon discarding certain core metaphysical assumptions of modernity, such as human exceptionalism, human stewardship of nature, human creation outside of evolutionary processes, humans as exclusive owners of souls to the exclusion of other animals, and belief in a transcendent afterlife. Perhaps the most commonly cited example of such a problematic vision is that of the Cartesian *cogito*, which led Western modernity in the misguided direction of understanding

56 | Grounding God

the human being as an exclusively "mental substance" and thereby separate from its own body and from the environment. Callicott focuses on the modern insistence on intrinsic value, which blinds the West from seeing the relational nature of all that exists (1999:246). Indeed, such an insistence on mental substances considered to be real solely in and of themselves is also incapable of understanding science, since biology has overcome its "selfish gene" pathology and come to share with ecology an understanding of the earth and evolution as deeply symbiotic and interdependent (predator–prey).[1] Quantum physics, biosemiotics, symbiogenetics, and ecology all seem to confirm the relational nature of the cosmos, and thus to justify one of the fundamental metaphysical assumptions of Eastern philosophies.

Because the metaphysical paradigm of most Asian philosophies does not include these dichotomies, nor the human exceptionalism and separation of the human from natural processes, many scholars maintain that such philosophies could provide inspiration and could assist in undermining the presuppositions of modernity and replacing them with ecocentric ones. Philosopher Bruno Latour expresses this well in his book *Politics of Nature*, when he notes that nature as an autonomous entity separate from human existence simply does not exist in a-modern cultures. Studying such cultures can thus provide Westerners with the "detox" that they need in order to finally discern the relationalities that were hidden from view by ideological boundaries. As Latour observes: "Other cultures, precisely because they have never lived in nature, have conserved for us the conceptual institutions, reflexes, and routines that we Westerners need in order to detoxify the idea of nature. . . . These cultures offer us indispensable alternatives to the nature–politics opposition by providing us with ways of grouping associations of humans and nonhumans that utilize a single collective, clearly identified as political" (1999:64, my translation).

Comparative philosophers J. Baird Callicott and Roger Ames assert that Asian traditions can thus provide "an alternative place to stand . . . from which the West can more clearly discern the deeper substrata of its inherited intellectual biases and assumptions," while at the same time providing the "metaphor, simile and symbol" needed to articulate the abstract ideas of contemporary science that contradict the modern paradigm and tend to be in harmony with Eastern philosophical presuppositions.[2] Often-cited examples of this confluence between contemporary science and Eastern ideas can be found in the ideas of interdependence intrinsic to Taoist and Buddhist ideology (the Jewel-net of Indra, *pratītya samutpāda*, the Tao), the attribution of soul or Buddha-hood to all beings, the interspecies relationships intrinsic to the idea of reincarnation, and the Buddhist idea that all things lack inherent existence and are thus constituted through relationality.

Yet using ideas as though they can be extracted from their cultural contexts is problematic. Indeed, it might be deemed a form of cultural appropriation. As comparative philosopher Gerald James Larson points out, ever since colonial hegemony in the eighteenth century, the West has appropriated and commodified "raw materials" from the East. Are "conceptual resources" the last in a long line of disembedded resources the West has exploited from the East? By taking such ideas out of the contexts where they come to life and are put into practice, they become reified as things that can be extracted, mass-produced, commodified, and sold as isolated elements that in no way interfere with the modern status quo of resource depletion, environmental pollution, and capitalist commodification.

Larson notes:

> Since the eighteenth century, European nation-states have been utilizing Asia to supply a variety of resources: spices, tea, cotton, minerals, oil, natural gas, cheap labor, and hosts of other commodities. Now it seems that we are setting out again, only this time we are on the lookout for "conceptual resources." We appear to be using, in other words, an economic metaphor of raw materials. The needed "ideas" for environmental ethics are presumably in short "supply" in our own environment, but we recognize that there is an increasing "demand" for some new intellectual commodities. (1989:269)

Because ideas are always part of a worldview or cultural paradigm, Larson questions the motivation behind extracting ideas from their sociocultural contexts. He calls this the "fallacy of disembedded ideas," in which we reify ideas as though they were simply another commodified product on the market. He asks if we can simply retrieve from the attic and "dust off" "archaic notions such as the 'Tao,' *brahman-ātman,* Allah, God, *dharma,* or whatever" (273) and think that they can somehow remedy our contemporary environmental crisis even though they were developed in different times and different contexts to respond to different problems. The goal of comparative philosophy, then, is not "to offer up non-Western, alternative 'world views' for possible adoption" (277) but to study conceptual frameworks in their own life-worlds and seek to understand how such ideas condition and are conditioned by particular sociopolitical configurations.

One reason given for why Eastern traditions might nonetheless be helpful in developing a cross-cultural metaphysics for the Anthropocene Age is that, though such conceptions are at odds with the metaphysical assumptions of both Christian and modern metaphysics, they seem to correspond quite well with Western science. Quantum physics, biosemiotics, symbiogenetics, and ecology all seem to provide a scientific basis that can be interpreted as confirming many metaphysical assumptions of Eastern philosophies. The point is not then to appropriate such traditions and commodify them such that they can be one more "resource" to exploit and offer cheaply to Western markets (what Ron Purser has aptly called Mcmindfullness). Rather, the point is to appreciate the ways Asian philosophies corroborate rather than contradict science and convey religious and philosophical ways of being in the world that are capable of moving beyond anthropocentrism and espousing a more respectful relationship with the nonhuman world. Philosopher Rolston Holmes III puts it as follows: "Perhaps there is a metaphysics to which the West can be converted, though that seems unlikely. What seems more realistic to expect is that representative Eastern convictions will, in encounter with the West, provoke the West to reassess either its own theory or practice, resulting, for example, in a less anthropocentric framework and in a more sensitive ability to value nature" (1987:174).

This chapter will therefore seek to do two things. First, it will outline some aspects of Buddhist dogma that are ecocentric, namely the idea of interdependence, the attribution of Buddha-hood to all beings, the interspecies relationships intrinsic to the idea of reincarnation, and the Buddhist idea that all things are empty (*śūnyatā*) and thus lack inherent existence and are constituted through relationality. Then, to avoid the problem of appropriation, this chapter will show how such Buddhist ideas can found an environmental ethics that, rather than seeking to abstract itself from place to become commodified and universalized, as modern theories are wont to do, seeks to develop an intrinsic relationship to place, and even to locate subjectivity there. This is the Japanese theory of *fudo,* developed by twentieth-century Buddhist philosopher Tetsuro Watsuji. This theory deconstructs the Western understanding of environment altogether, and is thus able to move beyond the dualistic dilemmas of Western ideology to reenchant our relationship with the natural world and provide a promising response to the Anthropocene Age.

Ecocentric Buddhism

Buddhist ideology[3] seems ideally suited to confirm and give a philosophical foundation to the science of the ecosystem and of ecology more generally. The three most important ideas of Buddhism are dependent origination, impermanence, and the nonexistence (or emptiness) of intrinsic essence. All three are essential to developing an ecological awareness of planetary boundaries and dependencies. If human exceptionalism sees the human as somehow set apart from the world of impermanent transformation of interdependent entities, Buddhism denies that the human being, or any other being, has an intrinsic essence by means of which it can attribute to itself autonomy and an unchanging essence or soul. The repercussions of such a worldview are profound and linked to the fundamental notion of emptiness, which this chapter will set out to clarify.

Buddha experienced what are called the "Four Truths" during his life: that there is suffering, that the cause of suffering is craving (*tṛṣṇā*), that there is a way to end suffering, and that the way to end suffering entails following the Noble Eightfold Path of Buddhist morality.[4] Suffering is caused in Buddhism by misunderstanding reality, by taking it to be something that it is not. This misunderstanding, which is constitutive of conventional reality, involves the superimposition of autonomy, of permanence, and of intrinsic identity onto reality. Believing that the world should be this way creates ignorance and suffering, a constant struggle against accepting reality as it actually is. In order to overcome suffering, the Buddhist must awaken (Buddha, from *Bodhi,* means "the awakened one") to the nature of ultimate reality, which entails understanding that reality is impermanent, interdependent, and empty of intrinsic essence. It is this understanding of conventional reality that constitutes ultimate reality, when the nature of emptiness, in other words, that all selves and things are empty of intrinsic nature, is accepted. Following the ethical rules codified in the Noble Eightfold Path helps one to see conventional reality truly, and thus to see ultimate reality. This entails developing care for the welfare of all living beings (*karuṇā*). This care is the natural outcome of understanding the nature of reality, since realizing the impermanence and the interdependence of all beings means understanding that one's well-being depends upon the well-being of others.

In Buddhism such an inclusive ethical bond is not limited to humans alone. Buddhism adheres to the theory of reincarnation, believing that all beings are continually reborn until they reach nirvana (illumination, the

60 | Grounding God

snuffing out of existence on earth). Because rebirth is conditioned by action (karma), and beings have no intrinsic souls, karmic seeds can return in any bodily form. There is thus a very clear continuity between different animal forms and different forms of consciousness. All humans have been other animals in different lifetimes. Indeed, the Jataka tales that recount the many lives of the Buddha depict the Buddha as a turtle, a parrot, a monkey, and a lion, among other animals. In each lifetime, whether as a turtle or a human being, the Buddha performs a virtue, doing a good deed to help another living being. The Jataka stories thus make clear that all animals, humans included, are capable of virtue, and there is no ontological break between the virtue demonstrated by a lion and that demonstrated by a beggar, a princess, or a sage, other rebirths of the Buddha. In Buddhism each being longs to be born in human form because it is only in human form that nirvana can be reached, owing to the particular characteristics of human self-consciousness. Such a distinction is not used by Buddhists as a form of anthropocentrism that would radically separate human animals from all others, but rather as a responsibility humans have during their human life span, perhaps a chance in one thousand years to reach enlightenment and practice the Noble Eightfold Path. But this human consciousness is not different in kind from other beings but rather in degree, pointing to the continuity of all forms of life. Such an interspecies ontology is far more inclusive than that of Western modernity, founded as it is on an ontological chasm between human and other life forms, which is contradicted by the theory of evolution itself.

The interdependence at the heart of the Buddhist tradition, called "the entirety of Buddhist teaching" by the Dalai Lama (Garfield 2015:25), is often explained in the Mahayana tradition[5] using the example of the Net of Indra, a metaphor for the cosmos described in the Avatamsaka Sutra. In this sutra the cosmos is described as a great net, each knot holding a precious gem. In each gem is reflected not only the entirety of the net but also the unique brilliance of all the other individual gems, reflecting in their turn reflections of all of the reflections, ad infinitum. Thus each individual gem sustains and defines all of the others, in an interdependent web where micro and macro, individual and group, are connected and self-sustaining. Indra's Net is an instantiation of the fundamental Buddhist dogma of "dependent co-origination" (*pratītya samutpāda*). Each entity manifests itself in a particular space-time context in reciprocal interaction with others. In his book on the Prajnaparamita Heart Sutra, Zen monk Thich Nhat Hanh calls this relationality "interbeing." He opens his commentary with the fol-

A Buddhist Response to the Anthropocene | 61

lowing beautiful words: "If you are a poet, you will see clearly that there is a cloud floating in this sheet of paper. Without a cloud, there will be no rain; without rain, the trees cannot grow; and without trees, we cannot make paper. The cloud is essential for the paper to exist. If the cloud is not here, the sheet of paper cannot be here either. So we can say that the cloud and the paper *inter-are*" (1988:3).

The idea of interdependence undermines any idea of intrinsic selfhood that might be construed outside of relationality. Coexistence entails understanding the falsity of all metaphysical absolutes that ignore the transient nature of life on earth, what Joanna Macy calls "interweaving circuits of contingency" (1991:xii). Since one's existence relies entirely on the existence of others in the contingent space-time world one inhabits, the idea of intrinsic essence that is taken for granted in Western modernity makes very little sense. Thus one's identity cannot be construed alone, and the notion of the inherent existence of an enduring, unchanging self is shown to be false. Suffering arises from clinging (*tṛṣṇā*) to entities as though they were, or should be, autonomous and permanent, rather than accepting and celebrating the contingent, transient nature of reality, which allows each subsequent generation of life to develop. Buddhism thus adheres to a process philosophy, where everything is understood to be in movement, in flux, in a dynamic system of causal interactions. Biophysicist Harold Morowitz explains:

> Consider a vortex in a stream of flowing water. The vortex is a structure made of an ever-changing group of water molecules. It does not exist as an entity in the classical Western sense, it exists only because of the flow of water through the stream. If the flow ceases, the vortex disappears. In the same sense, the structures out of which biological entities are made are transient, unstable entities with constantly changing molecules, dependent on a constant flow of energy from food in order to maintain form and structure. This description stands as a scientific statement of the Buddhist notion of the unreality of the individual. (1989:48)

The ego is of course the root of this clinging to permanence. By claiming that there is no intrinsic self (*svabhāva*), no enduring soul, no permanent ego, in light of the continual flux of causes and conditions that is dependent origination (*pratītya samutpāda*), Buddhism interprets emptiness (*śūnyatā*) in terms of its most well-known tenet, that of no self

62 | Grounding God

(*anātman*). Entities are thus "empty" of intrinsic essence, and it is this notion of emptiness that is the central idea of Mahayana Buddhism. In the words of Koji Tanaka, emptiness, *śūnyatā*, means "anything which exists is empty of any essential property that is independent of anything else" (2014:56). If, according to Mahayana philosopher Nagarjuna, the founder of the Madhyamaka school and perhaps the most celebrated philosopher of the Mahayana canon, conventional and ultimate truths are both empty of *svabhāva*, or inherent existence, then we are left with the double negation of the tetralemma; neither A nor B is true, leading some scholars to accuse Nagarjuna of nihilism though he expressly refutes this position in chapter 15 of his *Mūlamadhyamakakārikā*.

> To say "it is" is to grasp for permanence.
> To say "it is not" is to adopt the view of nihilism.
> Therefore a wise person
> Does not say "exists" or "does not exist." (cited in Garfield
> 1995:40)

Rather than nihilism, what Nagarjuna is advocating is to refrain from dividing reality into oppositions. All things exist conventionally, but have no intrinsic inherent existence independent of all of the causes and conditions that brought them into being and keep them in existence for their given life span. It is only when transient beings and things are reified that they are clung to (*tṛṣṇā*) with hopes of unchanging permanence, and it is this that leads to suffering. Conventional truth is determined by language, and taken for granted in daily life. Ultimate truth, on the other hand, is not apprehended by ordinary consciousness, but entails having grasped the emptiness of conventional truth. In other words, the ultimate truth is simply understanding that things are empty of intrinsic inherent existence, and thus exist interdependently, impermanently, just as emptiness itself is empty of inherent essence, and thus is not to be transformed into a transcendental, absolute truth. As the Buddha explained to his disciple Kasyapa:

> It is not (the concept of) emptiness that makes things empty; rather, they are simply empty. It is not (the concept of) the absence of any ultimate cause that makes things lack such a cause, rather, they simply lack an ultimate cause. It is not (the concept of) the absence of an ultimate purpose that makes things

lack an ultimate purpose; rather, they simply lack an ultimate purpose . . . . Because, Kasyapa, emptiness is the exhaustion of all philosophical views. I call incurable whomever holds emptiness as a philosophical view. (cited in Huntington 1989:57–58)

So emptiness is also empty, otherwise one would cling to it as an absolute unchanging truth, an essence standing above conventional truth the way that the word God functions in Christian culture. To avoid such a risk, a famous Zen koan attributed to Lin Chi (866 CE) states: "If you see the Buddha, kill him!" in order to reinforce the danger of reification, and of clinging to absolutes and fetishes.[6] Garfield comments:

> We are driven to reify ourselves, the objects in the world around us, and—in more abstract philosophical moods—theoretical constructs, values and so on, because of an instinctual feeling that without an intrinsically real self, an intrinsically real world, and intrinsically real values, life has no real meaning and is utterly hopeless. Nagarjuna emphasizes . . . that this gets things exactly backward: if we seriously and carefully examine what such a reified world would be like, it would indeed be hopeless. But if instead we treat ourselves, others, and our values as empty, there is hope and a purpose to life. For then, in the context of impermanence and dependence, human action and knowledge make sense, and moral and spiritual progress becomes possible. It is only in the context of *ultimate nonexistence* that *actual existence* makes any sense at all. (1995:317–18)

Tetsuro Watsuji's *Fudo*

Instead of leaving these general foundations of Buddhist philosophy floating in a no-man's-land, ready for appropriation, this last section will show how such ideas can fruitfully provide the foundation for an Asian environmental ethics that avoids the pitfalls of modern dualistic ideology and offers a response to the Anthropocene Age that is in line with both science and ecology. This response is that of twentieth-century Japanese philosopher Tetsuro Watsuji's theory of *fudo*—climate or milieu. In this theory, Watsuji develops the ideas of interdependent origination, impermanence, and most

64 | Grounding God

especially emptiness into one of the most important ethical and environmental theories of the twentieth century, one where place, or milieu, allows the focus to move from the individual to the community or environment, and to the notion of embeddedness as an individuating process.[7] Drawing on Buddhism, Watsuji uses the concept of codependent origination to emphasize what he calls the "betweenness" (*aidagara*), which pertains to people but also to the relationship between people and their planet. Such relationship is made possible because beings are empty of inherent essence, and it is this concept of emptiness that is the key notion in all of Watsuji's works.

Although David Dilworth (1974) argued that Watsuji was not a Buddhist thinker, most scholars are in agreement that Buddhism is central to Watsuji's philosophy (Lafleur 1978; McCarthy 2017; Müller 2009; Mochizuki 2006; D. W. Johnson 2019), even if some scholars find his interpretation of Buddhism in terms of Western phenomenology (especially Husserl and Heidegger) original rather than traditional, and question the extent to which he transforms Buddhism to suit his own needs (Sevilla 2017; Isamu 981; Bein 2017).[8] Fumihiko Sueki, for instance, notes that Watsuji tends to ignore or downplay aspects of Buddhism that are not rational, treating them as nonessential superstition (Sueki 2004). He thus dismisses reincarnation, dharma, and communication with the dead, for instance, though all are central to the ways Buddhism is practiced, leading some practicing Buddhists to critique his reading of Buddhism as "areligious" (Sevilla 2017:244). Indeed, as a philosopher, Watsuji maintains that these ideas were simply adopted by Buddhists from their Hindu milieu, and thus were neither essential nor useful in understanding core Buddhist teachings.[9] His interpretation of these concepts inclines toward what Evan Thompson (2007) has called Buddhist modernism, a tendency to interpret Buddhism as areligious and scientific that many Westerners adopted when Buddhism moved to the West. Although those defending the "insider" position in religious studies assert that Watsuji missed the whole point of Zen Buddhism as a practice for reaching nirvana, the philosophical and historical study of Buddhist ideas is also essential for understanding the role they play in Japanese culture, from cuisine, to architecture, to literature. In this sense, the "outsider" position represented by Watsuji's study of Buddhism is also essential. Müller summarizes Watsuji's position as claiming that "from an intellectual point of view, the plurality of religious creeds obliges reason to favor a kind of secularized religion" (2009:118).

Notwithstanding Watsuji's distance from Buddhist practice, Buddhist ideas were central to his career as a philosopher, and his many published works on Buddhism were highly respected, widely read, and influenced many other Japanese scholars. Though he devoted his early works to Western existentialism (Nietzsche [in 1913], Schopenhauer [his doctoral dissertation, in 1914], and Kierkegaard [in 1915]), Watsuji had a change of heart and turned back to Asian and Japanese ideas, especially those rooted in Buddhism. This change of heart was recorded in his diary in 1917, where he writes of a shift of interest from Western idealism to the Buddhist culture of Japanese antiquity, perhaps prompted by a long trip to Nara that in 1919 inspired his first book about Buddhist temples, *Koji junrei* (*A Pilgrimage to Ancient Temples*) (Müller 2009:114), which was followed by nine subsequent books on Buddhism and Japanese culture whose publications spanned his entire life.[10] This return to Japan, and to the Buddhist ideas that form its conceptual structure, led Lafleur to assert that "Buddhist religious thought in general and the concept of emptiness in particular became the fulcrum for the structure of Watsuji's philosophy" (1978:241).

Watsuji began his academic career in 1925 teaching Buddhist ethics at Kyoto Imperial University, where he worked with Kyoto School philosopher Kitaro Nishida. He published his book on environmental philosophy, *Fudo*,[11] when he became professor at Tokyo University the following year. Though not pertaining explicitly to Buddhism as his ten volumes on Buddhist culture are, the Buddhist ideas of codependent arising, and especially of emptiness, inform his understanding of the environment and form the foundation for an environmental ethics that avoids the pitfalls of modern dualistic theory.[12] For this reason, Anton Sevilla has called Watsuji's ethics an "ethics of emptiness" (2016) in order to highlight the importance of Buddhist *śūnyatā* for his understanding of the human person and the milieu in which she abides. Indeed, emptiness is the idea Watsuji utilizes to explain ethics in his three-tome work of that same title (*Rinrigaku*). There he explains the emptiness of emptiness as enabling the return of the self in terms that have led Sevilla to call Watsuji's theory "Hegelian Buddhism" (2017:271).

Watsuji was inspired to write *Fudo* during 1927, his year abroad in Europe, while studying with Heidegger in Berlin. In his reading of *Sein und Zeit*, he was struck by two things: the individualistic focus of Heidegger's *Dasein*, and the focus on time to the exclusion of space (Watsuji 1961:v–vi). Watsuji notes:

> I found myself intrigued by the attempt to treat the structure
> of man's existence in terms of time but I found it hard to see,
> why time had thus been made to play a part in the structure

66 | Grounding God

> of subjective existence, at the same juncture space also was not postulated as part of the basic structure of existence. Indeed it would be a mistake to allege that space is never taken into account in Heidegger's thinking, . . . yet even so it tended to be almost obscured in the face of the strong glare to which time was exposed. I perceived that herein lay the limitations of Heidegger's work. (1961: preface, 1)

Though Heidegger had already postulated a spatial and social dimension in his being-with-others (*Mitsein*), he often described such a relation in terms of inauthenticity, and does not give it the same centrality in his work as Watsuji accords to relationality (*aidagara*) (this is also the point of view of Jean-Luc Nancy [1990:203] and Habermas [1988:24]). Heidegger's existential analytic of *Dasein* neglects the role of nature in the constitution of Being, what D. W. Johnson calls Heidegger's "near-blindness to the way the places and spaces of the natural world are part of the structure of human existence" (2019:151). Watsuji's *fudo* thus provides an important corrective to the Western focus on temporal ontology to the exclusion of space and place.[13]

Just as Watsuji accorded space the importance that it deserves in a phenomenology of life experience, he also avoided the individualism so typical of modern theory, since living in a milieu is always a shared experience, and others are thus essential to the constitution of individuality. If Watsuji dedicates *Fudo* to elucidating the relation between human experience and the space dimension so as to overcome Heidegger's first prejudice, his work on ethics, *Rinrigaku*, is devoted to overcoming Heidegger's second prejudice by showing that human existence has meaning only outside the scope of individuality. By focusing on being-toward-death, which is always one's own, Heidegger's subject was able to exit solipsism solely at the cost of alienation, the "they" (*das Man*), which Heidegger called inauthentic Being. Yet from the point of view of society as a whole, death is necessary to allow for renewed life, and need not, for a Buddhist, induce anguish and solitude. In this way, Watsuji develops Heidegger's notion of *Mitsein* into a proper interpersonal theory, where constitutive sociality as the very foundation of Being transforms Heidegger's being-in-the-world into a far more compelling being-in-a-milieu-with-others (D. W. Johnson 2019: 81, 123). *Fudo* is a reciprocal and constitutive relation, in which the self cannot be considered outside of its relationality to others.

Fudo is better translated as "milieu" (this is the translation of geographer Augustin Berque) than as "climate" because the Japanese word has connotations quite different from those in English.[14] *Fudo* is not weather in the sense of the study of the interactions of the physical forces present on planet earth. Rather, as Watsuji makes clear: "I use our word Fu-do, which means literally, 'Wind and Earth,' as a general term for the natural environment of a given land, its climate, its weather, the geological and productive nature of the soil, its topographic and scenic features" (1961:1). Unlike the term *climate*, *fudo* indicates a particular environment, and the many ways such particularities of climate, topography, rain, and soil patterns influence the lives of its inhabitants. As the environment that conditions human becoming both individually and socially, "climate is milieu, that which we find ourselves in the middle of" (Janz 2011:175). *fudo* thus refers to how such forces relate to the beings that are affected by them, transformed by them, acculturated by them. Climate, as *fudo*, "matters to someone, or to some species or ecosystem, and if there is no possible way of mattering (for example, with atmospheric phenomena on other, presumably lifeless planets), we do not yet have climate. Climate affords ways of being" (Janz 2011:174). Thus D. W. Johnson gives the example of Antarctica, which has climate but no *fudo*, since there are no human inhabitants who could be influenced by this milieu (2019:18). The human mind and body become what they are only through this acclimatization. As Johnson points out, the development of our palate is linked to the water, the temperature, and the flora and fauna of our milieu. Even the power of the imagination is climatic; Watsuji notes that Santa Claus was not invented in the tropics (Johnson 2019:28). Our emotions as well are influenced by climate, "so that, for example, there come to be a variety of ways in which human beings are brought together through bonds of affection" (28). As Watsuji makes clear, "It is essential to my position that the phenomena of climate are treated as expressions of subjective human existence and not of natural environment. I should like at the outset to register my protest against this confusion" (1961:v). So rather than representing the environment as a set design for the theater of human action, or an objectified nature somehow distant from human culture, *fudo* is implicated in culture and cannot be understood apart from it. Thus, instead of the nature–culture divide of Western modernity, *fudo* allows us to understand both terms as complicated and codependent.[15]

Watsuji calls this ontological experience of nature *fudosei*, stressing that this is the experience of subjectivization, and thus that the human being cannot be understood apart from its milieu. Lafleur uses Berque's translation of *fudosei* as *médiance*, "the sense of acculturated acclimatization" or "acclimatized culture" (Lafleur 1978:217) in order to clarify Watsuji's claim that

68 | Grounding God

"in the dual structure of man—the historical and the climatic—history is climatic history and climate is historical climate" (cited in Lafleur 1978:217). Lafleur explains: "Cultures arise in response to the environments in which they find themselves, and so when human beings engage in self-discovery, they always find themselves in a culture that has already been acclimatized, and a climate that has already been acculturated" (216). One of the major consequences of such a view is a rejection of universals to describe human beings, since human cultures and milieu are unique in their codependent symbiosis. This constitutes a third critique of modern Western ideology's attempts to constantly generalize and universalize being, outside of place as *milieu*. Watsuji critiques such a Western rejection of the earth in no uncertain terms: "Such a thing as the existence of human beings in general does not exist in reality. What was deemed universally human by Europeans, in the past, was outstandingly European-like" (*Rinrigaku*, 26, cited in Couteau 2006:280).

Since, in Watsuji's theory, *fudo* determines the being of the human being, it is an ontological concept. According to Berque, the concept of *fudo* is ontological because the word for "being" in Japanese, *sonzai*, is itself spatial. *Sonzai* originates in the Chinese character *zai*, which Berque translates as "being in a place" or "the place of being" (1996b:60). Similarly, *ningen*, human being, is a combination of *nin* and *gen*, *nin* meaning "human being" and *gen* being an alternative pronunciation of *ma*, meaning in-betweenness, and connoting, according to Berque, a spatial dimension in a house or among things. The human being for Watsuji, and in Japanese culture more generally, is intrinsically relational, a "between" that is constantly seeking its identity in its surrounding world and in the social world of others. So not only, in the words of Berque, "one cannot figure the properly human Being (the being-human, *ningen sonzai*) if not spatially" (60), but such relationality in space undermines the intrinsic autonomy of the individual subject in favor of a relational "we." Jin Baek explains: "Ningen thus brings to the notion of man a balanced perspective of individuality and communality. Further, it is not that the relational dimension of ma between man and man is secondary to his individual dimension; Watsuji saw the linguistic construction as indicating that man is fundamentally inscribed with the dimension of 'we.' In fact, Watsuji went so far as to claim that 'every trace of the notion of independent existence must be voided'" (2010:383).

Just as Watsuji focused on the *ma* or in-betweenness to understand the meaning of *ningen*, so he focused on betweenness (*aidagara*) to understand ethics. Since both *nin* and *gen* are empty of intrinsic existence, they

A Buddhist Response to the Anthropocene | 69

exist only in a dialectical dependence. It is thus only betwixt or between that ethics exists (*aidagara*), rather than in the mind of an autonomous individual. Watsuji writes: "The context of ethical problems is not to be found within the consciousness of the isolated individual, but rather within the mediating space or 'betweenness' that exists between one person and another. . . . Without seeing ethics as the study of this dynamic mediating space, which exists between one person and another, we will not be able to unravel the nature of virtue, responsibility, obligations, and of the good and the bad within human actions."[16]

In his interpretation of Watsuji's *Rinrigaku* (*Ethics*, 1937), Lafleur explains that *nin* and *gen* exist in dialectical tension in Watsuji's philosophy, the human being attempting to affirm itself over and against relationality or "betweenness," while relationality seeks to dissolve the individual human being in a collective "we." Indeed, for Watsuji, *nin* and *gen* exist only in this codependent dialectic relation, and thus each negates the other in order to affirm its own nature. From this seemingly Hegelian conflict emerges *ningen*, as a socialized individual that has negated the other and then negated its own separate existence, in what Watsuji calls a "dialectic of double negation" (Lafleur 1978:219).

For Watsuji, the individual is "emptied" of her nature by society, and society is "emptied" of its nature by the individual, in a continuous movement of negation. In its kenotic justification of codependent origination, such a movement can never reach the stasis of the Hegelian synthesis.[17] "The self-return of the Absolute is realized endlessly, and has nothing to do with a static and absolute destination" (*Rinrigaku*, 1996:121). It also undermines those interpretations that see Watsuji's ethics as a capitulation to communitarianism, since society, or what Watsuji calls totality, is also negated of any independent existence that would override the individual.[18]

> The standpoint of an acting "individual" comes to be established only in some way as a negation of the totality of ningen. An individual who does not imply the meaning of negation, that is, an essentially self-sufficient individual, is nothing but an imaginative construction. . . . [But, similarly,] a totality that does not include the individual negatively is also nothing but a product of the imagination. These two negations constitute the dual character of a human being. . . . The true reality of an individual, as well as of totality, is "emptiness. . . ." (Watsuji 1996:22–23)

70 | Grounding God

We see here a classic example of his use of the Buddhist term for emptiness, *śūnyatā*. The concept of *śūnyatā* is meant to undermine the idea of inherent existence, or self-existent reality (*svabhāva*). We are mistaken when we isolate entities and attribute individual ontological existence to them. Rather, in the Buddhist system, each entity is dependent upon others to be, according to the fundamental idea of codependent origination (*pratītya samutpāda*). In his *Rinrigaku*, Watsuji clarifies: "Man's existence in relationships is an existence which comprises both the individual and society through mutual negation. Therefore, human existence cannot be explained as a situation in which we first have individuals and then the establishment of relationships among them; nor can it be explained as first a society and then the emergence of individuals out of that society. In both of these explanations it is the 'priority' which is the impossibility" (vol. 1, 107, cited in Lafleur 1978:245).

The being of the human being is thus a movement of negation, constantly demonstrating the emptiness of intrinsic essence that is its very foundation. It is for this reason that Lafleur sees emptiness as codependent origination as the central tenet of Watsuji's philosophy, and hence of his critique of Western thought, founded as it is in the ontological autonomy of individual entities. Couteau clarifies the role of negation in the foundation of *fudo* as follows: "Fūdo itself is thus the space of those reciprocal co-determinative interconnections between milieu and human existence that operate in the dynamic of self-negation" (2006:282). Watsuji confirms this reading when he asserts in *Rinrigaku* that "the true reality of an individual, as well as of totality, is 'emptiness,' and this emptiness is the absolute totality" (1996, 23, cited in Sevilla 2016:606–7).[19]

In his book *Fudo*, only the first chapter deals with *fudo* and *fudosei* as general concepts, the following chapters being devoted to *kokumin jikaku*, revealing the climate character of different nations. Watsuji tended to generalize those cultures he was least familiar with, describing the people of the Indian monsoon as typified by passive resignation (1961:19), those of the desert as typified by struggle and an aggressive spirit (57), and the Chinese as typified by a calm lack of emotion (61). His analyses regarding the meadow typology of Europe, and the typhoon typology of Japan, are far more subtle, however. Watsuji was nonetheless accused of geographical determinism, and since he was instrumental in creating imperial ideology during the war, rejecting Western modernity and celebrating Japanese ritual and the cultural specificity of the emperor, his reputation was tarnished after the war and his book gained little recognition.[20] But for Watsuji it is not so much that geography causes individual or state character, but that geography gives rise to particular values. Watsuji's intention was to help his readers move away from the Western focus on individualism by showing that values are always shared, and embedded in a milieu. Both Berque and Johnson have described these critiques as largely misplaced because they misinterpret *fudo* as an environment directly determining a culture, rather than understanding *fudo* as human existence in a milieu (Berque 2010; D. W. Johnson 2019). According to Berque, poor translations of Watsuji's work were often to blame for interpreting *fudo* in a deterministic light, as was the case for him when he read the English version before reading the original Japanese (2010).

Notwithstanding this problematic essentialism and nationalism and his difficulty in accounting for individual responsibility and the plurality of subjects within the same milieu (Mochizuki 2006:53), Watsuji successfully uses *śūnyatā* or emptiness to deconstruct the dualism of Western ideology along with the inherent existence of its subjects. Emptiness can thus provide the important function of opening theory back up to the earth and to other people, and overcoming the Western dualities that separate us from our own bodies, from the earth, and from others. In developing a Buddhist theory of the self that is codependent on its milieu and empty of intrinsic essence, Watsuji successfully undermines the nature–culture divide intrinsic to Western ontology.

Today, when human culture has finally reached the ends of the earth in what has come to be called the Anthropocene Age, this antithesis between nature and culture has lost all credibility. Indeed, *fudo* seems to both foreshadow and explain the concept of the Anthropocene that we have been seeking to come to terms with since atmospheric chemist Paul Crutzen coined the term in the year 2000 (Crutzen and Shwägerl 2011). We are now in a position to trace this dissolution of the nature–culture divide back to Watsuji's philosophy of *fudo,* and to realize that, seventy-five years before its official decree, he had given us an understanding of the world that Westerners are only now being told they must accept as true. Like *fudo,* the Anthropocene concept has undermined modern ontology by showing that nature and culture cannot be separated and that they are coconstructed and interdependent. *Fudosei* thus expresses the very meaning of the Anthropocene. Nature without culture, culture without nature, are empty.

Indeed, by foreshadowing the Anthropocene concept in a Buddhist framework in Japan, before World War II and the Great Acceleration, Watsuji's interpretation sheds light on aspects of the Anthropocene that are often

72 | Grounding God

overlooked in the West and allows us to consider solutions to the climate crisis from a different perspective. If our experience of ourselves and of the earth is threatened by the modern conception of nature that separates us from our milieu and blinds us to the changes such an ecological crisis has imposed on who we are, Watsuji's *fudo*, and the Buddhist ideas that undergird it, can help us to overcome this estrangement. Beneath our objectification of our environment lies the interdependence of all beings and their milieu, which should inspire care (*karuṇā*) for all living beings and for our planetary home (*fudo*). Once we reinhabit our milieu, we can recognize that human value is continuous with its world, and thus that desecrating such a world destroys the value of the human being itself.

D. W. Johnson has called the human estrangement from its milieu "disenchantment," and in both the introduction and conclusion of his book *Watsuji on Nature* he maintains that Watsuji's *fudo* can enable "the reenchantment of nature" (2019:4–5, 205). Johnson's vision of *fudo* as a reenchantment is felicitous, but his understanding of *fudo* as a rejection of science and a nostalgia for the premodern is both erroneous and misleading. For Johnson, it is the scientifically objective understanding of nature that leads scientists to disregard our direct experience of the world, and thus our lives as embedded and experienced through and in a specific milieu. Thus Johnson understands the reenchantment of *fudo* as a return to the past, to what he calls a "premodern conception of experience" (16, 209) that can achieve a "reconciliation with the world," only if we are able to return to the world before the advent of modern science and the objectivist stance. This rather old-fashioned vision does not do justice to the revolutionary nature of *fudo* and its correlation with the Anthropocene Age. *Fudo* appears today not as a nostalgia for the past, but as one of the most prophetic interpretations of the twenty-first century. *Fudo* is postmodern, not premodern, in line with the relationality and interdependence at the heart of Earth System Science, and not opposed to it. *Fudo* gives Earth System Science a philosophical foundation by developing the values that science cannot provide. In conclusion, I will emphasize a few of these values that could ensure the reenchantment of our world and point toward a resolution of the climate crisis.

The self as a sovereign and exclusive ego or soul, cut off from the natural world and encased momentarily in a body, is a dangerous and false understanding of selfhood. *Fudo* reveals human nature to exist only "betwixt" and "between" (*aidagara*), and never in a stagnant intrinsic essence, which does not allow for evolutionary change. If the being of being human is codependent upon its milieu and upon the community of others living in such a milieu, such a milieu must be understood as constitutive of human development and flourishing.

Though Westerners take for granted an absolute dichotomy between nature and culture, *fudo* can help us to "detox" (Latour 1999) from such an erroneous ideology and open our experience to the relational nature of the real. The Anthropocene concept demands this transformation of us, without giving us a strategy to enact such a metamorphosis. *Fudo* is just such a strategy, and the idea of emptiness at its heart is essential in order to reject both the intrinsic self and the autonomous world as obsolete, and embrace nature/cultures for the continuous and interdependent processes that they are.

Because different milieus, specific ecosystems, are unique, they cannot be universalized. We therefore need to reinhabit our milieu so as to deconstruct the homogenizing universals exported by Western nations. Informed by the experience of community, the inhabitants of each milieu must develop a unique response to a unique milieu, choosing the laws necessary to safeguard this specific reciprocal relation.

If nature and culture, subject and object cannot be separated as *fudo* and the Anthropocene concept both imply, this entails a way of experiencing both the subject and the object of cognition as constitutive of human existence. It entails waking our senses to the many ways in which a frightened deer, rain on the windowpane, or a lilac flower constitute our very experience. To use this last example of the flower, Watsuji goes so far as to claim in his *Rinrigaku* that the beauty of the flower is intended for the human gaze: "The *way* that a flower is beautiful is based on human existence; it is not a property of a thing called a 'flower' which is separate from human existence. Rather, in the feeling of a flower's beauty, human beings receive their own existence as coming forth from the origin of this flower" (*Watsuji Tetsurō zenshū, Rinrigaku,* 11, 106, cited in D. W. Johnson 2019:199).

If the flower exists *as* our experience, its beauty constitutes who we are. From a scientific point of view, the flower's perfume, color, and shape are intended for the bee and the bird, and without them, there would be no flower. But the useless beauty of the flower is there for us. The flower exists for the bee and the bird, regardless of human spectators, but its beauty does not. What is required of us to receive the beauty of the flower as intended for our gaze is a certain decentering of subjectivity, in order to include the being of the flower, the rain, and the deer, *in* our experience, *as* our experience.

74 | Grounding God

The Buddha's last teaching, called the Flower Sermon, was given without words. The Buddha, who was teaching near a pond, simply reached into the water and plucked a lotus flower. He simply held up the flower, dripping mud and water to the ground, for all to see. Only disciple Mahakasyapa smiled, and was thereby granted dharma transmission. What did Mahakasyapa see in the lotus flower? Perhaps he recognized the formless form of the flower as a gift, the gift of his own perception. Mahakasyapa's smile is the smile of a painter who has relearned how to see. John Berger comments on this gift that the painter is not a creator but a receiver. "Creation is the act of giving form to what is received" (2001:17–18). If "emptiness is form, and form is emptiness" (the Heart Sutra), giving form to the formless, then, can occur only when our gaze, and the gaze of the flower, meet. There can be no creation, and no beauty, unless we can receive the gaze of the lotus flower.

While such an enlarged subjectivity is typical of Japanese animism (Rambelli 2019), Watsuji's *fudo* transforms this animism into a phenomenological reenchantment available to all of us, insofar as we can recognize the object of cognition as intrinsic to our subjective experience. When we can receive the gaze of the flower, and its gift of beauty, we have reenchanted the world. The world can then demand reciprocal consideration from us. Science is essential in seeing the world from the point of view of the bee, and the bird, and the flower. But without the flower's gift of beauty, and our ability to open our gaze to receive it, human existence will go extinct along with the birds and the bees.

Chapter Four

Neopaganism and the Grounding of the Sacred

Though there is much to praise in Pope Francis's encyclical *Laudato si'* (2015), and one may hope that it will have a profound influence on reforming the Catholic tradition, Pope Francis nonetheless retains the human exceptionalism inherent in humanism and warns against pantheisms that divinize the earth, which he claims lead to an "asphyxiating closure within immanence" (117).[1] After so many attempts in the twentieth and twenty-first centuries to rehabilitate matter, such as "new materialisms," and to understand matter as itself holy, such as the Gaia movement, why does the Pope retain the modern interpretation of immanence as asphyxiating closure? What exactly about immanence might lead one to find it asphyxiating? Typically, Christianity has denigrated the material world by associating it with the Fall, and thereby with sin and mortality, from which a Christian must separate herself in order to reach salvation understood in terms of the transcendent dimension of God and heaven. But the Christian God is flesh and blood, and his humanity belies this transcendental focus, as much recent scholarship has shown (see, for instance, Wallace [2018]; Keller and Rubenstein [2017]). Just as the *Imitatio Christi* is lived in immanence, by applying Christian moral principles to the material conditions of our immanent lives we experience transcendence only as embodied animals here on earth, and a scientific understanding of the world precludes the dualism that pits the soul against the body, and culture against nature. As we come to understand the mind as reliant on the body and brain, and culture as an expression of nature, such dichotomies are no longer tenable, and are today held responsible for much of the climate crisis we are currently facing. So how might we rehabilitate immanence, and find it liberating rather than asphyxiating?

76 | Grounding God

Such a rehabilitation could go far toward redressing the harms the Western tradition has enacted toward women, colonized populations, and animals, all of which were deemed inferior by being associated with embodiment rather than reason. While much research in the fields of brain science, cognitive science, and ethology has shown that reason itself is entirely embodied, we will focus here on the scholarship demonstrating that for many people, the material earth, what we commonly call nature, can itself be considered divine, and thus that the divine does not need to be associated with transcendence. Scholars Carol Christ and Judith Plaskow express this well in their work developing an embodied theology:

> Throughout our book, we have considered the widespread dissatisfaction with the God of traditional theologies who rules the world from outside it. We have suggested that this God no longer answers our questions about the meaning of life and does not provide the guidance we need as we face the urgent social, political, and environmental issues of our time. Traditional ideas about divine transcendence turn us away from this world, which is the place where our lives and decisions matter, while understanding divine power as omnipotence does not adequately explain the evil in the world or the nature of human freedom. In addition, traditional images of God fail to affirm diversity and difference and legitimize domination and oppression. (2016:287–88)

Though much scholarship has attempted to redress the transcendental interpretation of Christianity and point toward its immanent message, this chapter will move beyond the bounds of Christianity to focus on one of the fastest-growing religious groups today, neopaganism. Because its adherents celebrate diversity, neopaganism is notoriously difficult to define. With its adherents estimated to number between eight hundred thousand and one million in the United States alone (Clifton 2006:11; Cowan and Bromley 2015:166–67), neopaganism comprises a bewildering variety of traditions, lineages, and schools of thought. Tending to eschew monotheism because of its patriarchy and its historical intolerance, dogmatism, and violence, neopagans call themselves polytheists, pantheists, panentheists, Mohists, henotheists, animists, goddess-feminists, religious naturalists, Gaians, agnostics, and even atheists, and are happy to practice together notwithstanding these differences (G. Harvey 1994:38). Similarly, they have no single scripture, no dogmatic creed, and no central authority. Neopagans call themselves Witches, Druids or Norse, Heathens, Asatru, Shamans, or Gaians, yet by choosing to place all of these religious traditions under the banner of neopaganism, they all share central attributes. If none of the elements constitutive of monotheistic faiths, neither scripture nor deities, neither creed nor hierarchical authority, can be considered essential to neopagans and their religious practices, what is it that brings these different groups together and makes them all neopagan? What they all share is a veneration for and celebration of the living earth (39), a belief in the immanence of the divine (40; Cowan and Bromley 2015:162), and the conviction that they can interact and communicate with the energies of the universe (162).

Neopagans often trace these three core characteristics back to pre-Christian religious traditions of Europe such as goddess worship, Druid traditions, and northern shamanism, finding in antiquity and indigeneity the pagan ideals that lend their traditions authenticity (Rountree 2016:6). Seeking to retrieve and revalorize the pre-Christian folk traditions of Europe, neopagans often call for cultural revival, sometimes allying themselves with national independence movements (particularly in Iceland, Lithuania, and Ukraine [Roundtree 2012:309]). In light of challenges from hegemonic Christianity, many neopagans feel the need to stress the antiquity of their tradition and to call it "the old religion" so as to gain legitimacy and resist being labeled a new religious movement, since such movements are often considered less serious and respectable than their older, more established counterparts (G. Harvey 2011:172). Their approach to these ancient traditions is not, however, scholarly, but can be traced to the nineteenth-century Romantic movement, and is in continuous evolution and transformation marked by creative improvisation. In this sense neopaganism is clearly part of New Age spirituality, a new religious movement that integrates both ancient and New Age teachings from a variety of traditions and periods. It emerged toward the end of the twentieth century with a purpose: to counteract the modern alienation from the natural world and provide a means to reenchant the world. Jones and Mathews explain: "Paganism has re-emerged within Western twentieth-century society for a good reason, for though it draws upon the past, it is designed for living in the present. Its reappearance at this time is a spiritual corrective to what many see as the head-long hurtle towards planetary destruction" (1990:13, cited in G. Harvey 2011:187).

The diverse pagan circles often resemble other New Age traditions in their interest in the occult and their combinations of different religious rituals and beliefs as suits their needs. Thus we can find pagans deliberately borrowing aspects of Buddhism, Hinduism, voodoo, Kabbalah, or even Sufism

78 | Grounding God

or Christianity in their practices, and transforming these borrowed elements to fit local cultures, seasons, and deities (Rountree 2016:5). Though Graham Harvey differentiates neopagans from New Age based on neopagan distrust of consumerism and the selling of spiritual practices (2011:2015–21), this is an unnecessarily restrictive and very recent interpretation of New Age movements, which ignores their historical development among the social movements rejecting monotheistic dogma and patriarchy and engaging in more eclectic, occult practices that share much with neopaganism.

Neopagans borrow from many traditions to develop ritual practices and festivals that enable their members to "interact with the subtle processes and energies by which the universe is established and maintained" (Cowan and Bromley 2015:162). Because these energies flow through the world and animate its many living beings, neopagans often focus their ritual activities on trying to regain lost sensibility and intuition in order to sense and communicate with a world pulsing with subtle energy. This often takes the form of honoring and "feeling" the sun and the moon in its various phases of movement, and in practicing what our chapter on animism will call "ontological boundary crossing": seeking to identify and feel oneself into other beings, in order to transfer energy.

Because neopaganism's adherents feel that they are a part of the living earth, neopaganism allows them to explore "a spiritual context for ecology" (G. Harvey 1994:40). We have shown in our chapter on Christian traditions that becoming ecological has not been an easy transition for monotheists, and has demanded both effort and repentance as monotheists seek to revalorize minority traditions or seek out new interpretations of old texts (38). In neopaganism, however, this ecological consciousness constitutes what Harvey calls a "natural growth from its already ecological roots. Modern Paganism is primarily a Green Spirituality, a Natural Religion, a Religion with roots in Nature" (38). For many scholars, this ecological focus itself constitutes a critique of modern techno-scientific "progress" and digital alienation from the living earth and the animal nature of the human being. Giving a modern Western voice to an animist ontology of kinship allows neopagans to embody a counterculture that seeks to learn from the past and correct the aberrations of modernity. Rountree notes:

> In this visionary rather than representative sense, [neopaganism] may be seen as a religion for the times: an ecological religion for societies confronting critical ecological challenges. I am not, of course, suggesting that neo-Paganism is the only religion

currently concerned with ecological issues and human relationships with the rest of the natural world. . . . Neo-Paganism is distinctive, however, in that ideas about human relationships with other-than-human beings in the natural world constitute the fundamental plank of its religious beliefs and worldview. (2012:306–7)

Because all neopagans believe in "love and kinship with nature" (the definition of the Pagan Federation), they can be considered animists as well, since kinship with other beings includes other animals in the order of familial relationships (Roundtree 2012:305). Many scholars have noted this correspondence with indigenous religious traditions, Roundtree going so far as to call the movement "neo-pagan animism" (313). She justifies this association in light of the deconstruction among neopagan animists of the nature–culture divide, and the attribution of personhood to more than human animals and ecosystems. Because most neopagans live in industrialized nations, their communion with nature is often limited to ritual and religious festivals and events, solstice and moon celebrations and special gatherings, rather than being part of everyday life as is the case for most indigenous animists. Roundtree points out, for instance:

A large number of modern Pagans (not all) are animists of one sort or another, for whom all of the earth's visible inhabitants— trees, rocks, rivers, mountains, caves, insects, animals (including humans), fire, snow, particular tracts of land or indeed the whole earth itself (or Herself)—are conscious and en-souled or en-spirited. . . . Embracing a new animism by neo-Pagans is, potentially, a means of influencing a shift in the dominant Western worldview towards nature, to suggest a different way of thinking about and acting within and towards the world and all its people. (2012:307–8, 317)

In considering the earth to be alive, pagans attribute life not only to animals and trees but also to clouds and water. They thus believe in what Harvey calls an "ecology of souls" (2011:140). In this sense, neopaganism is part of what could be called "neoanimism." Neopaganism has adopted an animistic kinship ecology, while at the same time providing a tendentious rereading of history in order to claim animism for its own, as intrinsic to its own pre-Christian European traditional practices and beliefs. This is what

Harvey calls the "indigenizing" of paganism (231), a strategy developed in order to undermine the dichotomies of modern culture and especially the separation of nature from culture. In this sense, Harvey sees animist neopagans as confirming Latour's claim that "we have never been modern" by undermining Cartesian dualism and showing that the separation between sacred and profane, mind and body, and human and animal are failed attempts to separate human beings from their very humanity, and that this premodern unity belongs not only to non-Western indigenous peoples but also to pre-Christian European indigenous groups.

In this sense, neopaganism provides a spiritual counterpart to scholarly movements like new materialism (see Conty 2018) that point toward a new Western paradigm, one that has finally left behind the dualities set up in modernity to avoid the implications of the relationality and interdependence of all matter (subject–object, nature–culture, matter–mind, human–nonhuman). Like these scholars, neopagans seek to celebrate the materiality of our world and its nonhuman actors. And because the human being is no longer understood as exceptional, and set over and against a world of objects, many neopagans share with new materialists a posthumanist stance, thereby undermining the humanist understanding of exceptionalism that set the human apart from other forms of life by an unbridgeable ontological chasm. These two enemies are indeed allies, since it is the belief in humanist exceptionalism that informs the human subject against a world of objects, human culture against a world of nature, and human reason against a world of matter. Studies from disciplines as diverse as biology, physics, cognitive science, information technology, anthropology, sociology, philosophy, political science, paleontology, archaeology, primatology, geology, and indigenous studies have confirmed the neopagan conviction that rather than an autonomous creature somehow standing apart from material conditions and relations, the human being is part of and dependent upon a web of material relations. But neopaganism contributes something essential that new materialisms and scientific ecology and climate science cannot provide. Instantiating Rudolf Otto's definition of religion as inspiring awe and mystery, neopaganism includes a veneration for nature and religious ritual practices that allow such an understanding to leave the mind and itself become embodied. This chapter, in considering some different movements—Wicca and Gaianism as forms of religious naturalism—seeks to reveal the similarities between these movements so as to understand them all as belonging to the general religious category of neopaganism, largely defined.

Wicca

One of the fastest-growing neopagan movements in the Western world, Witchcraft or Wicca is largely a Caucasian heterosexual female movement (89 percent Caucasian, 60–70 percent women, and 65 percent heterosexual [E. White 2015:167–68]) based on polytheistic initiatory practices centered on worshipping nature through its envoys, typically a mother goddess and a horned god (Wallis 2003:81). After emerging in Britain in the early twentieth century, the movement came to the United States, and these two countries host the majority of witches. Though Wiccans trace their traditions back to pre-Christian forms of witchcraft and paganism, they practice what most take to be modern and postmodern forms of religiosity influenced by nineteenth-century Romantic interpretations of paganism.

Though some Wiccans are monotheistic, believing in a single goddess, most are polytheists, focusing on a mother-goddess and horned-god pair, or integrating many gods and goddesses from different pagan traditions (Norse, Greek, Celtic, Egyptian). Often these deities are understood to be immanent, incarnating the power and forces of nature, which can be channeled through magic and incantation. Notwithstanding the great diversity of Wicca practices and beliefs, they all share a creation myth: the myth of the "mother-times" (Starhawk 1987:32) before the advent of patriarchy, consequently destroyed by Christianity during the Inquisition, which burned thousands of witches and is thus called the "burning times" (Barner-Barry 2005:41). Though witches have faced severe repression by Christian hegemony since the Middle Ages, and continue to be discriminated against in America, particularly by fundamentalist Christians, a slow movement toward mainstream acceptance has been facilitated by popular culture, and such books and films as *Harry Potter, Charmed, Buffy the Vampire Slayer*, and *Sabrina the Teenage Witch*.

Tracing their traditions back to a pre-Christian history, particularly that of Anglo-Saxon England and Iron Age Celtic communities, is important for many Wiccans because it gives them a sense of authenticity and historical continuity. The ideas and ritual practices of Wiccans, however, were largely invented by British witches of the early twentieth century interested in esoteric lore, such as Gardner (the "father of Wicca") and Murray (the "grandmother of Wicca"), and developed largely in contestation of mainstream modern culture. Witches often seem to hesitate between defending weak historical antecedents ("Just because there are no historical traces doesn't mean it isn't true") and celebrating the inventive storytelling that allows them to

82 | Grounding God

create their own tradition, an amalgamation inspired by growing awareness of ecology, feminism, and sexual freedom, along with New Age self-help psychology and rituals (Starhawk 1979/1999:224). Often this past is so idealized and universalized that one wonders if witches themselves actually believe it is anything more than a myth. Starhawk, a witch who provides a good example of this idealization, writes:

> The Goddess, who is the soul of earth, of sky, of the living being in whose body we are cells, once was awake in us and all knew and honored her in women and men, in nature, in the turning cycles of the seasons and the shifting cycles of our lives, in the works of mind and hand we created, in the plants and animals, in moon, sun, and ocean, in tree and stone and the intricate dance all living beings do together. We lived in balance on the earth. Women were free, and men too, for we had not yet learned how to oppress each other. And because we lived in harmony with the earth, we understood the earth's ways and her mysteries. (1987:310)

Witches locate this matriarchal past without oppression and violence in Europe and England, where it is highly unlikely that witchcraft was ever a dominant matriarchal religion. Anthropologist Lynne Hume notes that witches often prefer a "romantic past-as-wished-for, rather than an historical past-as-known," reflecting a "romanticism of a long forgotten, fairy-like Celtic past" that is "based on sketchy historical facts rather than any rational piecing together of the jigsaw of history" (cited in E. White 2015:85).

Though the nostalgic myth of European witchcraft has little historical veracity, witchcraft was dominant in other cultures and remains so in many cultures even today. While witchcraft continues to be prevalent in much of Africa, where it is thought of as the cause of most human deaths among both tribal and urban groups, no modern Western witches ever draw on this heritage to my knowledge, even though it is based on both anthropological and contemporary history, unlike their Edenic myth. Seemingly, the reason actual witchcraft practices and beliefs are ignored is that modern Anglo-American witches are in need of an idealized feminist, politically correct, Western version of witchcraft that shares next to nothing with traditional witchcraft, other than the power of incantation and magic. Modern witches are interested in using their spirituality to resist and free themselves from the patriarchy and dualisms of modern Christian ideology.

Neopaganism and the Grounding of the Sacred | 83

They therefore prefer to invent a tradition borrowing from indigenous ecology, Romanticism, New Age spiritualism, and feminism, rather than from actual witchcraft as it was and is still practiced.

To counteract the patriarchy of modern ideology, the witch becomes a "positive antitype" (E. White 2015:78) whose power is expressed through contestation of Christian Enlightenment ideology. This role comes naturally to the witch, since it was this very Christian culture that diabolized the witch as a child-devouring, devil-worshipping enemy of Christian morality. Wicca identity is thus constructed oppositionally, by marking itself out from mainstream Anglo-American culture. White explains that historically, "there was a real Wiccan process of whitewashing the image of the historical witch so that it would better suit the purposes of modern Wiccans themselves" (79). Thus the witch self-identifies in opposition to institutional religion, to bureaucratic subservience, to mainstream consumer capitalism and its rape of the natural world, and to puritan and life-denying Christian morality. Contrary to this restrictive normative tradition, the witch is self-sufficient, close to nature, and most importantly, free.

This freedom is largely expressed as a rejection of patriarchy. Describing oneself as a witch is often taken as a feminist statement in and of itself, since the witch is a symbol of what Roundtree describes as "female power which lies outside male control" (cited in E. White 2015:79). Though many of the early witches and founders of covens were men, the movement has become predominantly female, integrating core ideas of feminism and rejection of patriarchy into its rituals and beliefs. This has historical precedent, since most of the witches burned at the stake by the Inquisition were women. The question Starhawk pragmatically puts to patriarchal monotheisms is thus: "What's in it for me? What does this spiritual system do for women?" (1999:222).

Indeed, to the extent that a male deity is attributed both omniscience and omnipotence, whereas the female figure Mary serves her husband and son as devoted wife and mother, one can understand Starhawk's impatience with Christian patriarchy. This impatience is extended to an ideology that posits a male deity presiding over the earth from a heavenly sphere not of this world, and giving humans the duty to exploit the earth and its many beings solely for human gain, in the hopes of abandoning the earth at death for a heavenly realm. It is for this reason that Wicca proclaims the immanence of the divine. Because it is inherently sacred, the earth and all its creatures must be approached with the same numinous awe and respect that Christians show to their transcendent deity. And because the beings of the

84 | Grounding God

earth are not sinful, they do not require salvation and they are reincarnated again and again, into the many forms of living matter on the earth. For this reason, "those who live in the present have a much more personal stake in what their policies will do to future generations" (Barner-Barry 2005:29).

The immanence of the divine is often thought to incarnate itself into the forms of the Great Goddess and her consort, the horned god. In most covens the female goddess is considered more powerful than her male consort, and many female covens have eliminated the male god altogether. "Known by many names and in many aspects, the Great Goddess represents the divinity of the natural world and her consort the principle of fertility" (Cowan and Bromley 2015:171). Unlike the monotheistic God, the goddess does not rule over the world, for she *is* the world (Starhawk 1979/1999:33). Identified with nature, the goddess is often symbolized as maiden, mother, and crone, and is identified with the waxing, full, and waning moons, the regenerative life cycle that regulates life on earth. As Barner-Barry notes:

> The concept of the Goddess as deity is not a mere feminist device aimed at asserting the value of the feminine in the face of the patriarchal Christian traditions into which most contemporary Pagans were born. Although it does that, it does much more. Primarily, it places, at the center of religious consciousness earthly life, procreation and the passing of the phases of life, as well as the changing of the seasons. This is not the idea of the sacredness of human life and procreation that energizes the "right to life" movement. It is more broad and subtle. The central value is not some absolute "right to life" for human beings, but the celebration of life in all of its diversity—human and nonhuman. (2005:32)

As the totality of nature, the goddess is within each human, just as it is within each toad, and each mountain, inspiring respect and kinship among all living beings. Thus the High Priestess, speaking as the goddess, says: "For I am the soul of nature, who gives life to the universe. From me all things proceed, and unto me all things must return. . . ." (Farrar and Farrar 1984:43; also Starhawk 1989:90–91). And the Druids of Ár nDráiocht Féin (ADF) refer to "our Holy Mother Earth" (New Member's Guide 1990), and teach new members that "in keeping with our reverence for and worship of the Earth Mother, we advocate and practice ecological and environmental research, education, and activism" (New Member's Guide

1990:4). Ecology is thus central to Wicca. Starhawk notes that "the model of the Goddess, who is immanent in nature, fosters respect for the sacredness of all living things. Witchcraft can be seen as a religion of ecology. Its goal is harmony with nature, so that life may not just survive, but thrive" (1979/1999:34–35; also 1987:8).

Such a sacralization of immanence entails that destroying or transforming the natural world be done solely out of necessity. Barner-Barry (2005:34) thus notes that killing for food is allowed, but not for sport or for luxury garments. Interference in the natural cycles of change is to be limited to the utmost, in order to avoid the horrific effects of climate destruction we are witnessing today, and to seek to redeem the harm already caused. Witches often turn to indigenous traditions and borrow their ecological rules, such as explaining to prey why its death is required, in order to honor the kinship structure of life.

In order to commune with the goddess and God, witches practice incantation and seek to enter altered states of consciousness, channeling the divine cosmic energies that give modern witches their power to work magic. Though there are a wide diversity of practices, which are being continually reinvented, all witches follow two principles: Rede, and the Rule of Three. Rede is simply the rule of freedom, so long as no one is harmed: "an it harm none, do as thou wilt." The Rule of Three states that whatever magic one does in the world, the results will return threefold.

Though many witches practice alone, they often form covens, support groups for community ritual practices. "The coven," writes Starhawk, "is a Witch's support group, consciousness-raising group, psychic study center, clergy training program, College of Mysteries, surrogate clan, and religious congregation all rolled into one" (1989:35). Though covens can and do convene for other purposes, the most important rituals they mark are the eight annual sabbat festivities to celebrate the cycles of nature, the two solstices and the two equinoxes and the midway points, as well as the esbats or lunar gatherings, which follow the thirteen-month lunar calendar. The sabbats involve channeling cosmic energy as related to the elements and the planets, in order to overcome the alienation from nature so typical of Western modernity. The sabbats are as follows:

- Samhain, Halloween—October 31
- Yule, Winter Solstice—December 21
- Imbolc, Candlemas—February 2
- Ostara, Spring Equinox—March 20

86 | Grounding God

- Beltane, May Day—May 1
- Litha, Summer Solstice—June 21
- Lughnasagh, or Lammas—August 1, beginning of the harvest
- Mabon, Autumn Equinox—September 23

The sabbats are performed in a sacred circle, either fully clothed or "sky-clad," using symbolically laden ritual objects such as the chalice (the womb), candles, an altar, and incense. In a rite known as "drawing down the moon," the deities of the coven are invited into the circle to share their energy and power with the participants. Often the goddess enters into the High Priestess during this ceremony, and it is thought that an altered state of consciousness is reached that transcends the ego. Also important is the Great Rite, which ritualizes the union between the male and female, either "in truth" meaning they have sex, or "in token" symbolically. This symbolic ritual involves the male priest offering a chalice (symbolic feminine) to the priestess, who pushes a dagger (male principle) into the chalice enacting the union. Witches also practice Wiccanings, similar to baptism, hand-holdings, a form of marriage, "as long as love shall last," and "crossing over" rituals for those who die and pass into another form.

Though magic has a bad reputation, both regarding the historical bias of Christianity toward medieval witchcraft and in contemporary witchcraft in Africa today, by abiding by Rede and the Rule of Three, Western witches consider their actions ethical and geared toward abetting divine energy of the cosmos. Cowan and Bromley have surveyed definitions of magic, such as that of Cunningham, who defines magic as "the projection of natural energies to produce needed effects" (1988:19). They also cite Lisa McSherry, High Priestess of an online cybercoven, who defines magic as "the art of consciously directing energy through focused will and effort to affect the things around us" (McSherry 2002:6), and Starhawk, who defines magic as "the art of sensing and shaping the subtle, unseen forces that flow through the world, of awakening deeper levels of consciousness beyond the rational" (1989:27, cited in Cowan and Bromley 2015:172).

In order to channel such energy, intense willpower is required, which is why becoming a High Priestess is quite rare and requires many years of practice. Channeling cosmic energy allows a witch to redirect cosmic energy toward achieving goals by the witch. In this sense, magic is not supernatural, but rather a part of the natural order of the universe. Though not recognized by the scientific establishment, many witches feel that quantum mechanics

Neopaganism and the Grounding of the Sacred | 87

can be interpreted in such a way as to at least not contradict Wiccan magic. Other, more scientific-minded witches explain magical successes by means of the placebo effect (G. Harvey 2007:52). As Cowan and Bromley explain: "Humankind in the late modern world has simply forgotten how to access these energies, but through modern Pagan ritual and spellworking can learn, indeed must learn to do so again" (2015:172) in order to participate in a reenchanted world.

Religious Naturalism: Gaia

Though polytheism is popular among Pagans attracted to Wicca, the most common religious tradition espoused by pagans is pantheism, "the view that Deity and Cosmos are identical" (Yandell 1998:202). The *Stanford Encyclopedia of Philosophy* similarly defines pantheism as the "view that God is identical with the cosmos, the view that there exists nothing which is outside of God, or else negatively as the rejection of any view that considers God as distinct from the universe."[2] In addition to Chinese Taoism, pantheism has a long history in the West and is the religious view of some of the greatest minds of its tradition, from the pre-Socratics, Plotinus, Giordano Bruno, Spinoza, and Hegel to Goethe, Ralph Waldo Emerson, Walt Whitman, Carl Sagan, and Einstein. Because the immanence of the divine constitutes a defining trait of neopaganism (G. Harvey 1994:40; Cowan and Bromley 2015:162), most pagans are thus pantheists.

Because the cosmos constitutes a unity, and that unity is divine, or sacred, individual entities are thus modes or attributes of this totality, this unity. Pantheists thus deny that the divine can exist separately from the world and the matter of the cosmos, and also that the divine could be a transcendent person, since pantheists agree with science that all persons have bodies made of matter. The divine cannot transcend the cosmos, nor have an autonomous existence separate from the matter of the cosmos. The divine is immanent in the world.

This view was propounded most famously by Spinoza, who rejected dualism in favor of understanding mind and matter as two sides of a single coin. By famously writing "Deus sive Natura"—God or nature, he clearly defended the view that the divine could not be separated from the cosmos, understood as everything that is. If God is everything that is, then God is just another word for nature. As a contemporary example of this position,

88 | Grounding God

the architect Frank Lloyd Wright stated: "I believe in God, only I spell it nature" (cited in Rue 2011:122).

Pantheists conflate body and mind, world and God, thus undermining fundamental dogma of monotheistic religious traditions. Indeed, such conflations have made pantheism one of the most hated and feared heresies in the Christian tradition, inspiring what Mary-Jane Rubenstein has called the "monstrous." We will follow Rubenstein in understanding the deconstruction of these dichotomies as a spiritual and philosophical contestation of modern ideology. The ideology of modernity is constructed upon a hierarchical division between male–female, transcendent–immanent, mental–physical, reason–irrational emotion, eternal–mortal, human–animal, where the first term is understood as superior to the second. Pantheism makes these dichotomies redundant; hence its danger and the "monstrosity" of its risk. As Rubenstein points out, the first terms of these dichotomies are those associated with the disembodied divine in Western metaphysics, understood as worthy of veneration, over and against the world, associated with the second terms of these dichotomies (2018:3). By collapsing the dichotomy between God and world, the privilege of "spirit, masculinity, reason, light and humanity" over "matter, femininity, passion, darkness, and animal-vegetal-minerality" is also undone (11–12, citing Jantzen, *Becoming Divine*, 267).

In the eighteenth-century Enlightenment, this pantheistic position was adopted by Unitarian universalist creeds, becoming religious naturalism. Religious naturalism thus plays a role in our postmodern era similar to Deism during modern history. Just as Deism sought to undermine superstition and belief in miracles by postulating a religiosity in harmony with the laws of nature, so religious naturalism understands the natural world in terms of science, and finds beauty, holiness, and wonderment in its absolute immanence. Both pantheism and religious naturalism thus provide a religious life without belief in a transcendent God, and without an afterlife or an eternal soul. The main difference between the two is that, whereas pantheism deifies the cosmos, religious naturalism adheres to a religious response to the cosmos without requiring that the cosmos itself be divine. In this sense, just as Spinoza was accused of atheism during his own time, religious naturalism is often conflated with atheism as well. The difference between religious naturalism and atheism lies in the way one relates to the world: as a unity capable of inspiring wonder, thankfulness, veneration, and grace. In his explanation of the differences between atheism and religious naturalism, Donald Crosby emphasizes a "distinctively religious commitment, namely commitment to nature itself as the fit focus of profound religious awe and devotion, and as the ultimate source of religious assurance, demand, and empowerment" (2013:3). Herself a pantheist, Mary-Jane Rubenstein expresses her outlook in a similar fashion: "Try and penetrate with our limited means the secrets of nature and you will find that, behind all the discernible concatenations, there remains something subtle, intangible and inexplicable. Veneration for this force beyond anything that we can comprehend is my religion. To that extent I am, in point of fact, religious" (2018:162). Scientists such as Einstein and complexity theorist Stuart Kauffman also espouse this view, honoring the "ceaseless creativity in the natural universe" as "so worthy of awe, gratitude, and respect, that it is God enough for many of us" (Kauffman 2010:xi; 6). By giving ecology a religious motivation, pagan pantheists are more likely to engage in respectful practices toward earthly environments and their many inhabitants since it is through drawing close to nature by means of religious ritual and veneration that they engage in "reverential communion" with the divine (Levine 1994:227).

In his attempt to discredit religious naturalism, theologian John Haught correctly lists the essential traits that it shares with science:

1. Outside nature, which includes humans and their cultural creations, there is nothing.

2. It follows from #1 that nature is self-originating.

3. Since there is nothing beyond nature, there can be no over-arching purpose or transcendent goal that would give any lasting meaning to the universe.

4. There is no such thing as the "soul," and no reasonable prospect of conscious human survival beyond death.

5. The emergence of life and mind in evolution was accidental and unintended.

6. Every natural event is itself the product of other natural events. Since there is no divine cause, all causes must be purely natural causes, in principle accessible to scientific comprehension.

7. All the various features of living beings, including humans, can be explained ultimately in evolutionary, specifically Dar-winian, terms. (2006:116–17)

90 | Grounding God

Haught uses this description to claim that nature is not enough, and that only a transcendent teleology can provide the religious answers that humans need. Philosopher of religion Loyal Rue rightly concludes that perhaps nature is not enough for everyone, since some people, like Pope Francis, lacking an intimate relation with nature, might experience it as "asphyxiating" and hence require a transcendence not of this world. But for more and more people, and Loyal Rue is convinced the number will continue to grow, nature is anything but asphyxiating, and transcendence often appears as mere escapism.

But there is another response to Haught's contention that only theism can respond to the human need for teleology, one that comes from within science, and thus overcomes the opposition between religion and science. I am thinking here of the most widespread form of religious naturalism today, namely, devotion to Gaia, often called Gaianism in reference to the scientific theory of the same name invented by astrochemist James Lovelock in 1972, when, "in deference to the ancient Greek tradition," he chose to "refer to the controlled atmosphere-biosphere as 'Gaia'" (Margulis and Lovelock 1974:471). Like religious naturalism, Gaia falls under the naturalistic model of pantheism. Many Gaians thus understand the earth as eliciting wonder and devotion, and equate the living earth with the Greek earth goddess Gaia. Understanding the earth as Gaia is also a form of panpsychism, the view that holds that mind inheres in matter. Gaianism is panpsychist in that it holds that the earth's ecosystems exhibit a will to sustain life, and an experiential awareness, or consciousness, that constitutes the whole as greater than the sum of its parts (on panpsychism, see chapter 6). This panpsychist element within Gaia posits a teleology to the atmosphere-biosphere, in that it understands the earth as a living organism, actively seeking to regulate the conditions for the thriving of life. With the theory of Gaia, religious naturalism responds to Haught's critique from within science, and without requiring transcendence from the material world. The earth itself is teleologically driven to sustain life.

It was while Lovelock was working for NASA to develop ways of detecting life on Mars that Gaia suddenly came to him as an epiphany. He wrote: "It suddenly dawned on me that somehow life was regulating climate . . . suddenly the image of the Earth as a living organism able to regulate its temperature and chemistry at a comfortable steady state emerged in my mind" (2000:253).

Today the theory of Gaia is well established in the scientific community, as attested by the Amsterdam Declaration on Global Change, which confirms that "the Earth System behaves as a single, self-regulating system comprised of physical, chemical, biological and human components" (cited in Tyrrell 2013:3). But using a pagan earth divinity to name the theory, and giving the earth what at first appeared to be anthropomorphic agency, prompted negative appraisals of the theory among many scientists in its early days. And though many Gaians do indeed venerate the earth, often as a divine mother goddess, such beliefs are not part of the theory of Gaia and were firmly condemned by its founders Lovelock and Margulis, who used the term Gaia only metaphorically. As Rubenstein points out, such goddess worship "connotes what one author calls 'vague New Age mysticism,' what another dubs 'new-age goddess worship,' what Lovelock dismisses as 'Pagan goddesses and things,' what Margulis herself calls 'Earth Mother crap,' and what Sagan admits are 'scientifically unwelcome teleological, feminist, and animist connotations'" (2018:101). Indeed, both scientific authors go to some length to dissociate their theory from such New Age connotations, speaking in no uncertain terms. Thus Lovelock writes: "I am not thinking in an animistic way, of a planet with sentience, or of rocks that can move by their own volition and purpose. I think of anything the Earth may do, such as regulating the climate, as automatic, not through an act of will, and all of it within the strict bounds of science" (cited in Rubenstein 2018:123). And Margulis adds: "I cannot stress strongly enough that Gaia is not a single organism. My Gaia is no vague, quaint notion of a Mother Earth who nurtures us. The Gaia hypothesis is science" (Margulis 1999:123). Yet notwithstanding Lovelock and Margulis's attempts to separate Gaia from paganism, attributing teleology to the earth and calling it Gaia, a mother goddess sustaining life, fostered an immediate overlap between Gaia theory and fundamental pagan elements. This confluence led to what Glenys Livinstone calls PaGaianism, which she describes as follows:

> This is Gaian spirituality—taking on the mind of the universe, participating in the dream of the Earth, beginning to know from within the perceptive of Earth, Moon, Sun, Tree—our home and habitat. I have named such a perspective a "PaGaian" cosmology, to adequately express this integral sense of Gaia as Self-Earth-Universe, combining as the term does, the Pagan/indigenous sense of country/place—that we belong here, with an extended vision of GaiaMother, the larger primordial country of whom we are part. (2016:133)

92 | Grounding God

Such a pagan appropriation of course sparked a scientific backlash against the theory, many scientists refusing to take it seriously. Ford Doolittle's scathing attack on the Gaia hypothesis was duly titled "Is Nature Really Motherly?," and because the theory undermined the mainstream idea of the "selfish gene" and nature "red in tooth and claw," attacks only doubled when Margulis's theory of endosymbiosis confirmed the Gaia hypothesis, undermining neo-Darwinian atomism. As Strick points out, such an ideology of neo-Darwinian selfish genes "reinforces social-atomist, every-man-for-himself ideology that incentivizes continued depredation of Gaian life-support systems" (2015:102), thereby focusing on atomistic intrinsic essences rather than understanding interdependent symbiogenesis. Though Lovelock reiterated that the name Gaia was meant as a metaphor (just as the "selfish gene" was), metaphors of female figures that smacked of interdependent solidarity were somehow deemed more problematic than metaphors in line with capitalist ideology that postulated a selfish, brutish nature with each entity caring only about itself and seeking to outcompete and destroy others (Dawkins's "selfish gene" metaphor had a happier fate in the scientific literature). The animist and feminist connotations of Gaia were too much for the largely white, male, aging, scientific establishment, forcing Lovelock to consider changing the name of his theory. For a while he advocated calling it geophysiology, but it was not until people began referring to his theory under the name Earth System Science that it finally reached consensus and became mainstream science and the norm for studying the climate (Strick 2015:90). After the 1988 conference of the American Geophysical Union, the journal *Science* titled its article on Gaia "No Longer Willful, Gaia Becomes Respectable" (Strick 2015:87).

As John Lawton has pointed out, Earth System Science developed thanks to Lovelock's understanding that the thermodynamic disequilibrium of an interdependent biosphere is necessary for life: "James Lovelock's penetrating insights that a planet with abundant life will have an atmosphere shifted into extreme thermodynamic disequilibrium, and that Earth is habitable because of complex linkages and feedbacks between the atmosphere, oceans, land and biosphere, were major stepping stones in the emergence of this new science" (cited in Strick 2015:92). Because mainstream science continues to adhere to an ideology that understands biological processes to be mechanistic, attributing agency to ecosystems appeared to many to be slipping the supernatural into science by the back door. But as biologists Margulis and Guerrero have shown, the idea "that bacteria are simply machines, with no sensation or consciousness, seems no more likely than Descartes' claim that

Neopaganism and the Grounding of the Sacred | 93

dogs suffer no pain" (cited in Rubenstein 2018:123). Furthermore, the idea that organisms have agency cannot be misunderstood for a supernatural claim, since, as Rubenstein rightly points out, the theory can be accused of pantheism, of deifying the material earth, but certainly not of introducing the supernatural (101). Once the misunderstanding of Gaia as possessing autonomous agency was corrected, scientific reception of the theory improved, and conferences on Gaia were organized to assess the scientific merit of the Gaia hypothesis, attended mostly by scientists seeking to understand the origins of life on planet earth and the possibility of life on other planets. Lovelock had successfully predicted that no life would be found on Mars by noting that its atmosphere was in equilibrium, which would not be the case were there living organisms on Mars.

Lovelock first published his theory in a 1972 article titled "Gaia as Seen through the Atmosphere" in the journal *Atmospheric Environment*, where he wrote that "the purpose of this letter is to suggest that life at an early stage of its evolution acquired the capacity to control the global environment to suit its needs and that this capacity has persisted and is still in use" (1972:579). This paper was followed rapidly by two other papers that he coauthored with biologist Lynn Margulis in 1974, "Atmospheric Homeostasis by and for the Biosphere" in the journal *Tellus*, and "Biological Modulation of the Earth's Atmosphere" in the journal *Icarus*. In these papers, the authors showed that as a self-renewing, living organism, the earth adjusts to changing conditions through feedback loops in order to maintain stability, especially of the atmosphere and temperature. Not only does Gaia maintain stability, but it seeks conditions favorable to life. In their own words, they sought "to develop the concept that the earth's atmosphere is actively maintained and regulated by life on the surface, that is, by the biosphere," which they understood to be "the total ensemble of living organisms" (Lovelock and Margulis 1974:3) including the oceans and the climate, and that even "temperature, gas composition, and alkalinity have been actively modulated by organisms, especially microorganisms" (Margulis and Lovelock 1974:471, 479). Such interactions among parts form a "hypothetical new entity with properties that could not be predicted from the sum of its parts" (3).

Because they are constantly codependently interacting together, it is these minute self-propagating organisms (including the microbes and their metabolic by-products discovered by Margulis) that create macro ecosystem effects through their symbiotic interdependencies. In this way, Lovelock and Margulis were able to show that reciprocal relationality is essential to life on planet earth, living things producing and sustaining the very conditions

94 | Grounding God

that produce and sustain them in return. "It is in this sense," notes Rubenstein, "that Gaia can be said to be alive: 'her' innumerable, interlocking, and non-totalized systems do the active work of regulating the climate" (2018:122). Intrinsic essences so favored by Western metaphysics thus find no reality in the natural world, which evolves in symbiotic relationality. Often-cited examples include the gut bacteria that digest our food, keeping us alive. Mitochondria in animal cells have their own RNA and a separate existence within the cell. Fungus is essential to the root structures of trees. Lichen is constituted by two different entities: algae that allow it to photosynthesize, and fungi that allow it to eat. Coral polyps use zooxanthellae algae to photosynthesize sunlight. All of these examples show that the ecosystem is constituted by sets of interdependent relations, none of which could exist intrinsically outside of these relations. Since the earth is populated by microbial multitudes, "it is symbionts all the way down" (Hird 2009:26). Only human artifacts stand outside this web of relations, as extensions of the human being that enable human beings to understand, influence, and communicate with myriad other beings.

The earth is a living organism for Lovelock rather than an inanimate object because it has stabilized the climate for the last four and a half eons. If it were inanimate, it would have followed the variations in solar output, decreasing temperatures by 25 percent (below freezing), which has never occurred. Slowly feeding off of the carbon blanket for food would have caused a cooling of the planet; or the planet could have overcompensated by producing another greenhouse gas like methane, which would have resulted in rapid warming of the earth, unsustainable for life.

Instead, Gaia developed a control system to optimize the conditions for life on the planet. Slowly, because of photosynthesis, oxygen would have accumulated in the air. This would have been a fatal catastrophe for life when it occurred, but Gaia quickly adapted to this new poison and found ways to transform enemy into friend. For Lovelock, the chemical changes in the earth's surface and atmosphere that keep stable a highly improbable distribution of molecules conducive to life are proof of Gaia. Just like an oven thermostat that keeps temperatures constant, so the earth has kept temperatures on earth stable for life, never changing more than a few degrees even though the sun's output is not constant and the composition of the early atmosphere has changed drastically.

Indeed, the earth's atmosphere is such an incompatible mixture that it could not have arisen by chance. Normally, there would be much less methane and much more CO_2 in the atmosphere than there actually are.

So the atmosphere is kept far from equilibrium, and it is this negentropy that allows for life on planet earth. Mars has a steady-state atmosphere in equilibrium, and harbors no life. If we were to imagine the world at equilibrium, it could not produce life, since life requires a constant energy source from the sun to sustain it. We know that methane is caused by ancient organisms called archaea, and oxygen is produced by plant photosynthesis. Without them, there would be half the oxygen and up to one hundred times the CO2 (Lenton and Dutreuil 2020:169–70). Over time, plant life has transformed this dominating scenario into one that favors life forms. This means that rather than adapting to a climate, plants have actively created and maintained a climate suitable for their propagation (173).

The apparent incompatibilities of biological cycles and inorganic equilibria are actually proof of a symbiotic living planet. Life's biosphere is held in extraordinary disequilibrium thanks to the living organisms that transform chemicals to produce oxygen and methane. Though not itself alive, strictly speaking, "the atmosphere can now be seen as an extension of life 'like the fur of a mink or the shell of a snail.' This insight redefined our conceptions of Life and the environment" (Lenton and Dutreuil 2020:179; see also Dutreuil 2020:183). As climate scientists Lenton and Dutreuil explain:

> This is what makes the providential story so improbable: without the very activity of life forms, Earth's atmosphere would be closer to chemical equilibrium, much richer in CO2, would contain barely any O2, and would even have greater atmospheric pressure because living beings have progressively locked up its main constituent, N2. A story using geology as a stable frame for organisms that do nothing in it would mean only one thing: planet Earth would be simply uninhabitable, just as Venus and Mars are. Organisms have given a new twist to the saying "God (or rather Geology) helps only those who help themselves." (2020:170)

In order to prove his theory, Lovelock invented a computer simulation called Daisyworld. In a world with white and black daisies, the white daisies reflect back the sunlight, the black ones absorb it. When he manipulated the temperature in Daisyworld, when it got too hot, the world made more white daisies, and when it got too cold, more black daisies. The digital ecosystem would regulate the temperature by changing the prominence of white or black daisies.

96 | Grounding God

Though Daisyworld was successful, proving the viability of temperature regulation by life forms on planet earth, some scientists remain unconvinced of Gaia. Toby Tyrrell, for instance, has summarized Gaia as implying three theses: that the environment is well suited for life, that biota have shaped the environment and its chemical disequilibrium, and finally, that Gaia has kept the global environment stable for life. Tyrrell is willing to grant Lovelock only the second point, as he believes that Lovelock has convincingly proved that life forms shape their environments rather than being passively shaped by them. But though the earth's environment has remained habitable, it has neither remained stable nor well suited for life, for geological history clearly marks the rapid onset of past ice ages ("snowball earth") and other climate disasters that made most life forms go extinct (2013:203).

Lovelock's point is, of course, that in light of these climate disasters, and the force of entropy, we would expect the result to have been equilibrium, and the extinction of life on earth as is the case on Mars and Venus. But though it appears to be far more likely in terms of both the theory of entropy and other planets in our cosmos, that did not happen on earth, which managed to regulate climate in order to always retain disequilibrium, allowing life forms to thrive. The disequilibrium that is sustained by life forms is, however, fragile. For Lovelock the most important ecosystems, home to most microorganisms sustaining life on planet earth, are the continental shelves (under the oceans, about the size of Africa) and the wetlands (bogs and marshes in Brazil, Bolivia, Paraguay, the Camargue in France, the Wasur Park in Papua New Guinea, the Kakadu in Australia, the Okavango Botswana, the Amazon basin, the Kerala backwaters, the Florida Everglades, and the Bangladesh Sunderbans). Yet the highest rate of environmental degradation is currently in the wetlands. Lovelock fears that the devastation of tropical ecosystems may diminish the capacity of Gaia to autoregulate. The loss of tropical forest ecosystems and of wetlands because of overexploitation will lessen the capacity to thrive of all creatures on earth. If we do not carefully protect the tropics, the wetlands, and the seas close to the continental shores, we could sap the vitality of Gaia until we reach a point of no return (Lovelock 2016:114).

If the theory of Gaia received scientific respectability by separating itself from all animist and pagan connotations, it became famous and immensely popular outside the bastions of science, among the general public whose awareness and consternation regarding the climate crisis found a response in the theory of Gaia. For these people, Gaia was a means of venerating the absolutely unique, vibrant beauty of life on planet earth, and respecting the earth as far more than a mechanistic, utilitarian end. In line with Pachamama and Earth Mother traditions, Gaians can adopt a scientific understanding of the world that itself provides them with a spiritual sense of appreciation for and participation in the natural world.

Such an interpretation of the earth as capable of inspiring awe and veneration points toward Gaia and religious naturalism more generally as being religious in the archetypal way theorized by Rudolf Otto. In his classic work *The Idea of the Holy*, Otto maintained that religion could be understood as the feeling of *mysterium tremendum* and *fascinans*, the feeling of awe, mystery, and fascination humans feel before the divine. Religious naturalism holds that it is only the universe itself that can inspire such feelings, and thus that warrants our devotion. For religious naturalists, the power and glory of God is really the power and glory of nature, and scriptures usually describe God's power in naturalistic terms such as thunder, fire, earthquakes, and plagues, or more positively, food, healing, dreams, and children. If we are neither masters nor stewards of nature, "managing a property for the absent master, God" (Harrison 2013:55) but rather kin in a web of life, Gaians are well placed to heal the earth and hold her continuing vitality as sacrosanct.

Chapter Five

Animism in the Anthropocene

Je suis devenu un peu animiste, il m'arrive de dialoguer avec les oiseaux.

—Philippe Descola

In a play on Bruno Latour's famously destabilizing claim that "we have never been modern," Professor of Religious Studies Graham Harvey recently added, "but perhaps we have always been animists" (2014:11). Indeed, these two comments are more closely linked than one might at first infer. It was the anthropology of non-Western cultures that inspired Latour's intellectual journey and his famous claim since it is precisely this discipline that treats the empirical, the social, and the linguistic as a continuous whole. It is through studying comparative anthropology that Latour was able to understand the nature of technology and undermine the dualities of subject and object, nature and culture,[1] natural science and social science. Because we cannot access the motivations and goals within other agents, modernity typically separated the human as active and the rest of matter as acted upon. Showing how a-modern cultures had no trouble attributing agency to objects, subjects, spirits, and tools helped Latour to separate agency from its supposed cause in a uniquely human interiority characterized by intentionality and purposive action, and thus to look more objectively at the forms of agency at work in the world. It is time, Latour famously pointed out in his book *We Have Never Been Modern*, to see ourselves the way we are able to see the natives of nonmodern cultures, and to send ethnologists to study the modern tribe of "scientific researchers or engineers." The ethnologist (Latour himself) would notice that his modern informants adamantly refuse to see their projections onto nature and would therefore conclude that "for social reasons . . . Western scientists require a dualist attitude" (1991:102). If Western scientists assumed one nature and many different cultures, non-modern peoples take for granted one culture and many different natures. This ideological reversal represents what Latour calls a "bomb with the potential to explode the whole implicit philosophy so dominant in most ethnographers' interpretation of their material" (cited in Turner 2009:27). It is this bomb that we will be seeking to detonate by defending an animist ontology in which agency is attributed to all of life.

But if "we have always been animists," then objectifying the world from the position of a subject was always merely a projection, a reification. Latour's a-modernism thus represents a "return of the repressed" since we are now forced to acknowledge what was pushed below the surface to constitute what he calls "the unconscious of the moderns" (1993:37). Indeed, studies in genetic and developmental psychology have shown that animism is a natural predisposition in the human being, unlearned only through a long process of socialization.[2] According to Kate Wright, the repression of animism in modern thinking represents a major pathology. An animistic renaissance could thus function as an alternative to and a cure for the divisions and dichotomies founded in the human exceptionalism at the core of modern values. It constitutes what Wright calls "an attempt to address the systemic pathology of a species disconnected from the conditions of its world. Becoming-with offers a metaphysics grounded in connection, challenging delusions of separation—the erroneous belief that it is somehow possible to exempt ourselves from Earth's ecological community" (2014:278). If animism has thus been repressed and unlearned, this is largely due to the modern categorization of animism as belonging to the primitive past of indigenous populations,[3] populations that would eventually accept the "*mission civilisatrice*" of the West and the forward march of progress (Rosengren 2018). Anthropologists Marisol de la Cadena and Orin Starn comment:

> A century ago, the idea of indigenous people as an active force in the contemporary world was unthinkable. According to most Western thinkers, native societies belonged to an earlier, inferior stage of human history doomed to extinction by the forward march of progress and history. . . . History has not turned out that way at all. Many tribal societies have indeed been wiped out by war, disease, exploitation, and cultural assimilation over these last centuries. But far from vanishing as the confident

predictions once had it, native peoples today show demographic strength, even growth. (2007:1)

Though there are still diehard modernists who continue to identify animism with the past, such views testify to what Gisli Palsson has called "environmental orientalism" (1996:69), the hubristic attitude of colonizers responsible for the desecration and oppression of peoples and ecosystems across the world. Equating animistic cultures with nature, such moderns saw animists as virtually subhuman, since they assigned social roles to the nonhuman world. Along the arrow of progress, such primitive peoples could be subjugated and expropriated just as natural resources were, or else educated to recognize the separation of nature from culture, and thereby enter the domain of humanity proper. Anselme Franke explains how animism functioned for modernity as what he calls a "negative mirror image" (2012b:169) in order to construct its identity over and against an identity it could relegate to the primitive past.

In her book *Environmental Culture: The Ecological Crisis of Reason*, environmental philosopher Val Plumwood calls this extirpation a "remoteness" promoted by "sado-dispassionate science," which uses an "ideology of disengagement to wall itself off from ethics" (2001:53). Plumwood traces a continuous line between such remoteness from nature and a similar remoteness the male elite established between themselves and women, slaves, and colonized others, who were deemed lacking in human reason and thus part of exploitable nature.

> Many regimes, and many oppressions have since lent their colour to this hegemonic imaginary of reason and nature. In patriarchal thought, men represent reason and rightfully control the world as well as the dangerous emotionality, irrationality and reproductivity of women, who are "closer to nature." In the colonizing, racial supremacist version, it is inferior and "barbarian" others who are closer to nature, an earlier and more primitive stage of our own rational civilization, who receive only benefits when more advanced masters of reason, the colonisers, come to take away their land to put it to proper, rational use. (2001:21)

It thus becomes impossible to separate anthropocentrism from other problematic centrisms, such as androcentrism, ethnocentrism, and eurocentrism. All of these centrisms use a binary structure to exclude human and nonhuman

102 | Grounding God

others by isolating values to the realm of human reason alone. If such a model was useful for the Western conquest of the rest of the world and its expropriation of peoples and resources to produce what sociologist Jason Moore calls "cheap nature" (low-cost food, labor power, energy, and raw materials) (2015:53), in the age of the Anthropocene it is revealing itself to be nothing less than suicidal.

But in our postcolonial and emancipatory age, the tables have turned, and "new materialisms" (Conty 2018) and "new animisms" (Halbmayer 2012:9) are gaining recognition as we do our best to repress and unlearn Cartesian dualities in order to heal our ailing planet. Anthropologist Eduardo Viveiros de Castro expresses this reversal well:

> But now, in these poststructuralist, ecologically-minded, animal-rights-concerned times, everything has changed. . . . Instead of having to prove that they are humans because they distinguish themselves from animals, we now have to recognize how *in*-human *we* are for opposing humans to animals in a way they never did: for them nature and culture are part of the same sociocosmic field. Not only would Amerindians put a wide berth between themselves and the great Cartesian divide, which separated humanity from animality, but their views anticipate the fundamental lessons of ecology which we are only now in a position to assimilate. . . . Formerly, it had been necessary to combat the assimilation of the savage mind to narcissistic animism, the infantile stage of naturalism . . . now, as we have seen, animism is attributed once more to savages, but this time it is proclaimed . . . as the correct (or at least "valid") recognition of the universal admixture of subjects and objects, humans and nonhumans, to which we modern Westerners have been blind, because of our foolish, nay, sinful habit of thinking in dichotomies. (2015:240–41)

Latour himself is guilty of such a modernist bias in his book *Facing Gaia*, where he insinuates that indigenous populations don't really respect nature, but rather their small size and inability to use technology to manipulate matter gives the impression of ecological respect that would better be understood as redundancy in terms of numbers and power. "Maybe, if only we could be sure that what passes for a respect for the earth is not due to their small numbers and to the relative weakness of their technology.

None of those so-called 'traditional' people, the wisdom of which we often admire, is prepared to scale up their ways of life to the size of the giant technical metropolises in which are now corralled more than half of the human race" (2013:128).

But there are 370 million indigenous people alive today and they neither face the threat of disappearing because of modernization, nor, when given the chance, have they chosen to "scale up their ways" in mimicry of "technical metropolises." Anthropologist John Bodley makes clear that Westerners have become so ethnocentric and arrogant that they cannot imagine another culture having value for its members, and readily assume that such members desire Western modernization. But if we were to ask the question: "How do autonomous tribal peoples feel about becoming participants in the progress of commercial civilization?," we would have to acknowledge that tribal peoples

> would rather pursue their own form of the good life undisturbed. . . . Indeed, it can perhaps be assumed that people in any autonomous, self-reliant culture would prefer to be left alone. Left to their own devices, tribal peoples are unlikely to volunteer for civilization or acculturation. Instead, "acculturation has always been a matter of conquest . . . refugees from the foundering groups may adopt the standards of the more potent society in order to survive as individuals. But these are conscripts of civilization, not volunteers." (2014:33–34).

Though today anthropologists speak of "indigenous modernities" to reflect the fact that indigenous communities have adapted to modern tools, nation-state sovereignty, and capitalist economies in multifaceted ways, these communities continue to reject modern capitalist resource extraction and the placing of profit over shared kinship values intrinsic to animism. As anthropologist Dan Rosengren explains:

> Indigenous people have not succumbed to the temptations of the West; nor have they surrendered to the bliss of development and the capitalist market system that Westerners once thought inevitable. . . . On the contrary, they have now, at the beginning of the new millennium, achieved a position from which they challenge the powers and "truths" of the conquerors not as minorities or locals or any other special interest group but as

104 | Grounding God

indigenous people. . . . From the refusal to accept the dictates of modern Western hegemony emerge visions of the world and its future that are not only in opposition to Western modernity but that also present alternatives that become increasingly attractive as the consequences of Western modernity become evident. (2018:98–99)

Now that we have become aware that the problems of overconsumption, accumulation, commodification, and appropriation lie with technologically advanced peoples, instead of forcing indigenous peoples to modernize we should be pressuring modern societies to reduce energy consumption, de-grow their economies, and perhaps even learn to reinhabit localities and re-form communities. Danowski and Viveiros de Castro write:

It seems to us that Latour fails to consider the possibility that the generally small populations and "relatively weak" technologies of indigenous peoples and so many other sociopolitical minorities of the earth could become a crucial advantage and resource in a post-catastrophic time, or, if one wishes, in a *permanently* diminished human world. Our author does not seem prepared, himself, to accept the highly likely possibility that *we*—the people of the (capitalist) Core, the overweight, mediatically controlled, psychopharmacologically stabilized automata of technologically "advanced" societies that are highly dependent on a monumental consumption (or rather, waste) of energy—that we, when the chips are down, might be the ones who will have to *scale down* our precious ways of living. As a matter of fact, if someone needs "to be prepared" for something, that someone is us, the ones who are crowded together in "giant technical metropolises." (2017:95–96)

Since we now know that the West has never been modern, and no society has ever been primitive, anthropology can cease to function according to the illusory dichotomies of modernity and accept its new mission, "that of being the theory-practice of the permanent decolonization of thought" (Viveiros de Castro 2009:4).

The irony of such a return of the repressed has not been lost on anthropologist Alf Hornborg, when he asks "how shall we be able to reintroduce morality into our dealings with our non-human environment, now that we have invested centuries of training and discourse into convincing ourselves that Nature lies beyond the reach of moral concerns?" (2013:30). Might such a reintroduction of morality entail a "return" of sorts to premodern ways of thinking? If the West has always denied reciprocity and kinship with the natural world, is adopting such animistic views and attributing agency to the entire ecosphere feasible? If the illusory nature of the divide between nature and culture has finally been brought to light, and nature can no longer be made cheap, indigenous populations who never adhered to this divide in the first place can inspire an ontology not founded in human exceptionalism. Replacing the asymmetrical relation between nature and culture currently in place with a symmetrical one will require enlarging the scope of our values and thus of culture to the entire biosphere, and it will also require understanding the human species as an interdependent part of evolutionary natural processes. If Cartesian dualism has thus become implausible, it is perhaps time we sought to understand animism both anthropologically in terms of the dominant way of life of indigenous peoples and philosophically in terms of a new conceptual paradigm for the Anthropocene Age.[4] Now that we have used philosopher Bruno Latour's understanding of modernity as a general framework for a reevaluation of animism, the next section will employ anthropologist Viveiros de Castro's interpretation of perspectivism to describe the ontological presuppositions of indigenous animist societies, and the following section will elucidate philosopher Félix Guattari's notion of "machinic animism" as a new ideology for the Anthropocene Age.

Indigenous Animism

As a conceptual system, animism entails four interrelated ideas: personhood, relationality, location, and ontological boundary crossing. Graham Harvey defines animism as the belief "that the world is full of persons, only some of whom are human, and that life is always lived in relationship to others" (2006:xi). When constituted in terms of relationality, personhood is no longer the exclusive property of human beings. All animals are persons, meaning they all share consciousness and soul. In the terms of anthropologist Eduardo Viveiros de Castro, to be a person "is to be conscious and self-conscious, to act intentionally, with agency, and to communicate intelligently and deliberately" (2017:187). Thus Descartes's narcissistic motto "I think, therefore I am" needs to be replaced in animistic cultures by the far more inclusive motto "It exists, therefore it thinks" (Viveiros de Castro 2015:187). All

106 | Grounding God

material forms are ensouled, and thus, in the words of Viveiros de Castro, "subjectivity is not an exclusively human property, but the basis of the real" (cited in Melitopoulos and Lazzarato 2012b:248).

According to this first characteristic, personhood is redistributed from the exclusively human domain to the entire biosphere (see Mbembe 2017). Persons, bears, and koalas, ants and nematodes all have their own complex cultures because nature is culture all the way down. Indeed, the idea of nature does not exist among indigenous peoples, for the entire environment is filled with cultural meanings invested in it by indigenous tribes. Anthropologist Deborah Bird Rose explains: "The evidence of life in action shows us that other beings have and follow their own ways. They have their own foods, foraging methods, forms of sociality and seasonality; they have their own languages and their own ceremonies. According to one Elder: 'birds got ceremony of their own—brolga, turkey, crow, hawk, white and black cockatoo—all got ceremony, women's side, men's side, . . . everything'" (2013:100). Since all animals testify to personhood, what differs is embodiment, since different shapes, sizes, limbs, and sensory organs embody consciousness or soulhood in different ways. Rather than supporting the mind–body dualism of modernity, such an animist attribution of subjectivity to all agents transforms the meaning of immanence, for "subjectivity" and "thinking" are not transcendent categories in animism, but rather inhere in material bodies that transversally communicate with each other and coconstitute each other. As such, all entities, not just humans, have purposive agency and express themselves, and through enunciating, assemble and dissemble subjectivities and collectivities. Learning to recognize persons can thus cultivate an appreciation for the ways they reveal themselves and communicate with us, but can also, according to anthropologists Danny Naveh and Nurit Bird-David, "counteract the current destructive tendency to understand and engage with things/persons according to a utilitarian understanding" (2014:37).

In an ironic twist to Anthropocene discourse, Viveiros de Castro has taken the study of animism a step further in his research on Amazonian tribes, maintaining that not only are all living beings subjects, but they are *human* subjects.[5] Since being human entails placing oneself at the center of the world and interpreting the world in terms of one's own bodily form and needs, all animals take themselves to be human. For the jaguar, as the Runa people put it, blood is manioc beer (Kohn 2013:27). It is thus not nature that all entities share, but rather humanity as the ability to interpret the world from a subjective point of view, for, as Viveiros de Castro puts it, "the basis of humans and non-humans is humanity" (cited in Melitopoulos and Lazzarato 2012b:248). Describing the Raramuri peoples in the Eastern Sierra Madres of Chihuahua, Mexico, indigenous scholar Enrique Salmon calls this shared humanity "a kinship ecology," in which all the natural elements of an ecosystem are treated as kin. He explains: "In a previous world, people were part plant. When the Raramuri emerged into this world, many of those plants followed. They live today as humans of a different form. Peyote, datura, maize, morning glory, brazilwood, coyotes, crows, bears, and deer are all humans. Raramuri feel related to these life-forms much as Euroamericans feel related to cousins and siblings (Levi 1993)" (2000:1328–29).

It is this humanity as common ground that allows for a shared politics, because in enunciating, in expressing its humanity, each human is able to think itself beyond the boundary of the unitary and enclosed self of the Western tradition into a shared world. To refuse "to see as" is thus a refutation of humanity, for it is precisely this ability that is humanity's defining trait. As Viveiros de Castro notes:

> Typically, in normal conditions, humans see humans as humans, animals as animals and spirits (if they see them) as spirits; however animals (predators) and spirits see humans as animals (as prey) to the same extent that animals (as prey) see humans as spirits or as animals (predators). By the same token, animals and spirits see themselves as humans: they perceive themselves as (or become) anthropomorphic beings when they are in their own houses or villages and they experience their own habits and characteristics in the form of culture—they see their food as human food (jaguars see blood as manioc beer, vultures see the maggots in rotting meat as grilled fish etc.), they see their bodily attributes (fur, feathers, claws, beaks etc.) as body decorations or cultural instruments, they see the social system as organized in the same way as human institutions are (with chiefs, shamans, ceremonies, exogamous moieties etc.). (cited in G. Harvey 2005:470)

In such a worldview, humanity is both universal and subjective, since each species sees itself as the center of the world and other species cannot occupy the deictic position of the "I." Yet each species knows that other species see themselves in a similar way, and thus all interrelations are

108 | Grounding God

political, or function as what philosopher of science Isabelle Stengers calls a "cosmopolitics" (2002:249). Politics cannot be limited to human beings as Plato's philosophy has bequeathed to us; instead, Stengers asserts, it "should entertain the problematic togetherness of the many concrete, heterogeneous, enduring shapes of value . . . that compose actuality, thus including beings as disparate as 'neutrinos' (a part of the physicist's reality) and ancestors (a part of reality for those whose traditions have taught them to communicate with the dead)" (249). Because human persons see peccaries as game, while for peccaries humans are dangerous predators, just as jaguars see human persons as game and humans see jaguars as dangerous predators, all of these different perspectives must be taken into account when one lives in a world that includes multiple desires and multiple intentions, multiple cultures and multiple modes of communication. "It thus follows that every trans-specific interaction in Amerindian worlds is an international intrigue, a diplomatic negotiation, or a war operation that must be undertaken with maximum circumspection: cosmopolitics" (Danowski and Viveiros de Castro 2017:70–71).

For animists, such persons are defined relationally, our second trait, because they share their world with many other persons with whom they enter into complex forms of communication. Such a relational ontology entails that communication is always what Lévy-Bruhl called "participation." In a polis understood in a participatory framework, persons can never be understood in isolation and language is always dialogic. Because personhood is not understood in terms of ontological intrinsic essences, such relationality is essential for the constitution of a person.[6] As anthropologists Philippe Descola and Gisli Palsson explain in reference to indigenous animist tribes in South America, "the entities of which our universe is made have a meaning and identity solely through the relations that constitute them as such" (1996:99). In a relational ontology, there is no way to justify intrinsic differences between nature and culture, us and them, since neither element has an intrinsic identity outside of its relation to alterity. In the words of anthropologist Anna Tsing, "Human nature is an interspecies relationship" (2012:144).

Persons exist only through their relations, because they are all dependent upon a shared ecosystem, or location, our third trait, that grounds and gives meaning to their communication. So all persons are relational, and all relations are situated, and the location determines the communication and thus the persons that depend upon it. A relational ontology is possible only because beings are immersed in specific and irreplaceable localities that allow specific beings, cultures, and ecosystems to thrive. Harvey explains how these concepts work together: "Animists' contributions to ecological thinking and acting are rooted in the firm insistence that not only is all life inescapably located and related, but also that the attempt to escape is at the root of much that is wrong with the world today. Animism's alternative promise is a celebratory engagement of embodied persons with a personal and sensual world" (2005:186).

Finally, the ability to cross ontological boundaries entails the ability to "adopt the perspective of nonhuman subjectivities" in order to understand how they conceive of themselves as the center of their own worlds. This ability, which is essential for empathy and is wired into many animals via mirror neurons, allows a person to feel as, and think as, another. From the perspective of neurobiology, sharing intentional states is made possible because exactly the same neurons are activated in our brains when another person performs an action in front of us as when we perform the action ourselves (we have all experienced the spontaneous impulse to laugh when surrounded by laughter, and to sneeze when others sneeze). Political representation, as well as other forms of imaginative transference, develop out of this biological predisposition, making relationality constitutive of being human. "Men, as social beings, live in a world that is humming with empathy, such that they permanently adopt, almost involuntarily, the perspective of others" (Breithaupt 2009:8).[7] Anthropologist Maurice Bloch (2013) is thus correct when he asserts that the ability to "read the mind of others" and thus to share intentionality is a biological trait of the human species correlated with the firing of mirror neurons in the F5 cortex, but he is wrong to isolate this capacity to the human species alone. The sharing of intentionality with nonhuman others demonstrated in animist cultures has been widely corroborated by the science of ethology and the study of mirror neurons in other species (for animal cognition, see Bekoff, Allen, and Burghardt [2002] and the work on mirror neurons in chimpanzees and other apes in Rizzolatti and Sinigaglia [2008]). John Zerzan relates anthropologist Laurens Jan van der Post's astonishment when studying the bushmen in the Kalahari Desert who "seemed to know what it actually felt like to be an elephant, a lion, an antelope, a steenbok, a lizard, a striped mouse, mantis, baobab tree, yellow-crested cobra or starry-eyed amaryllis, to mention only a few of the brilliant multitudes through which they moved" (2012:14–15). Though such a capacity is available to all beings to different degrees, those

110 | Grounding God

persons who master this ability to cross ontological boundaries are called shamans, the "active interlocutors in transspecific dialogues" (Viveiros de Castro, cited in G. Harvey 2005:150).

Danowski and Viveiros de Castro call such indigenous animists terrans, and they claim that no matter how numerous (they cite 370 million indigenous people across seventy nations), such terrans will never replace the moderns because they will never form a majority and become "responsible for a hegemonic ideology that could control peoples. That is not their role" (2017:94). Yet such peoples can launch what they call, citing Deleuze and Guattari, a "resistance to the present" and create "'a new earth,' the world to come" (95). Danowski and Viveiros de Castro understand such a project of "re-becoming indigenous" (122) as one of "uncivilization," characterized by "a *technology of slowing down, a diseconomy* no longer mesmerized by the hallucination of continuous growth, *a cultural insurrection* (if the expression may be pardoned) against the zombiefication of the citizen–consumer" (97–98). Rather than testifying to backwardness, such a rebecoming indigenous delineates the possible "subsistence of the future" (123). Only such a new people can create a new world from the ruins we will have left them.

Machinic Animism

What might it mean, then, for us moderns to rebecome indigenous and become "uncivilized"? Should we prepare darts for our blowguns and set up camp in a yurt or Earthship in abandoned industrial zones, or join the *Zones à défendre* in France or the Earth Liberation Army elsewhere? That is certainly one way; but Westerners are also rebecoming indigenous in more subtle ways.

As the natural sciences seek to prove animist presuppositions scientifically, and moderns come to realize that sentience, consciousness, and culture are intrinsic to all of life, perhaps an animist ontology will become the new normal. But for this to happen, the values of solidarity and kinship will need to replace economic competition and consumer satisfaction as the sole values of modern culture. In his book *The Three Ecologies*, philosopher and psychoanalyst Félix Guattari expresses concern over this lack of solidarity in modern culture, and looks to animist cultures in order to cultivate kinship and develop a "transversal" response he calls ecosophy.[8] In a passage written in 1989 that has come to sound almost eerie, he noted:

Animism in the Anthropocene | 111

> Now more than ever, nature cannot be separated from culture; in order to comprehend the interactions between ecosystems, the mechanosphere and the social and individual Universes of reference, we must learn to think "transversally." Just as monstrous and mutant algae invade the lagoon of Venice, so our television screens are populated, saturated, by degenerate images and statements. In the field of social ecology, men like Donald Trump are permitted to proliferate freely, like another species of algae, taking over entire districts of New York and Atlantic City. . . . How do we regain control of such an auto-destructive and potentially catastrophic situation? . . . It is not only species that are going extinct but the words, phrases and gestures of human solidarity. (2000:43–44)

Because indigenous peoples never objectified the nonhuman world, preferring to attribute subjectivity universally to all entities in order to develop reciprocal and interdependent relations, Guattari asks us to "pass through animist thought" (2000:48) so as to develop a politics of nature in which subjectivation, and thus the political, inheres in all matter. By replacing behavior with assemblage (*agencement*),[9] and conscious subjectivity with preconscious subjectivation, the world is constantly opening itself up to being politically reconfigured by human and nonhuman subjects in a shared world. Attributing spirit to all beings like a Mexican Cuandero or a Bororo[10] could help us, Guattari claims, to develop the solidarity that is so sorely lacking in our Anthropocene Age.

Rather than involving intrinsic essences, and exclusive rationality, subjectivity is fluid, traveling from body to body by means of enunciation, or what Guattari called an a-signifying semiotics, whether gestural, aesthetic, or linguistic. It is only when subjectivity is imprisoned within a dominant human form in order to further the ends of economic competition and state power that communication ceases and subjects lose their singularity and can no longer be transformed by their encounters with other subjects. "We must ward off," Guattari asserts, "by every means possible, the entropic rise of a dominant subjectivity. Rather than remaining subject, in perpetuity, to the seductive efficiency of economic competition, we must reappropriate Universes of value" (2000:68).

Understood in this light, we might surmise that modernity represents precisely such an entropic dominant subjectivity, caused by the rapid extermination of subjectivation as the possibility of becoming other and communicating otherwise. If such a reconsideration of humanity is to be taken seriously today, it will require the development of a transversal ecosophy, which is able to take into account the ways natures and cultures coincide and communicate, the many ways subjects become other to themselves through ontological trespassing. Guattari calls it "machinic animism," the ability of souls to reassemble and become other to themselves, and he sees the return of pre-Columbian polyvocal subjectivities as a fitting reversal of capitalist globalized unicity. "And now it is Capital that is starting to shatter into animist and machinic polyvocity. Would it not be a fabulous reversal if the old aboriginal African subjectivities pre-Columbus became the ultimate recourse for the subjective reappropriation of machinic self-reference? These same Negroes, these same Indians, the same Oceanians many of whose ancestors chose death rather than submission to the ideals of power, slavery and the exchangism of Christianity and then capitalism?" (2012:15).

In this sense, machinic animism can help us see the many ways that even today, and even in the West, we can reassemble our identities and cross ontological boundaries in order to "see as another." Though we live in a world where the influence of the capitalist utilitarian system has meant that students choose to study business instead of anthropology, engineering instead of philosophy, the humanistic disciplines are nonetheless built upon the capacity to "see as other." Indeed, not only theater but reading itself, in the words of philosopher Frédéric Lordon, "is to leave the self" (2016). We can practice such a transference through literature, for instance, and imagine ourselves as men or women, beggars or emperors, Maggie Tulliver or the Princesse de Clèves. Or even as a fox, elephant, or eagle, phenomenautical projections that author Emma Geen was able to brilliantly bring to life in her novel *The Many Lives of Katherine North*. In this sense, studying the humanities can foster ontological boundary crossings similar to animistic traditions. And though we can never totally incarnate a raven, since humans will always project human complexity from the perspective of the human body, human plasticity is such that we can indeed approximate other life forms. Magician, philosopher, and shaman apprentice David Abram was indeed able to join a raven in flight: "And I'm balancing, floating utterly at ease in the blue air. As though we're not moving but held, gentle and fast, in the cupped hands of the sky. Stillness. Through a tangle of terrors I catch a first sense of the sheer joy that is flight. Falling, yet perfectly safe. Floating. Floating at the heart of the feathered thickness that is space. Aloft

Animism in the Anthropocene | 113

at the center of the world mandala, turning it beneath us, the whole planet rolling this way or that at the whim of our muscles" (2011:251).

Historian Dipesh Chakrabarty has claimed that "the questions of justice that follow from climate-change science require us to possess an ability that only the humanities can foster: the ability to see something from another person's point of view. The ability, in other words, 'to imagine sympathetically the predicament of another person' " (2016:378). For Chakrabarty, a solution to the Anthropocene depends upon the ability to enter other embodiments and see the world from their perspective, an ability very similar to the ontological boundary crossing of animism. We might indeed assert with novelist J. M. Coetzee that the humanities foster the inclusion of all other beings within humanity, just as indigenous animism does, and that such an inclusion is indeed constitutive of what it means to be human. Though his book *The Lives of Animals* does not directly address the Anthropocene, Coetzee imagines a world where nonhuman forms of life have been genetically and biologically reengineered to serve human ends, and where such a loss of other ways of being in the world incurs a loss of humanity, because "the sympathetic imagination" is dulled. For Coetzee, to become human we must be able to "think ourselves into the being of another," to be more than one. Thinking, that is to say, is always thinking alterity, and thus always about sharing a world. And if we can think ourselves into the fictional characters of literature, Coetzee's protagonist Elisabeth Costello claims that we can think our way "into the existence of a bat or a chimpanzee or an oyster, any being with whom [we] share the substrate of life. . . . There are people who have the capacity to imagine themselves as someone else, there are people who have no such capacity (when the lack is extreme, we call them psychopaths), and there are people who have the capacity but choose not to exercise it" (1999:35). Sympathetic imagination, rather than rational calculation, is required to see things from the point of view of a jaguar, a flying ant, or a forest.

Indeed, such a capacity for ontological boundary crossing may very well be essential to politics as well. If such "thinking as" is essential to thinking the polis and organizing ways of living together that can fulfill the human potential, it is because without the ability to put oneself in the place of the other, to see things from his or her perspective, one cannot develop moral judgments in a plural world of competing worldviews. In order to adopt universal norms that refer to and represent all persons equally, one must consider each normative concept from the points of view of all persons,

114 | Grounding God

irrespective of gender, ethnos, religious affiliation, political affiliation, or even species. This ability to consider multiple points of view, to put ourselves in the place of others, is thus a requirement in order to sustain democratic governance. It is central to philosopher John Rawls's "veil of ignorance," by means of which a citizen applies the *epoché* to her own experience and status so as to imagine herself in the place of others. And it is essential to what philosopher Hannah Arendt calls representation, by which she means "making present to my mind the standpoints of those who are absent. . . . The more people's standpoints I have present in my mind while I am pondering a given issue, and the better I can imagine how I would feel and think if I were in their place, the stronger will be my capacity for representative thinking and the more valid my final conclusions" (1977:241). For Arendt, because "political thought is representative" (241) through and through, such feeling and thinking in the place of others constitutes the very meaning of politics.

If politics has been considered a uniquely human sphere in Western modernity, this is due to the hegemony of symbolic communication. To develop a more inclusive cosmopolitics, we will need to master other semiotic systems, particularly biosemiotics (including zoosemiotics and phytosemiotics). If icons and indices are signs shared by all animals, and if biology itself can be interpreted as a semiotic system (cells and the genetic code are semiotic signs for Kalevi, Emmeche, and Hoffmeyer [2011] and for Barbieri [2008]), acknowledging such a biosemiotics will allow a cosmopolitics to include *all* social relations, not only those between human beings privileged by Arendt. If we have been witnessing the slow and unfinished attempts to include other human genders and ethnicities in political representation, relations with nonhuman beings, such as elephants, mountains, and rivers, have been excluded from the political sphere and relegated to science (which objectifies them) or to folklore, tourism, or ecology. Anthropologist Marisol de la Cadena addresses this political reductionism in her remarkable book on the Runa shaman Nazario's attempts to have his people's relationship with the Ausangate mountain recognized by the Peruvian state:

> Analogous to dominant science, which does not allow its objects to speak, hegemonic politics tells its subjects what they can bring into politics and what should be left to scientists, magicians, priests, or healers—or, as I have been arguing, left to dwell in the shadows of politics. Because mountains cannot be brought to politics (other than through science), Nazario's partnership with Ausangate is all but folklore, beliefs that belong to another

Animism in the Anthropocene | 115

"culture," that can be happily commodified as tourist attraction, but in no case can it be considered in politics. This exclusion is not just racism; it expresses the consensual agreement foundational to politics. The exclusions that result from it are disabled from their translation as political disagreement because they do not count—at all. (2010:359)

Though Bruno Latour has called for the enlargement of democracy to include nonhuman others, he specified that these others required scientists to speak for them, thereby retaining the objectification of nature and the limitations of its potential political claims. If relations with nonhuman others are to be represented politically, all interlocutors (including Nazario and the Ausangate mountain) must be represented. For Nazario, blowing up the Ausangate mountain to find gold is wrong. The mining industry could reply to Nazario that mountains are not sacred, and that scientifically speaking, they are made of rocks, which have no sentience, and therefore are worth next to nothing as compared to the gold. But if Nazario were to retort that the Vatican is also nothing but a pile of dead stones, the modern would quickly retort that indeed, to quote Viveiros de Castro's brilliant example: "the Vatican is made of stone, but it has a sacred value, in other words, it is not just stones. And the indigenous tribe would reply, it is the same for us at home, the mountain is made of stone, but it is not just stone" (2019). Though the value of the Vatican is not in the stones, destroying the stones would nonetheless also destroy its value. And in the same way, the sacrality of the Ausangate mountain does not lie in the individual stones, yet destroying these stones would indeed breach the sacrality of the human–mountain relation. Destroying the mountain also destroys a culture and a way of life. By shifting the focus away from the scientific truth and toward the pragmatic concern that according sacrality to the mountain is a way of protecting it and the cultures it enables, the truth becomes a secondary attribute of justice and flourishing. Such a cosmopolitics can be a powerful tool in decolonizing not only anthropology but also the natural sciences.

Such work has been taken up in the field of law in organizations such as Indigenous Governance Systems, Earth Jurisprudence, and Wild Law (founded by Cormac Cullinan), which adhere to laws where "the Earth itself is the source of law" (Hosken 2011:25–26, cited in Alberts 2015:136). Such a nonanthropocentric legal basis has enabled animist communities to give legal personhood to nonhuman entities such as rivers (New Zealand's Whanganui River, India's Ganges and Yamuna Rivers, the

116 | Grounding God

Vilcabamba River in Ecuador, as well as the Atrato and Amazon Rivers in Colombia). In these cases, the rivers were indeed allowed to defend themselves in court, with the help of "negotiators" or "legal guardians" who were in all cases interlocutors and not Western scientists. In the case of the Whanganui River, its negotiator, Gerrard Albert, defended the river as an ancestor: "We consider the river an ancestor and always have . . . treating the river as a living entity is the correct way to approach it, as an indivisible whole, instead of the traditional model for the last 100 years of treating it from a perspective of ownership and management" (cited in Roy 2017). The Vilcabamba River defended itself as plaintiff, with the help of legal guardians Richard Frederick Wheeler and Eleanor Geer Huddle, calling for its own right to "exist" and to "maintain itself" over and against the Loja government, which wanted to build a highway that would interfere with the river's flow. The river won. Ecuador decided to recognize the intrinsic value of its ecosystem legally in its constitution in 2008, establishing in article 255 the principles of "harmony with nature, defense of biodiversity and the prohibition of private appropriation for use and exclusive exploitation of plants, animals, microorganisms, and any living matter" (cited in Avelar 2013:270). Bolivia then similarly passed the Ley de Derechos de la Madre Tierra (Law of the Rights of Mother Earth) in 2010. These examples reveal the political implications of ontological boundary crossing, which will need to both stretch and deconstruct legal categories.

Nazario can think with the Ausangate mountain, just as the Maori can think with the Whanganui River, and the Runa can think with the forest (Kohn 2013). It is this ability to "think with" that allows us to "live with," rather than over and against, the natural world. In a world "humming with empathy" (Breithaupt 2009:8) we can adopt the perspective of both human and nonhuman persons. As part of our biological evolution and the social nature of our species, empathic "thinking with and as another" can explain our capacity for political representation and help us to learn "appropriate etiquette and protocol" from animists (G. Harvey 2006:19) in order to open our political worlds to nonhuman persons and ecosystems.

Such "thinking as other" will need to be explicitly cultivated in the world of the Anthropocene and in the solutions developed to address it. In a world where wild animals and indigenous communities are being pushed to extinction, we may be left with no alterity to imagine at all. This was indeed the dream of the Tyrell Corporation in the sci-fi film *Blade Runner*. The Tyrell Corporation produced androids "more human than human." The more human trait entailed precisely an utter lack of empathy, particularly empathy toward nonhuman forms of life. Philosopher James Stanescu well expresses the stakes of this lack: "These androids are completely interchangeable with humans, except for one test. This test measures a person's empathy, particularly their empathy toward other animals. These replicants have managed the feat of cutting the human away from the animal. And this is the promise that the Tyrell Corporation is making with their slogan, 'More Human Than Human': to produce a humanity that is disconnected from the finitude of humanity's very real animality" (2013:144–45). However ironic, the "new age of the human" might very well herald a world inhabited by a mono-species more human than human. Such an android "more" heralds a loss of the humanity we share with all other "earth beings" (de la Cadena 2015). To respond to such a loss, we may need to cultivate a form of machinic animism that would privilege solidarity over technological manipulation and put into practice ontological boundary crossing alongside specialized learning. Perhaps such a revalorization, capable of incorporating the perspectives of other thinking subjects into a shared cosmopolitics, will be capable of providing us with the sympathetic imagination capable of making the Anthropocene Era truly human.

Part II

Philosophical Responses to the Anthropocene

Chapter Six

Panpsychism

A Metaphysics for the Anthropocene Age

Mind is no other than mountains and rivers and the great wide Earth, the sun and moon and stars.

—Dōgen

Coined by Italian philosopher Francesco Patrizi in the late sixteenth century (Skrbina 2017:7), the term *panpsychism* can be defined, in the words of the *Cambridge Dictionary of Philosophy* (1999), as "the doctrine that the physical world is pervasively psychical, sentient, or conscious (understood as equivalent)." Philosopher Thomas Nagel gives us the best-known definition of the term: "By panpsychism I mean the view that the basic physical constituents of the universe have mental properties, whether or not they are parts of living organisms" (1979:181).

In its religious form panpsychism is a kind of religious naturalism, since it holds that the entire universe has mentality, or sentience, and that, when taken as a whole, this sentient universe can be considered divine. The gods have always been attributed mentality, so the originality of religious panpsychism lies in identifying the mentality of the divine with the matter of the universe, and in this it can be considered a form of pantheism, or even a philosophical foundation for Gaianism. Though many famous panpsychists have been religious, the panpsychist position stands on its own, the divinity of the material universe being more a question of axiology than of ontology. Often referencing the "sacred depths of nature," religious

121

122 | Grounding God

panpsychists share with Gaianists and religious naturalists the veneration of nature for "its beauty, terror, scale, stochasticity, emergent complexity, and evolutionary development" (Wildman 2014:41). Yet notwithstanding its many religious adherents, panpsychism is a philosophy, not a religion, and its validity remains intact from an atheist position. It thus gives us a general philosophical foundation to make sense of and universalize many of the religious intuitions that have been developed in earlier chapters. In particular, this chapter will present a coherent metaphysics to show that reality is inherently monistic rather than dualistic, and that mind does not inhere in the human mind alone but is intrinsic to nature itself.

Though this philosophical position has a long history, going back to the Neoplatonists, to Giordano Bruno, Goethe, Leibniz, and Paracelsus, and in the twentieth century to Whitehead, Hartshorne, and David Ray Griffin, it has remained fairly marginal in the philosophical tradition, often considered counterintuitive since it effectively puts into question the binary thinking constitutive of modern ideology that distinguishes between a transcendent deity and a conscious human soul over and against an immanent material world devoid of mental attributes. If the difference between religious and areligious forms of panpsychism relates to the attitude one has toward the material earth, and whether or not it inspires awe, reverence, and devotion, the distinctions between religious theism and religious panpsychism are more acute. Since energy can be construed as mental and mentality is as eternal as matter itself[1] (as Einstein's $e=mc^2$ has shown), the separation of the divine from the matter of the universe makes little sense. Religious panpsychists thus reject belief in a transcendent world (the afterlife) and a transcendent God, seeking scientific explanations of matter that belie modern distinctions such as nature–culture, body–mind, immanent–transcendent. It is this dissolution of the notion of a transcendent deity and a transcendent soul so important for anthropocentrism that has roused the ire of both traditional theists and secular humanists intent upon retaining human exceptionalism even at the cost of ignoring cognitive and brain sciences, as well as biology and physics, and attempting to discredit panpsychism by falsely claiming that panpsychists believe that rocks think (to cite just one example). Rocks do not have abstract thoughts the way humans do, but science can trace sentience and mental properties like choice at least as far back in evolutionary time as bacteria, and it is more logically feasible to think that all of matter, including such things as neurons and other cells and even electrons, are sentient than to claim that sentience appeared all of a sudden out of nonsentient matter. The main point that panpsychism makes is therefore that matter and mind are one and the same, and hence that the dualities of modern theory, between body and soul, are mistaken.

Now that we have entered the new geological age of the Anthropocene, much research has gone into undermining such modern dichotomies. From DEET-resistant mosquitoes to the ozone heavens, there is no nature untouched by culture, making classical substance dualism appear both unsustainable and irrelevant. Though such efforts can be traced back to biosemiotics and theories such as Uexkull's lifeworld (*Weltbild*), Watsuji Tetsuro's *fudo*, or Charles Peirce's semiotics, today such efforts have become mainstream as scholars seek to understand the social causes of climate change and seek ways of conceptualizing nature–cultures beyond the confines of Western dualism. Thanks to many recent scholarly attempts to view Western dichotomies as regional anthropological contributions rather than universal objective criteria, binaries such as "nature" and "culture" and "mind" and "matter" have come to be understood as the product of a particular historical process and express the specific distribution of ontological properties developed and structurally maintained by Western modernity.

But habits die hard, and many academic disciplines remain entrenched in ideological presuppositions that take for granted a human identity as soul substance separate from the material world. According to panpsychist philosopher David Ray Griffin, many continue to support mind–body dualism simply because they have the emotional need to believe in life after death, such that "the wish (or the fear) may be the parent of the paradigm" (1998:11–12). Indeed, interpreting matter as inert was necessary in order to contrast atheism and animism, which held that the universe was capable of self-organization. If matter was considered inert, Boyle and Newton could show the necessity of a Prime Mover external to the universe itself (Griffin 1998:12–13). When such views were later turned on their head and replaced with materialism, the dualism intrinsic to the religious view remained intact. For materialists, matter remained inert, and the mental remained somehow metaphysically distinct from matter even if no longer attributed to an external divine cause. From Descartes's substance dualism, which celebrated soul over and against body, to Bacon's separation of culture from nature (which man could "put on the rack, and do to as he would"), such dualisms have become endemic to a world divided against itself.

It is through such an understanding of the natural world as empty of symbolic meaning and sentience that the Western world could dissociate it

124 | Grounding God

from ethical consideration, and thereby justify the destruction and deple-tion of the ecosystem.[2] According to this modern separation, all entities either have subjective mental properties that inhere in human beings alone or objective material properties, and hence no intrinsic value. Indeed, as Leonora Cohen Rosenfield points out, "Descartes's denial of experience to 'nature,' which included all nonhuman animals, was used to justify exploit-ative practices such as hunting and vivisection" (1941:15–16). One might think of the often-quoted example of Western medical experimentation done on dogs in the nineteenth century, which used no anaesthetic since Descartes had established that animals are automata and can't feel. The doctors nonetheless felt the need to cut the dogs' vocal cords so as not to hear the simulacra of pain.

Because Western science has focused exclusively on understanding the external material world, how spatially extended matter relates and interacts with unextended mind has become an aporia in Western thought. Does everything that happens in the mind correspond to neurons firing in the brain, or is free will itself a causal agent of material change? Is consciousness identical with brain function, or might it exist separately from the brain? How can we have subjective experiences like tasting cardamom if the brain is purely objective? But if the mind is separate from the brain, how can it transmit consciousness to the brain? Can worms, jellyfish, or even molecules be conscious without a brain? Does consciousness emerge in evolutionary history because of complex neuronal systems, or might consciousness inhere in all living systems, or even all matter?

In order to answer these questions, the mental must be granted scientific reality alongside matter, and scientific knowledge must include nonmeasurable phenomena such as consciousness and feelings. To do this, however, science must reform its epistemological assumptions regarding the meaning of matter itself, and how such matter can be known. Instead of reducing all of reality to insensate matter driven by mechanical forces, science must engage with the qualitative alongside the quantitative, and undergo what philosopher Christian de Quincey calls an "epistemotherapy" (2002:6) to cure the pathologies of Western dualism. Our task, he claims, "is to transcend the artificial Cartesian split between mind and body, and to reintegrate the subjective and the objective, the psychic and the physical, the qualitative and quantitative, meaning and mechanism, order and chaos, unity and multiplicity at all levels of our being-in-the-world" (6).

Today, such an epistemotherapy is underway. Panpsychism has under-gone a recent revival, and a growing number of philosophers of mind now consider it the most realistic theory to explain the presence of consciousness in the world. Matter has thus come to be understood as possessing the very subjective mental properties attributed in modernity to mind or soul, and hence as capable of experience, self-regulation, and relationality.

Such a revival in the philosophy of mind has been in large part inspired by paradigm shifts that have taken place in the natural sciences. Since matter is indeed energy, in constant relational flux, the matter–mind dichotomy makes little sense in physics. In quantum theory, these events are both waves and particles, bundles or quanta that can act across distance and defy prediction. Because such events are random and nonlocal, space-time cannot be understood as being causally determined by outside forces, and therefore at some level, such events "choose" to happen. Such quantum conundrums have led many physicists to adopt a panpsychist position (Jeans, Sherrington, Wright, Rensch, Walker, Cochran, Bohm, Dyson, Rohm, and Hameroff). In David Bohm and B. J. Hiley's ontological interpretation of quantum theory, for example, "even an electron has at least a rudimentary mental pole, represented mathematically by the quantum potential" (1995:387). Similarly, medical scientist Stuart Hameroff states that "quantum spin networks encode proto-conscious 'funda-mental' experience" (cited in Skrbina 2017:259). This "quantum potential" is also called "quantum choice" by many scientists to emphasize that a certain form of awareness can be deduced (de Quincey 2002:28).

Similarly, biologist Lynn Margulis's epigenetic revolution undermined the genetic determinism that had given an ontological status to the gene outside of relationality to its environment, inspiring new research on symbiogenesis and the interdependency of all species on the planet earth. Inspired by her work, de Quincey looks to biology to trace this primal consciousness back to the arrival of ribonucleotides in evolution, when cells evolved to locate sources of energy in their environment by means of receptors and signal transduction cascades. Whether stimulated by photons or vibrations or molecular motion, receptors are aware of different shapes, energies, wavelengths, and intensities that are useful or harmful for their propagation. From an awareness of physical and chemical properties, to an evolved awareness of prey or predators of symbionts, to the recognition of procreation partners, de Quincey notes that "much of biological evolution can be said to entail the evolution of what organisms are aware of." If this is already the case with all sexual eukaryotes, it becomes the central feature of the neuron, which he describes as "a cell type specialized for awareness, and this made possible the avenue of awareness called consciousness" (2002:89–91; see also Dombrowski 1988; Varela 1992).[3]

126 | Grounding God

If such agency and intentionality is as widespread as these scholars claim, the idea that mind and matter must somehow be coextensive becomes far more convincing than substance dualism, which is unable to account for the interaction between the physical and the mental, and thereby imprisons the physical world in a deterministic closure, leading to various untenable theological implications. The rejection of substance dualism leaves us of necessity with various forms of monism, capable of giving us a united theory of nature that can account for both mind and matter. Yet understanding how mental qualities could appear in evolutionary history from a world of nonmental elements has proved quite difficult. Ontogenetically, during the nine months of fetal growth, when does the fetus acquire consciousness? And phylogenetically, where is one to draw the line between animals that are conscious and those that are not? Dolphins and cats cause little trouble, but what about goldfish, earthworms, and wasps? As philosopher David Skrbina points out, almost everything on our planet has emerged, but does consciousness function like an organism or more like time and space, which cannot evolve and have always existed (2017:18–19)?

Scholars have sought to resolve this dilemma in one of three ways: either qualia emerge at a certain level of complexity (mental emergentism), or the basic constituents of the cosmos *are* conscious qualia (idealistic monism) or *have* such qualia as attributes or qualities from time immemorial (metaphysical monism or dual-aspect monism). Those scholars who adopt a form of idealistic monism (Ells)[4] maintain that the physical is derived from the mental. If, on the contrary, the mental is understood as evolving from the physical, one must adopt a form of mental emergentism (O'Conner and Wong, Popper, Humphrey, Chalmers, Dennett, Rosenberg, Brüntrup) that must explain how something mental can be derived from something material. Scholars who adopt the emergentist position hold that consciousness emerged from nonconscious matter at a certain ill-defined moment of evolutionary history, as an epiphenomenon that was caused by the evolution of complex life systems equipped with nervous systems and brains. Just as solidity emerges when liquids cool, so consciousness emerges from an embryo without being present in the nutrients that feed the embryo (Popper 1977, cited in Skrbina 2017:254). This position was famously defended by Lucretius as follows: "Since we perceive that the eggs of birds change into live chicks, and that worms come seething out of the earth when untimely rains have caused putrefaction, it is evident that the sensible can be produced from the insensible" (cited in Wilson 2006:177). Updating Lucretius's position to take into account nonequilibrium thermodynamics, philosopher Lawrence

Cahoone explains how the emergentist position allows scientists to focus on emerging complexity over time: "The more complex has generally come later in cosmogenesis, enabled by the fine-tuning of physical forces and pockets of non-equilibrium thermodynamics" (2008:56–57). If complex configurations of matter are syntheses of their components upon which they depend, the entential phenomena they give rise to cannot be reduced to their parts. As an epiphenomenon, consciousness was neither willed nor destined, though for many it serves the important evolutionary function of abetting social cohesion by allowing certain animals to put themselves in the place of others, and see themselves as they are seen by others (Tomasello 2019). Indeed, if experience is not understood in emergentist terms, the distinction between matter that is capable of conscious experience (entential phenomena) and matter that is not still needs to be explained. Neuroanthropologist Terrence Deacon explains the inconclusive results obtained from forms of panpsychist monism in explaining entential phenomena as follows:

> Making mind as ubiquitous as space and time is no more of an answer to this dilemma than was Aristotle's concept of final causality. If everything is entential in some respect, then we are nevertheless required to specify why the absential properties of life and mind are so distinctive from the properties exhibited in the non-living world. We still need to draw a line and explain how it is crossed. Is experience a feature of the interactions of elementary particles? . . . Wherever we place the threshold distinguishing entential phenomena from the rest of natural processes, we need an account of what is involved in crossing that threshold. (2012:40)

Other scholars find the emergence of consciousness from nonconscious matter unconvincing. As Skrbina explains, mental emergentists incur "the burden of explaining how the experiential can arise from, or emerge from, a wholly non-experiential physical reality . . . *how can it be* that something like experience can possibly emerge from that which is utterly devoid of experience?" (2011:18). De Quincey believes it is inconceivable "that sentience (subjectivity, consciousness) could ever emerge or evolve from wholly insentient (objective, physical) matter" (2002:45). Using the work of philosophers Whitehead and Hartshorne, philosopher David Ray Griffin claims that the assumption that conscious experience has emerged out of insentient matter constitutes what he calls the "actual-possible fallacy" (1998:75). To

128 | Grounding God

avoid such a fallacy, Griffin asserts that the physical and the mental must be understood as coeval and equiprimordial, leading to metaphysical monism or dual-aspect monism (Peirce, Whitehead, Hartshorne, Skrbina, Strawson, Nagel, de Quincey, Ruyer, Griffin). These scholars prefer the position that matter and consciousness are coextensive and thus that sentience is an intrinsic quality of matter "all the way down." Similar to Spinoza's understanding of matter and soul as two aspects of the same reality, consciousness is understood as a nonmaterial attribute of matter (dual-aspect monism). Semiotician Charles Sanders Peirce clarifies this Spinozian position well when he calls matter "specialized and partially deadened mind" (1892:533). In his well-known article published in *The Monist* in 1892, he explains: "It would be a mistake to conceive of the psychical and the physical aspects of matter as two aspects absolutely distinct. Viewing a thing from the outside, considering its relations of action and reaction with other things, it appears as matter. Viewing it from the inside, looking at its immediate character as feeling, it appears as consciousness" (1992 reprint: 349). Another scholar who agrees with Spinoza that there can be no distinction between substance and attribute, and that the experiential "can't emerge from the wholly and utterly nonexperiential," is philosopher Galen Strawson, who claims that "there is no good reason to believe that anything nonexperiential exists." Since "all concrete reality is necessarily experiential," he concludes that "we should favor panpsychism over all other substantive theories of the fundamental nature of reality" (2017:80, 82, 98, 104, 105).

Understanding consciousness as a continuous and fundamental quality of the universe itself, whose "emergence with the birth of the universe is neither more nor less mysterious than the emergence of matter and energy" (Velmans 2014:371), has led some scholars to follow philosopher and physicist David Bohm in equating it with quantum field theory, a sort of "swarm intelligence," "hive mind," or "property of the breathing earth" (Abram 2017:222). Philosopher David Abram espouses this approach, since it offers a resolution to the Western separation of the human mind from brute nature. For Abram, attributing consciousness to the earth itself could help overcome anthropocentrism, or what he calls "the era of human arrogance . . . that has now brought the current biosphere to the very brink of the abyss" (2017:241). Suggesting "that mind is not at all a human possession but rather a property of the breathing Earth—a property in which we, along with the other animals and plants, all participate" could bring to light "the thorough dependence of human culture upon the continued creativity and flourishing of the more-than-human natural world" (223).

Such a panpsychist understanding of the earth can have important ethical consequences, in that the human mind is integrated into a universe with which it shares sentience or even what Skrbina calls "the quality of enmindedness" (2017:5). Instead of taking for granted, as the modern paradigm has done, that mind is what has set us apart from the rest of nature, sharing mind with the earth can in itself overturn human exceptionalism and replace it with more empathetic and ecological values. For philosopher Patrick Spät, in light of our climate crisis, "the formulation of 'human dignity' is without a doubt very important and one of the greatest intellectual and ethical achievements in human history, but the present situation calls for widening its scope to all participants in the planetary ecosystem" (2009:175–76).

The Night in Which All Cows Are Black: Is All Matter Equally Sentient?

If panpsychist views can provide an ethical reorientation for the Anthropocene Age, such views can also be used to do just the opposite, by undermining the distinction between animate and inanimate matter, between made and evolved entities. Philosopher Freya Mathews is a good example of such a trend. Though she espouses dual-aspect panpsychism, rather than using it to undermine anthropocentrism in order to further the health of the ecosphere, she uses panpsychism to problematize the very possibility of making ecological moral judgments. Reducing the meaning of matter, or what she calls "nature" to physics, and thus to particles, she claims that "nature will not be of particular interest to environmentalists, since such a nature cannot be threatened, and does not, on the face of it at any rate, stand in need of human protection or conservation" (2005:26). If environmentalists focus exclusively on the biological definition of nature, "since it is this biological realm which is clearly under threat from the engines of industry and the appetites of global markets today" (26), they are unable, she asserts, to defend inorganic elements of the environment like rivers, caves, and mountains. When ecologists seek to defend "elements or aspects of the world that have not been created or unduly modified by human agency" (27), they divide matter over and against itself, as if the matter of a vacuum cleaner were somehow different from the matter of a kangaroo. But since panpsychism endows the entire material world with what she calls "an internal or subjective aspect," no distinction can be drawn between the

130 | Grounding God

agency of the living and the nonliving, the human and the nonhuman, the made and the evolved. And she concludes:

> All material form is to some extent, from a panpsychist point of view, a manifestation of mentality; therefore to regard trees and rocks and animals, not to mention webs, hives, termite mounds, and coral reefs, as falling within nature, and cars and fax machines and cities as falling outside it, seems to be a case of oversimplifying the issue, to say the least. Any form of environmentalism resting on such a dichotomization of the human and the nonhuman will undoubtedly end up reinstating dualistic fault lines in the terrain of modern thought and practice, despite its own best intentions. (27)

Once nature has been reduced to matter and matter to conscious molecules, there is indeed no distinction between a human artifact like a car and naturally evolved forms of matter like forests. Indeed, once she has reduced nature to molecules, Mathews is justified in claiming that letting a forest regrow is equivalent to letting a city go derelict, and indeed, this is precisely what she calls for: to allow ghettos to disintegrate, cars to rust, and weeds to grow.[5] Mathews's inability to differentiate between human-made artifacts, created by exterior aggregation to serve particular human purposes, and planetary evolution, developed to secure the present and future equilibrium of ecosystems, leads her to diminish the importance of social welfare and ecological efforts to remediate climate change.

To treat structures created by humans for particular human uses as identical to structures evolved to sustain themselves as essential elements in the ecodependent flourishing of an entire ecosystem constitutes an inability to judge what can and should be corrected and improved by humans (like tenement buildings) and what cannot (like forests), what is good for life on the planet and what is not. If panpsychism is used as an argument to claim that we are unable to differentiate the living from the nonliving, the natural from the artifactual, we will be unable to develop critical judgments and work together to develop an ethics to address climate change. Cars don't suffer, and are not going extinct. Trees and rivers, mountains and prairies are necessary habitats for the biodiversity of the planet and regulators of planetary CO_2 levels. Slums should be improved, forests should be protected.

Mathews is not alone in seeking to undermine not only the human–nonhuman divide, but also the living–nonliving and made–evolved distinctions.[6] Generalizing agency to the nonliving is a central component of the Actor–Network theory developed by Bruno Latour, and accepting the equal value and agency of nonlife is central to the work of philosophers Jane Bennett and Isabelle Stengers and anthropologist Elisabeth Povinelli. Since life depends upon nonlife, and, as Povinelli puts it, "life is merely a moment in the greater dynamic unfolding of Nonlife" (2016:176), devoting oneself to defending neutrinos or ancestors is as equally commendable as defending forests and rhinos. And if neutrinos, ancestors, and hair dryers are also sentient according to panpsychists, how are we to avoid indifference toward the destruction of the living earth, since, after all, everything has to die and decay at some point or another?[7] If we are to treat a rock with the same consideration as a jaguar, and a washing machine as equivalent to an indigenous Anuar, it is difficult to avoid a certain moral nihilism intrinsic to commodity fetishism. Such an attribution of sentience to human artifacts makes it difficult to differentiate between those beings with agency that can suffer and whose death is a loss for the ecosystem, and those things made to serve human ends that decompose without suffering and without participating in ecosystemic equilibrium at all. Though Mathews is correct at a very abstract level that the entire planet—petrol, hair dryers, streams, forests, and tadpoles—is made of molecules that may be sentient to varying degrees, shifting from ontological essences to relational degrees does not create a "night in which all cows are black," as Hegel put it. The fact that all of matter is sentient does not entail that it is all equally so, nor that it therefore demands a similar ethical response.

Just as Mathews uses panpsychism to maintain that all matter is sentient and thus that we cannot differentiate between artifacts and evolved beings, philosopher Jane Bennett similarly applies the living criteria of health indiscriminately to all matter. She asks: "What would happen to our thinking about politics if we took more seriously the idea that technological and natural materialities were themselves actors alongside and within us—were vitalities, trajectories, and powers irreducible to the meanings, intentions, or symbolic values humans invest in them?" (2010c:48). Overcoming the modern distinction between the human and other forms of life, and replacing such a distinction with the materiality and health of bodies is certainly necessary and beneficial, since, as she puts it, "it can inspire a greater sense of the extent to which all bodies are kin in the sense of being inextricably enmeshed in a dense network of relations (2010a:47–48). But Bennett goes too far when she proceeds to treat "technological and natural materialities" as synonymous and include human artifacts like cars and computers in the

132 | Grounding God

network of vibrant and healthy bodies. In what sense is a hammer's vitality irreducible to the uses humans invest in it? A chair is not vibrant the way a dog or a daffodil is, and a vacuum cleaner does not require the same type of care that a homeless person or an ecosystem does. By not distinguishing between "technological and natural materialities," Bennett adopts a position similar to that of Mathews who used panpsychism to draw a parallel between forests and slums, anthropomorphizing the nonliving and using language usually reserved for the living—"vibrant," "kinship," "healthy," and "enabling"—to describe inanimate matter. Bennett has admitted that her work has "a touch of anthropocentrism,"[8] but claims this is essential in order to replace passive descriptions of objects with active ones. Yet objects can be understood as active agents, without needing to be described in terms of "health" and "kinship." How can human artifacts and natural living materialities be treated as equivalent in light of the physiological criteria of health she uses? Does she really think that animating a car as more or less healthy, and thus more or less alive is a good idea? There are bodies that enter into kinship relations, are healthy or ill, enabled or hindered, and bodies that do not. There are bodies that we treat as means to an end, and bodies that we do not. If confined to life forms, Bennett's physiological criteria could be used to defend an embodied ethics that could go far in overcoming the exploitation not only of certain humans (those historically identified with the body and embodied functions) but also of other living organisms. But attributing the same vibrant enabling criteria to inanimate artifacts undermines her project from within by reinforcing commodity fetishism and concealing human labor and human power relations behind such "vibrant" commodities. As Bennett must herself be well aware, the advertising industry and capitalist market are happy to exploit the anthropomorphization of artifacts for greater profit at the expense of the environment and the sustainable living she advocates.

By attributing sentience and health to human artifacts that stand outside of evolutionary ecosystems, authors such as Mathews and Bennett undermine, perhaps unknowingly, the very possibility of moral engagement and judgment. The lack of distinction between living and nonliving entities makes political and ethical considerations obsolete, since it leaves us unable to differentiate between sensate, conscious beings who suffer, intend, and resist, and constructed entities devoid of sensation who carry out the programs they were designed for. Under these conditions, it becomes impossible to protect animals and ecologies from torture and destruction, since they are no different from paper cutters, computers, and trains. Isn't a technological tool made of human social relations in a way that a polar bear is not, and isn't such a distinction essential to understanding the nature of the tool and of the bear?

An Anthropology beyond the Human

Because scholars of AI have tended to anthropomorphize machines and mechanize humans, the tendency to not distinguish between different forms of matter has become a widespread form of alienation and has reinforced a misunderstanding of the nature of nature, as material configuration. Because of this growing tendency to generalize all agency as equal (Latour), all matter as vibrant (Bennett), and all matter as equally sentient (Mathews), many scholars have developed responses that seek to differentiate between different material forms and the levels of sentience and awareness their configuration enables them to express. We will discuss two attempts to overcome this alienation, those of anthropologists Tim Ingold and Eduardo Kohn. Where Ingold differentiates between living and dead organisms, Kohn's biosemiotics is able to extend life to entire ecosystems such as forests. Scholars such as Mathews and Bennett who are unable to differentiate between rocks and racoons have much to learn from these thinkers.

Anthropologist Tim Ingold holds Latour, Bennett, and Mathews to account for eliding the distinction between living organisms and inert matter and flattening all forms of matter to an external expression of agency, vibrancy, or sentience. Imagining a discussion between an ant (Latour) and a spider (himself), spider claims that "it is simply absurd to place a grain of sand and an aphid on the scales of a balance and to claim that they are equivalent" (2011:94). Aphids, he points out, have nervous systems, which gives them, and all other creatures with nervous systems, a capacity of "attention" that differentiates the grain of sand from the aphid, and the spider from a leaf. "It is the attentiveness of this movement that qualifies it as an instance of *action* and, by the same token, qualifies me as an *agent*. To put it another way, the essence of action lies not in forethought (as our human philosopher would claim) but in the close coupling of bodily movement and perception" (94). It is because of this attention that humans and spiders and other living beings can remember what they learn and develop skills over time to adapt to their environment, and these skills differentiate our actions from those of inanimate entities. A car or a rug does not have the attentiveness to context and the perceptual abilities to transform itself

134 | Grounding God

and grow in light of its context the way living agents do. And he concludes: "To attribute agency to objects that do not grow or develop, that consequently embody no skill, and whose movement is not therefore coupled to their perception, is ludicrous" (94). We are the particular animal that uses inanimate tools to increase our perception, and thus to modify our skills to respond to a world that speaks to us through the agency of myriad living entities, whose voices can be heard and whose health can be fostered, but only if we are able to differentiate between bodies that suffer, intend, and flourish and bodies that don't.

Ingold's analysis points to some important distinctions between perceptive organisms with nervous systems that grow and develop, but his distinction is unable to take into account the rivers and mountains that Mathews rightly mentions as requiring consideration. In the Anthropocene Age, when ecological concerns have become so crucial for the survival of the planet, we must develop a politics and an ethics that can engage with polar bears but also with glaciers, with clown fish but also with coral reefs. Hence, though nervous systems should certainly be an important criterion to help understand living animals and develop animal rights, it is not in itself sufficient to implement a politics and an ethics for the Anthropocene. The lives of spiders and aphids, as well as human lives, are to a large extent determined by inanimate forms of matter that do not have nervous systems, and we must find a way to account for their agency, their status as ends, and the ways they enter into an interdependent mesh with living bodies.

Anthropologist Eduardo Kohn has found a way to enlarge his definition of life to include animals, plants, and their habitats (he excludes the mineral and chemical) without sacrificing the distinction between living and nonliving organisms. Kohn's anthropology "beyond the human" extends thinking, and with it "strivings, purposes, telos, intentions, functions and significance" to entire ecosystems.[9] His book *How Forests Think: Toward an Anthropology beyond the Human* describes his fieldwork in the Colombian rain forest with indigenous peoples. In order to describe emergent meanings that do not revolve around the human, he uses Peirce's semiotic system to develop a system of signs to characterize selves. In this way he is able to convincingly explain what differentiates living and nonliving matter, and to develop a philosophy of life that includes not just the animals in the forest, but the forest itself. Because life is semiotic, and signs have meaning only for selves, a self is a living organism that maintains an individual form over time. Kohn agrees with Ingold that such forms "learn by experience, which is another way of saying that, through the semiotic process I've been describing, they can grow" (2013:77). But unlike Bennett he claims that materiality is not enough to confer vitality (92), for it is only thinking matter that is alive. He defines thought as the semiotic ability of form to remember the past and predict a future, and it is such thought that accounts for vitality and differentiates animate from inanimate matter. Rather than distributing agency to matter indiscriminately, Kohn asks us to understand agency as the unique attribute of animate selves that interpret and represent the world around them and therefore think: "Life thinks; stones don't" (100). Recalling Uexküll's famous explanation of the lifeworld of the tick, Kohn uses the example of the anteater to show that it is formed by past knowledge of ant tunnels, which are other to it yet essential to the form it seeks to maintain. Agency should not be attributed indiscriminately to all action but rather only to the action of an organism that "acts for itself" in order to maintain its form in relation to an otherness that it is not but that it depends upon to survive and project itself into the future. Anteaters therefore think, since thought is "the product of an expectation—of a highly embodied 'guess' at what the future will hold" (76), in this case ant tunnels similar to ones to which it adapted its snout in the past. In his own words:

> Living beings differ from snowflakes because life is intrinsically semiotic, and semiosis is always for a self. The form an individual anteater takes comes to represent, for a future instantiation of itself, the environment its lineage has come to fit over evolutionary time. Anteater lineages selectively remember their previous fits to their environments; snowflakes don't. . . . Any kind of life, be it human, biological, or even, someday, inorganic, will spontaneously exhibit this embodied, localized, representational, future-predicting dynamic that captures, amplifies, and proliferates the tendency toward habit taking in a future instantiation of itself. (77–78)

Kohn's biosemiotic system enlarges Peirce's semiotic system to include ecosystems and all organisms capable of using the past to inform the future. But Kohn is no panpsychist and he focuses on reflexively individuated, volitional entities made up of cells to the exclusion of nonliving matter. Such a biosemiotics is an excellent means of valuing life and differentiating sentient, volitional material configurations from nonsentient, nonvolitional ones. Panpsychist philosophers like Bertrand Russell and Alfred North Whitehead, however, grant rudimentary thought even to nonliving material

136 | Grounding God

configurations. Russell uses the same criterion of volitional memory as Kohn to grant thought to a riverbed:

> This [memory] also can be illustrated in a lesser degree by the behaviour of inorganic matter. A watercourse which at most times is dry gradually wears a channel down a gully at the times when it flows, and subsequent rains follow [a similar] course. . . . You may say, if you like, that the river bed "remembers" previous occasions when it experienced cooling streams. . . . You would say [this] was a flight of fancy because you are of the opinion that rivers and river beds do not "think." But if thinking consists of certain modifications of behaviour owing to former occurrences, then we shall have to say that the river bed thinks, though its thinking is somewhat rudimentary. (1956:155)

To fully address the challenge of Mathews and Bennett, a more complete schema of material forms of agency and experience is therefore needed in order to distinguish different material configurations, understand the relationship between parts and wholes, and differentiate between constructed and evolved entities.

Whitehead: Differentiating a Stone from a Stork

Working from the discipline of philosophy rather than anthropology, panpsychists have developed criteria to enhance our understanding of the gradations of difference between different forms of matter, and come to conclusions similar to those of Ingold and Kohn. For philosopher D. S. Clarke, for instance, the ability to experience requires an appropriate level of structure and internal organization as well as spontaneity of behavior, a qualitative aspect, and the ability to maintain oneself through homeostasis (2003:5). Thermostats and computers have organization but lack an interested point of view. Quarks lack internal organization of parts, being fundamental.

Though he never called himself a panpsychist, philosopher Alfred North Whitehead developed such gradations of difference into the most important and original response to those critics who are unable to differentiate between constructed and evolved entities. While his philosophy has remained at the fringes of the philosophical tradition because of the difficulty of his writing and his concepts, his theory is certainly one of the most important of the twentieth century and a major influence on philosophers such as Gilles Deleuze and Félix Guattari, Hannah Arendt, Maurice Merleau-Ponty, and more recently Isabelle Stengers.

Because Whitehead holds that there are no substances, only events, each event is only the accumulation of its effects on other events. In this way, our perception is not something enclosed inside a soul, or a self, but is part of the world, directly in contact with those events that cause its sensual organization of the world. Because subjects are not substances with inner qualities and states that might constitute an unchanging soul, independent ontological substances represent "the misconception which has haunted philosophic literature throughout the centuries. . . . There is no such mode of existence; every entity is only to be understood in terms of the way in which it is interwoven with the rest of the Universe" (1911:687, cited in Henning 2005:29). Whitehead calls this perception *prehension*, a general form of experience that can include unconscious sentience as well as conscious mental states. It is by including unconscious sentience within the category of prehension that Whitehead is able to extend experience to events that Western philosophy has categorized as unliving matter, and hence as falling outside the realm of moral considerability. Never merely representations of an external world or unfeeling physical events, prehensions are themselves experiential events in the world, and thus sentient subjects. By generalizing experience to all of matter, Whitehead is able to move beyond the divide between mind and matter, as well as that between subject and object, and thereby "lead to more penetrating ways of understanding" (1968:135).

Since all events are self-organizing and self-determining to varying degrees, all events can be considered organisms, and Whitehead does indeed refer to his philosophy as a "philosophy of organism." Yet rather than maintaining that all of matter is equally sentient, Whitehead clearly differentiates between different modes of organizing matter, detailing grada-tions of experience for different material configurations. Organisms that are entirely aggregative with no internal centralization form what Whitehead calls a nexus (and Ferré calls "aggregate entities"), whereas different degrees of organization between constituting parts create a "social order" (Ferré 1996a:337) constituting what Whitehead calls societies. As philosopher Joseph Bracken points out, these societies resemble "natural systems" in that they refer to what he calls organic, suborganic, and supra-organic systems—to trees, to molecules, and to human communities (1995:3). Nonliving soci-eties are typified by stable behavior, inherited from the past, and show next to no signs of spontaneity or change. Living societies, on the other hand,

138 | Grounding God

show signs of creative spontaneity (Henning 2005), conforming to Kohn's understanding of life in learning from the past to adapt and conform to their environments in order to predict a future and thus to project their own survival and well-being into the future. Such societies are often interdependent, living organisms working with unliving nexuses in order to create conditions of equilibrium (Armstrong-Buck 1986:247). There are thus no ontological differences among organisms, but rather differences of degree of organization and centralization. Susan Armstrong-Buck clarifies this point: "The differences then between inorganic material and the highest reaches of human consciousness are due to differences in the organization of the constituent actual occasions into nexus and structured societies. A conscious thought entertained by the dominant occasion of a human psyche is dimly foreshadowed by the conceptual prehensions of the simplest actual occasions in a piece of iron ore, tradition-bound though they are" (249). Though we cannot grasp the quality of their experience, feeling exists even in electrons and living cells. But an earthworm would, to cite Frederick Ferré, "seem a Mozart by comparison" (1996a:356). Likewise a sparrow experiences its environment far more intensely than does an earthworm, and a bonobo can achieve even more complex and rich experiences than a sparrow. The more developed brain structure of Homo sapiens means that humans are capable of more complex and hence even more valuable experiences than the bonobo.

Whitehead focuses on six primary configurations of matter: aggregate entities (for example, a rock), systematic entities (for example, an airplane), formal temporal and nontemporal entities (for instance, a species), organic entities (like a possum), compound entities (for example, a cell), and fundamental entities that cannot be further reduced (like water), all of which, as he puts it, "influence each other, require each other, and lead on to each other" (1968:156–57; Ferré 1996a:336–38). As composed of these different typologies, matter is constituted by differences, with varying degrees of internal relations and hence centralization. Since ontological entities do not exist as more than passing events for Whitehead, these differences are always a matter of degree. Though the molecules that constitute them may have a very basic level of unconscious experience, inorganic aggregates like rocks possess no centralization, and thus no subjective experience. Having no experiential unity that might allow for feelings and individual agential action, such aggregates are created from without, often in layers. Such aggregates can form into societies, such as billiard balls or mountains, that give them constitutive properties that a mere pile of sand does not have. But such properties do *not* give these aggregates experiential unity, and

Panpsychism | 139

lacking strong internal relations, they cannot respond to their environment as individuals. As Deacon explains:

> Only living organisms are truly individual in the sense that all aspects of their constitution are organized around the maintenance and perpetuation of this form of organization. It is the circularity of this consequential architecture—teleodynamics—that both delineates and creates the individuality that is organism self. Organism functions are in this way indirectly self-referential and self-projecting. In the inanimate world around us, we find no trace of this circularity of generative processes. Though bounded and unified, neither stones, nor drops of water, nor automobiles, nor computers, nor any other non-living artifact is reflexively individuated in this way. (2012:465)

Misunderstanding panpsychism by amalgamating these six different configurations of matter together is a category mistake. The different ways that matter is organized produce different modes of functioning, different teleologies and causes, different levels of sentience and awareness, and thus different explanations. If Nagel ascribes mental properties to the basic constituents of matter, this does not in any way presuppose that the composite entities formed by means of these basic constituents unify such mental properties into a sentient, thinking whole. This error is known as the "fallacy of composition." Philosopher Pierfrancesco Basile explains: "Surely, to believe that a whole (a rock) must have all the properties of its parts (the rock's ultimate constituents) is to be guilty of the mistake known as 'the fallacy of composition'" (2009:181).

Whitehead's organizational schema allows for a clear and convincing means of differentiating between material events, and explaining how consciousness and self-consciousness can be enjoyed only by those individuals whose molecules form cells that form nervous systems and brains capable of individualizing experience. So when scholars demean panpsychism by claiming that such a position holds that rocks can think, they misunderstand it. First, thinking must be redefined in order to understand those scholars such as Kohn (2017) and Russell (1927, 1956) who do indeed claim that thinking can be generalized to all entities capable of learning from the past to predict the future and adapt to the present. And second, if we choose to retain a definition of thinking that includes self-consciousness, then only those compound individuals possessing centralized experience are capable of

140 | Grounding God

it. For Whitehead, if all compound individuals do indeed have experience of varying degrees and some of them are capable of thought, aggregate entities do not, since their parts are not centralized in such a manner as to allow for individualized experience.

Conclusion

In this time of ecological crisis, it is essential to recognize the conceptual framework that has facilitated the commodification and expropriation of the nonhuman world. Mind–body dualism must be held accountable for justifying a hierarchy of values that placed the immaterial soul or mind over and against the material body, the world of culture over and against the world of nature, and human values over and against a valueless non-human world. Such dualities and antagonisms have created a world divided against itself, where nonhuman nature has been deprived of value, and the material, animal, sentient, mortal human being has falsely understood its identity as somehow transcendent, purely rational, and heaven- rather than earth-bound. Panpsychism could go far in overcoming these illusions, and replacing them with an organic monism capable of reintegrating mind into matter, culture into nature and value into the nonhuman world. If matter is enminded, then sentience, awareness, and relationality can be extended to the nonhuman world, and with them, the values and rights attributed to the human person.

It is thus essential to study material forms in terms of their causation, their relationality, their unity, and their intentionality in order to clearly differentiate between different material configurations. Natural living entities find their cause in evolution, which allows them to grow based upon auton-omous morphogenesis. They are transformed by adapting to an ecosystem and its many inhabitants, which they in their turn transform. They have united perception and intentional structures embedded in their morphoge-netic structure, and their actions are intentional, as they seek teleonomically to survive and reproduce. Natural nonliving forms are constituted by the four elements, find their cause in the Big Bang, but rather than evolving, they undergo geological and atmospheric transformation caused by outside sources, which can transform both their form and substance. They have aggregative structures and thus no internal unity that would allow for per-ceptual and intentional awareness, though their parts (molecules) may be sentient at a very basic level. Human artifacts are caused by human beings

Panpsychism | 141

to serve particular ends. They do not evolve nor constitute environmental ecosystems, though they can be programmed to relate to such ecosystems. They are transformed by geological and atmospheric pressures from without, but as aggregative structures, they have no internal intentionality that could allow them to grow by means of morphogenesis. They have no intrinsic teleonomic unity and cannot reproduce, though they may be constituted with a unitary structure given to them by the human beings who create them. As aggregative structures, they are not sentient, though their parts may be sentient at a very basic level. Natural nonliving forms and human artifacts differ in that such natural forms constitute the fundamental, elemental structure of the earth and its atmosphere. These elements are essential to ecosystems and the forms of life that inhabit them, whereas human artifacts are not. Human artifacts can destroy, abet, and transform living and nonliving natural forms, but are not necessary for the survival of either. Taking into account these different material configurations is essential to constitute the values that are so lacking in the conceptual attempts to address climate change. Contrary to the tendency we saw at work in the scholarship of Mathews, such differences cannot be sublated, for they allow us to understand how complexity evolves in particular ways that allow for the development of sentience, awareness, and intentionality.

Without studying the material configuration of each entity in order to understand its level of complexity and sentience, we tend to characterize the nonhuman world in the Cartesian terms of *res extensa*. Yet by claiming that there are no "brute facts," devoid of experience, Whitehead provides a necessary critique of what he calls the "vacuous actuality" of Cartesian dualism. Since the universe is a process that organizes itself to allow for greater complexification and thus greater awareness and sentience, all extension (*res extensa*) is vibrating subjective experience (*res cogitans*) and "apart from the experiences of subjects there is nothing, nothing, nothing, bare nothingness" (1978:167, cited in Henning 2005:38). Each experiential event thus seeks to sustain itself in order to reach its own goals. Whitehead notes: "If we discard the notion of vacuous existence, we must conceive each actuality as attaining an end for itself. Its very existence is the presentation of its many components to itself, for the sake of its own ends" (1929:30–31, cited in Henning 2005:39–40). In seeking to maintain itself, each entity is a self-valuing experiential event, leading to what Henning calls an "ontological democracy" where "everything has value in and for itself. To be actual is to have value" (39–40).

The stone, then, cannot feel, if by sentience we mean the intentional structure of subjective experience. As a nexus, it is an aggregative entity with

142 | Grounding God

no internal centralization, and thus no ability to respond to its environment as an individual. But perhaps, to repeat Bertrand Russell's point, "if thinking consists of certain modifications of behavior owing to former occurrences" (1956:155), then the riverbed, and the stone, have rudimentary thought. In an article on cosmopolitics, anthropologist Eduardo Viveiros de Castro (2013) repeats a comment from philosopher Michel Serres on the Myth of Sisyphus: "Everyone talks about Sisyphus, [Serres] points out, and no one says anything about the rock! 'The myth shows the continual fall of the rock,' yet we notice only 'the guilty, unhappy hero working like a slave.'" And Viveiros de Castro continues: "Indeed—what about the rock? . . . Panpsychism. That's what we should be moving to. Animals are just the first step. We'll get to the rocks eventually."[10] Riverbeds and rocks do not suffer, but perhaps, in their own way, they do think, as they remember, in the very event of coagulation of their aggregative parts, thousands of years of erosion, of wind and sun, of flood and flow.

Chapter Seven

Ecosophy

New Values for the Anthropocene Age

In the last chapter we explored a philosophy of life, that of panpsychism, that provides a response to the call to overcome the mind–body divide and the Western dichotomies that have always privileged a mental, male, transcendent dimension over and against a material, immanent, female one, and a human ontology over and against a life ontology that can include the nonhuman world. In understanding matter itself as minded, panpsychism can rehabilitate our material world without falling into the pitfalls of reductive materialism. And finally, panpsychism offers an analysis of different forms of matter, allowing us to differentiate between self-conscious animals, sentient beings, and nonsentient aggregational matter. In this way we can justify the cosmopolitics we developed in preceding chapters with a biocentric ethic, without falling into the common fetishism of human artifacts encouraged by technophiles and research in AI.

Panpsychism gives us the metaphysical grounding of an adequate philosophy for the twenty-first century, one that can include religiosity in deprofanizing nature so long as it does not privilege the transcendent over the materiality of our planet. If panpsychism gives us the metaphysical grounding for a philosophy of life, we will now propose several new values for this new philosophy, which we will call ecosophy. Though this term has been used by ecologists like Arne Naess, we will be elaborating on the meaning given to this term by philosopher and psychoanalyst Félix Guattari. Guattari devised the term *ecosophy* to show that nature and culture cannot be separated. Ecosophy is therefore interdisciplinary, placing together philosophy,

143

144 | Grounding God

anthropology, and ecology to demonstrate how important interdisciplinary research is in deciphering the nature of the real. Just as the new discipline of earth science has placed the disciplines of biology, chemistry, astrophysics, and geology together so as to better understand the earth, so can ecosophy place philosophy, anthropology, and religious studies together with ecology so as to develop a transversal response to the Anthropocene, and seek to overcome the disciplinary disjunctures within the academy. Guattari notes: "Without modifications to the social and material environment, there can be no change in mentalities. Here, we are in the presence of a circle that leads me to postulate the necessity of founding an 'ecosophy' that would link environmental ecology to social ecology and to mental ecology" (1992:23). Rather than always separating disciplines and studying them isolated one from the other according to the needs of academic specialization, these three ecologies must be understood as coimplicated and hence as transversal. For Guattari, it is only such a transversal ecosophy that might provide a new ontology that could give back to humanity the "feeling of fusion at the heart of the cosmos." He asks: "How do we change mentalities, how do we reinvent social practices that would give back to humanity—if it ever had it—a sense of responsibility, not only for its own survival, but equally for the future of all life on the planet, or animal and vegetable species, likewise for incorporeal species such as music, the arts, cinema, the relation with time, love and compassion for others, the feeling of fusion at the heart of cosmos?" (1995:119–20).

In his book *The Three Ecologies*, Guattari explains that the goal of these transversal ecologies is to develop the potential for a "new ecological democracy," where instead of competition and obedience to market despotism, we could develop "intelligence, solidarity, and an ethics of responsibility."[1] Mental ecology entails the creation and sustaining of subjectivities, and centers on what Guattari calls "respect for singularity" (2000:40) in that potentialities produce singularities rather than the universals of Western modernity. This singularity is Guattari's alternative to individualism, since singularities evolve in codependence upon their milieu rather than abstracted as intrinsic essences. The role of the ecosopher, therefore, is to recognize the ways in which these isolated singularities can become integral parts of a whole, once relationality has replaced intrinsic essences as the explanatory paradigm of human nature. Guattari writes: "Relationism has an ecosophical value because it dispels the belief that entities or people can be isolated from their environment. Talking about interaction between entities and their environment leads to misconceptions, because an entity is an interaction" (2018:33, 66).[2] Like a pack of wolves, our psyches are akin to rhizomatic multiplicities rather than unitary subjects, and reducing this multitude to one is emblematic of hegemonic violence. Such singularity "completely exceeds the limits of individualization, stagnation, identificatory closure" (Guattari 2000:47).

Social ecology seeks to bypass "ideas of race, nation, the professional workforce, competitive sports, a dominating masculinity, mass-media celebrity" (Guattari 2000:34) in order to rediscover solidarity and a shared social belonging. By pointing to unpredictable singularities that work for all of humanity rather than in competition, Guattari seeks to destabilize the status quo by freeing unknown potentials to inspire rhizomatic growth. Rather than allowing politics to be directed by what Guattari calls Integrated World Capitalism, politics must be reappropriated in order to work "for humanity and not simply for a permanent reequilibration of the capitalist semiotic Universe" (51). Politics must "organize new micropolitical and microsocial practices, new solidarities, a new gentleness" (51) so as to resist the "tyranny of the majority" and "become-minoritarian" (Guattari 1995:120). Such minorities function in Guattari's work much like the multiple worlds of anthropology, allowing for a schizoanalysis that respects multitudes, both without and within. There is also a political element in becoming minoritarian, which involves resisting majority rule and the homogenization that such rule ensures.

The third ecology, that of the environment proper, is similar to Watsuji's *fudo* in that it understands social ecology to be rooted in the environment, and inextricable from it. The self cannot exist independently of the environment. Rather, organisms can only become singularities in an environment that shapes them. To free up the "becoming animal" potential of humans, as well as the "becoming human" potential of other animals (Viveiros de Castro 2009), we must celebrate our own multiplicities made possible by rich and varied ecosystems. Milieus are thus assemblages of "animal-, vegetable-, Cosmic-, and machinic-becomings" (Guattari 2000:51). When singularities can sprout in natural environments, we are no longer constrained by convention to reduce our desire to the anthropocentric world, and can cross ontological boundaries like a shaman, developing schizoanalysis instead of psychoanalysis, and empathy instead of competition.

Though Guattari was not himself religious, by looking at the ways different religious traditions have sought to abandon the transcendental and ground themselves in earthly bodies and immanent flourishing, we should also consider religion as a fourth ecology, one particularly well suited to interdisciplinary cooperation with philosophy and anthropology for the benefit

146 | Grounding God

of ecological change. In this sense, this book has shown that responding to the Anthropocene and developing an ecosophy will also require a postsecular orientation, one that can resacralize nature or at least seek its deprofanization.

What remains to be done in this chapter is to draw out some of the philosophical presuppositions of previous chapters, so that, alongside the metaphysics furnished by panpsychism, we can formulate new values for this ecosophy. In particular, this chapter will maintain that in order to develop such a cosmopolitical ecosophy, we will need to espouse egalitarianism instead of perfectionism. Because the earth functions by means of interdependent relationalities, rejecting the dualisms of modern Western naturalism will also entail rejecting separate soul substances that somehow were thought to stand aloof from interdependent relationalities. Indeed, it was just such a rational soul substance that was used to justify perfectionism, the idea that humans were superior to other forms of life, and some humans (the colonial white males capable of reason) superior to other humans. In order to dispense with such forms of anthropocentrism, ethnocentrism, androcentrism, and eurocentrism, we will call for the adoption of an egalitarian ethic rather than a perfectionist one. Over and against Cartesian reductionism to the thinking substances of the *cogito ergo sum*, and molecular reductionism to "selfish genes," the section below on "Holobionts instead of Intrinsic Selves" will use the pioneering work of biologist Lynn Margulis to show that we are holobionts, living in cooperative interdependence with hundreds of other species, without which we could not live. Drawing a parallel between biology and philosophy, the following section on "Individuation instead of Individuals" will discuss philosopher Gilbert Simondon's theory of genetic individuation to show that we are events, rather than substances, continually becoming thanks to myriad alterities that enable our potentials to actuate themselves. Such an ontogenesis reinforces the event philosophy of Whitehead discussed in the previous chapter, as well as the theory of subjectivation propounded by Guattari in his ecosophical project. If, as Foucault famously stated, "the soul is the prison of the body" (1977:30), this chapter will seek freedom from this modern prison in its celebration of the symbiotic and dynamic nature of individuation.

If we value egalitarianism for all ecosystem participants, then we can no longer privilege one world ontology over another. Thus, instead of many different cultural interpretations of a single world, the section on "Cosmopolitics" argues that we need to protect multiple worlds, each with unique ontological boundaries. This is the only way to avoid the violence of imposing the truth of one world on all the others. Because truth claims are valid only within the parameters of a particular ontology, in order to avoid the hegemony of a "one-world world" (Law 2011) we will seek, in the final section on "Facing the Consequences," to privilege ethical consequences instead of truth claims. Such ethical consequences are valid not only for one particular human world, but across worlds and across species, for the entire planet earth and its ecosystemic equilibrium. Though truth matters, it cannot give value to mountains and rivers and polar bears. Only the consequences of their annihilation can reveal the need to defend them and the poverty of human existence without them. This entails adding an ethical dimension to science, so that rather than being misused by capitalist investors to rape the earth, it can be used to point to the culture in all of nature, and to the tragedy of reducing abundant ecosystems to strip malls and meat farms. Not only does such a reduction of life reduce the meaning of the human being and her potential, but it is inexorably leading to climate devastation and the extinction of life on planet earth.

All of the values promoted in this chapter are practiced in other ontological systems. But rather than calling for moderns to become animists or totemists, these values will be promoted here according to modern criteria, in other words in line with science, in order to show that such values are already available within the Western paradigm and can be adopted from within the West rather than borrowing from outside cultures. It is the alliance of such values between different ontological worlds that can allow global governance to put shared values at the forefront of international jurisdiction, instead of profit.

Egalitarianism instead of Perfectionism

Including nonhuman entities as legal persons and citizens in an enlarged democracy, as practiced by many indigenous peoples, should become the new normal. As long as we define personhood not as intrinsic substance but rather, in line with the research of anthropologist Eduardo Kohn, as an ability to learn from the past in order to interpret the future, then not only nonhuman animals but also rivers, mountains, and ecosystems should be given the right to flourish without interruption. A person is an organism that "acts for itself" in order to maintain its form in relation to an otherness that it is not but that it depends upon to survive and project itself into the future. The right to flourish of such persons should be protected by law.

Enacting such a legal change will require a moral transformation from perfectionism to egalitarianism. Moral perfectionism holds that the more rational, or the more self-conscious, the more worthy of moral considerability.

148 | Grounding God

It is certainly true that the life of the tick as described by semiotician Jakob von Uexküll is considerably less complex than the life of a baboon, and the life of a baboon less complex than that of a human, but complexity should not entail moral perfectionism, because each species plays a part in ecosystem equilibrium on an interdependent earth, and each species seeks to flourish and to live into the future.

During modern colonialism worth was defined in terms of male white reason, over and against colonized peoples and women. An indigenous person could be sacrificed for a Western person, just as in patriarchal cultures a female person can be sacrificed for a male one. Thanks to the political struggles of feminism and postcolonialism, this is no longer the case in many places. Today, notwithstanding the fact that these prejudices remain and enact injustices every day, we consider all human beings to have equal worth, regardless of the fact that some are ignorant and some brilliant, some black and some white, some female and some male.

But other forms of moral perfectionism are still practiced. All nonhuman animals can be and are sacrificed for human gain. Indeed, millions of sentient animals are tortured and killed in the most inhumane conditions in laboratories each year to further scientific understanding, which is considered a human good. And billions of sentient animals are caged, tortured, and killed in industrial farms each year to produce human food. These animals often never see the light of day, are inseminated only to have their children repeatedly taken away from them and killed, enclosed in cages so small they cannot move, genetically modified so that they cannot stand on their own legs, and branded and deformed to avoid any harm to the future meat.

As we saw in our chapter on animism, indigenous communities have been fighting to enlarge personhood to include not only nonhuman animals but also persons like Pachamama, rivers, and mountains. Many scientists and ethologists have also been active in seeking personhood for other animals, such as chimpanzees and other apes, elephants, dolphins, and octopi. And in some cases, these nonhuman persons have won the right to represent themselves legally with the help of legal guardians. If the ontology of naturalism cannot but find incongruous the recognition of a person like Pachamama that does not exist in its own ontology, little by little Western science and ethology are helping Westerners to enlarge the notion of personhood to many nonhuman animals and plants, in line with indigenous ontologies. Because many moderns lack phenomenological evidence of consciousness and agency in other animals because of their isolation from natural ecosystems, they may require scientific confirmation of the animist recognition of other animals as intentional, purposive agents. Such evidence is now readily available. Developments in ethology, cognitive science, and behavioral psychology demonstrate the intelligence, tool use, consciousness, and self-consciousness of many other animals (De Waal, Bekoff, Korsgaard, Oliver, Corbey, Godfrey-Smith, Coppens, Narby).

Studies have been published showing consciousness (Seth, Baars, and Edelman 2005) and "core emotions" (Panksepp 2005) to be intrinsic to all mammals equipped with a thalamo-cortico complex, and recognizing amniotes and octopi as capable of simulation and expecting consequences has enlarged the scope of conscious beings from mammals to all amniotes (Cabanac, Cabanac, and Parent 2009) and cephalopods (Merker 2005; Edelman and Seth 2009). For example, the "Cambridge Declaration on Consciousness," published by Cambridge University in 2012, states: "The weight of evidence indicates that humans are not unique in possessing the neurological substrates that generate consciousness. Non-human animals, including all mammals and birds, and many other creatures, including octopuses, also possess these neurological substrates."[3] This study was followed in 2017 by an INRA report on "Animal Consciousness" published by sixteen scientists, which concludes that:

> Livestock species, such as poultry, pigs, and sheep, exhibit cognitive behaviours that seem to imply levels and contents of consciousness that until recently were considered exclusive to humans and to some primates. That is even more the case for fish and invertebrates that until recently were not even considered as sentient. . . . It is thus likely that what matters to animals is rather similar to what matters to humans. We believe that human sentience is the capacity to suffer and to feel empathy for the suffering of others, and deserves ethical recognition. . . . Therefore, the same should apply to non-human beings.[4]

Similarly, a plethora of books on plant intelligence are now widely available, with titles such as *Plants as Persons*, *Plant Thinking*, *The Revolutionary Genius of Plants*, *The Language of Plants*, *The Imagination of Plants*, *The Hidden Life of Trees*, and *How Forests Think*, all of which point to the "repression of the living" typical of Western philosophy and science (Coccia 2018:24).

Botanist Matthew Hall gives the following reasons for the moral consideration of plants. To begin with, close observation of plant life-history demonstrates that plants are communicative, relational beings—beings that

150 | Grounding God

influence and are influenced by their environment. It also reveals that plants have their own purposes, intricately connected with finding food and producing offspring. Like other living beings, plants attempt to maintain their own integrity in changing environmental conditions. Plants display intelligent behavior in order to maximize both their growth and the production of offspring (2011:158). This moral inclusion of plants was confirmed by the Federal Ethics Committee on Non-Human Biotechnology (ECNH), which published a scientific study in 2008 ascertaining that humans do not have "unrestricted power over plants. We may not use them just as we please," not only because "we may influence or even destroy other players of the natural world, and so alter their relationships," but also because "individual plants have an inherent worth."

As the natural sciences seek to prove animist presuppositions scientifically, and moderns come to realize that sentience, consciousness, and culture are intrinsic to all of life, perhaps moral egalitarianism will become the new normal. Each life matters, and each life deserves moral consideration. It is time for us to adopt an egalitarian framework for moral considerability, built upon an enlarged category of personhood, informed by science as well as indigenous ontological worlds. Humans matter, but so does Pachamama, and so do forests, and frogs.

Holobionts instead of Intrinsic Selves

René Descartes, the founder of modern philosophy, famously claimed that the *cogito ergo sum*, "I think, therefore I am," was the only absolute certainty, thereby imposing the notion of the subject as an autonomous thinking substance on the modern world. This solitary thinking substance, or *res cogitans*, was of another kind than the extended matter, or *res extensa*, of the material world. The *res cogitans* included all thought, sensation, and feeling, whereas the *res extensa* was interpreted as an entirely mechanical world, devoid of thought and sentience. Since the category of the *res cogitans* included only the human being, the more-than-human world and its myriad living beings were understood to be machines, insensate and determinate.[5]

Such a freeing of subjectivity from embodiment would foster the mind–body dualism that plagues philosophy to this day. Modern Cartesian thought thus succeeded in creating the "brain in a vat" syndrome, a solitary identity absolutely autonomous from the material world, the material body, and all of its embodied nuisances. As philosopher Neil Evernden puts it:

Not only are we not a part of an environment, we are not even part of a body. We, the *real* we, is concentrated in some disputed recess of the body, a precious cocoon separated from the world of vulgar matter. Far from extending our self into the world as the territorial fish does, we hoard our ego as tightly as we can. The narcissistic Descartes created a "philosophy of solitude," and we suffer still from his success in "drawing a set of rigid boundaries around the *cogito,* and in withdrawing the ego from the world and the body." (Evernden 1999: 44–45)

Yet strangely enough, when such views were later turned on their head and replaced with materialism, Cartesian dualism was merely inverted, in order to propound a material narcissism instead of a metaphysical one. In mainstream deterministic biology we therefore find a very similar reduction of the human to its genetic inheritance, and eclipse of the body as a passive receptacle for the volitions of the gene, instead of the *cogito.* Where we might have expected to find the rehabilitation of embodiment, and an interest in how bodies incarnate cultures in different ways, instead we find a molecular reductionism replacing the ego with the gene that alone has volition, and directs the theater of life from a place withdrawn from both the felt body and the world.

This genetic Cartesianism finds its most ardent apologist in biologist Richard Dawkins, who famously claimed that we are machines made by our selfish genes for propagation purposes. Since our genes are "selfish," so are we. In a clumsy attempt at philosophy, Dawkins asserted that culturally speaking we could invent "memes," cultural units comparable to biological genes, that could seek to fight against our own natures in order to promote unselfish behavior.

We, and all other animals, are machines created by our genes. . . . I shall argue that a predominant quality to be expected in a successful gene is ruthless selfishness. This gene selfishness will usually give rise to selfishness in individual behaviour. . . . Be warned that if you wish, as I do, to build a society in which individuals cooperate generously and unselfishly towards a common good, you can expect little help from biological nature. Let us try to *teach* generosity and altruism, because we are born selfish. Let us understand what our own selfish genes are up to, because we may then at least have the

152 | Grounding God

> chance to upset their designs, something that no other species
> has ever aspired to. (1976:2–3)

Following such a molecular reductionism, Dawkins ignored the role of the living organism so central in Darwin's theory of evolution, and tried to reduce life to the algorithmic patterns of nonliving entities. Uncalculating sociability is thus rendered impossible for Dawkins since he cannot explain it in terms of the causal reduction to genes, forcing him to resort to metaphysical miracles for morality to be possible.

Ethologist Frans de Waal has shown how this propensity to interpret human nature in terms of selfish competition developed during the Industrial Revolution, based exclusively upon the preponderance of capitalist economic theory as developed by Adam Smith. Though law and business schools as well as political conservatives still try to convince us that social Darwinism is valid, and that we are selfish and competitive animals, thankfully much recent scholarship in biology, philosophy, and social sciences has been trying to undermine such a reductionist approach. Indeed, the moment we leave economics and consult anthropology, psychology, biology, or neuroscience, we are clearly confronted with a highly cooperative animal (de Waal 2019:1–26). Philosopher Mary Midgley has pointed out that instead of ruthlessly selfish animals, we find spontaneous cooperation everywhere in mammalian behavior, and even in birds (warning against predators, signaling food sources, engaging in collective defense, caring for offspring not their own, forgoing reproduction to care for nestmates), going all the way to self-sacrifice, especially in insect species (2010:15–33). Indeed, according to Darwin himself, we are social animals, "shaped for profound cooperation with others, living interdependently in friendly association" (Midgley 2010:24).

Thanks to the pioneering work of biologist Lynn Margulis, we have come to understand ourselves not as selfish genes but as holobionts, hosting a community of symbionts, without which we could not exist. Cooperation is thus a fundamental feature of evolution. "We are symbiotic complexes of many different species living together" (Gilbert, Sapp, and Tauber 2012:326–27). Bacteria, for instance, can constitute up to 40 percent of the material volume of some organisms. We maintain at least one thousand bacterial species in our gut microbiome. In light of such symbiotic interdependency, what constitutes an individual? Rather than being insular individuals, our identities include alterities and overflow organismic boundaries. As multispecies complexes, "animals can no longer be considered individuals in any sense of classical biology: anatomical, developmental, physiological, immunological, genetic, or evolutionary. Our bodies must be understood as holobionts whose anatomical, physiological, immunological, and developmental functions evolved in shared relationships of different species. Thus, the holobiont, with its integrated community of species, becomes a unit of natural selection whose evolutionary mechanisms suggest complexity hitherto largely unexplored" (334). From the point of view of our symbiotic natures, rather than a narcissistic *cogito* or totalitarian genes, "we are all lichen now" (Haraway 2015:8).

If such an intrinsic soul substance was essential to the modern framework of naturalism that upheld the nature–culture divide, now that the Anthropocene has shown such a framework to be a case of bad faith, it is time for us to propose an understanding of subjectivity in line with the symbiotic holobionts that we are. If there are no intrinsic substances as seats of subjective identity, then there can be no autonomous subjectivity outside of the relational nature of the real. The microbes in our gut, the beings that we eat, the environments and people who sustain us, all of these alterities allow us to be alive and thus to consider what dignity and freedom and value might mean. As Gibson-Graham and Miller point out:

> If we cease to think of ourselves as singular, self-contained beings and begin to think alongside, for example, the multiple communities of bacteria and bacterial symbionts from which we continually take shape and of which we are but fleeting, temporary manifestations (Hird 2009; Hird 2010); or if we place our activities in the context of the billions-of-years-old, emergent, planetary-scale process of biological self-construction known as "Gaia" (Lovelock 2000; Harding 2006; Volk 2003), it is no longer possible to identify a singular "humanity" as a distinctive ontological category set apart from all else. . . . Being-in-common—that is, community—can no longer be thought of or felt as a community of humans alone; it must become multi-species community that includes all of those with whom our livelihoods are interdependent and interrelated. (2015:10)

The values we attribute to the human species cannot be separated from this web of dependencies, and such values are thus not intrinsic and autonomous but relational.

Authors Clayton and Singleton have understood this dispute between an intrinsic and a relational ontology as fundamental to interpretations of

154 | Grounding God

the Anthropocene. "Indeed, the whole dispute between Gaia' advocates and their opponents could be reread as a battle between the world view or 'metaphysic' of interbeing and that of independent or substantial being" (2017:149). Humans have evolved in specific environments with particular climates and particular flora and fauna, all of which are constitutive of our being (*fudo*). Seeking to separate and purify organisms in the name of intrinsic substances or genes is a typically modern gesture that must be superseded if we can hope to adopt a more ecological future. Studying our biological nature can thus help us to deconstruct the modern notion of an autonomous identity, isolated from others within a soul substance that is somehow impermeable and unchanging. Once we recognize the interdependence of life forms and replant them in the soil of their environments, we start to notice how strange the myth of the modern self truly is. In his lovely biological musings in *The Lives of a Cell*, Lewis Thomas expresses this well: "This is, when you think about it, really amazing. The whole dear notion of one's own Self—marvelous, old free-willed, free-enterprising, autonomous independent, isolated island of a Self—is a myth" (1974:142).

Individuation Instead of Individuals

Though the autonomous modern subject is often conflated with the entire Western philosophical tradition, it is not just biologists but also many philosophers who have devoted their lives to overcoming such erroneous views, and providing relational ontologies in line with evolution. Both philosophers Alfred North Whitehead[6] and Gilbert Simondon were able to deconstruct the notion of the self as a substance in developing philosophies that replace substance with relational events. If we are events, we "happen" rather than existing as substantial stable identities over time. Because subjects are not substances with inner qualities and states that might constitute an unchanging identity, independent ontological substances represent a misinterpretation of experience.

Gilbert Simondon has provided one of the most important theories of the ontogenesis of individuation by deconstructing the notion of the self as a substance. Instead of beginning with a preformed and fully constituted individual, Simondon uses the term *ontogenesis* to describe the process of individuation from potential energy into individuated form. As Pascal Chabot put it, "Simondon sought a philosophy that could account for evolution" (2013:73). Individuation thus translates Darwinian evolution into a framework that takes into account psychic development, and ontogenesis translates adaptation into a philosophical framework that can take into account the birth and development of individuated entities: "Adaptation is a permanent onto-genesis," Simondon asserts (2005:235).

Such a psychobiological ontogenesis is meant to replace the substantialism and hylomorphism that for Simondon plague philosophy and limit its ability to understand human identity as a process of becoming rather than of stable being. Since for Simondon there are no first substances, no atoms that are irreducible to alterity, relationality itself becomes the foundation. Rather than isolating each entity as an autonomous and individual substance, Simondon studies the relations in the natural and cultural world that allow for the genesis of distinct psychobiological forms of life, and once this context is taken into account, the relational nature of all entities becomes evident. In the words of Chabot: "The relation is not an accidental feature that emerges after the fact to give the substance a new determination. On the contrary: no substance can exist or acquire determinate properties without relations to other substances and to a specific milieu. To exist is to be connected" (2013:77).

Just as hylomorphism is to blame for ignoring context, Simondon blames substantialism for ignoring the history and development of being, or as he puts it, for "considering being as consisting in its unity, given to itself, founded in itself, uncreated, resisting to all that is not itself" (2005:23). Rather than understanding the human being as having an essence that places it at the pinnacle of nature, or else outside of nature altogether, for Simondon, "nature is not opposed to Man, but rather the first phase of being" (1995:96). Extending the concept of subject to include other animals, Simondon seeks to understand the process of hominization from primate development to the transindividual instantiations of techno-cultural transmission. Instead of beginning with the individual as if it were somehow prefabricated, ontogenesis explains how preindividual life individualizes itself in order to become subjective. Simondon explains: "If, on the contrary, we were to suppose that individuation did not only produce the individual, we would not seek to rapidly pass over the phase of individuation to arrive at the last reality that is the individual: we would seek to grasp ontogenesis in the full development of its reality, and to know the individual by means of individuation rather than individuation by means of the individual" (2005:24).

Because both the substantialist and the hylomorphic theories presuppose "a principle of individuation anterior to individuation itself," they present a "reverse ontogenesis" by working backwards from a constituted

156 | Grounding God

individual to its conditions of existence. When the subject is understood as already constituted, and being already the being of the individual, the question is always regarding the "what" of its constitution—its properties and ontological status. When instead the focus is placed on the process of individuation, the question shifts to a "how," which emphasizes the relationality of subjectivation to a presubjective world. Ontogenesis thus substitutes for ontology in Simondon's work, and replaces the ontological focus on substance with a biological focus on processual development. According to Simondon's theory, there is no such thing as an individual, since such an entity ignores the process of time. Rather, there is only a process of genesis, of always incomplete individuation.

> Strictly speaking, we cannot speak of the individual, but only of individuation; we must get back to the activity, to genesis, rather than trying to grasp the already given being in order to discover the criteria by which we can know whether or not it is an individual. The individual is not a being but an act, and being is an individual as the agent of this act of individuation by which it shows itself and exists. Individuality is an aspect of generation, is explained by the genesis of a being, and consists in the perpetuation of this genesis. (1995:191)

If we are perpetually becoming who we are, in a genesis from beginning to beginning, then it is time to cease thinking of ourselves as ready-made soul substances, and open our awareness to the myriad influences, myriad symbionts, which enable our multiple potentials to bloom as epiphanous events, which grow, decay, and die with all of life.

Cosmopolitics: Diplomacy in the Multiverse

As the climate crisis deepens, the divide between moderns and a-moderns also deepens. On the one hand, we find the entrenched universalisms and notions of progress tied to techno-science leading many moderns to agree with García Linera when he claimed in 2007, in his defense of Bolivian extractivism, that "deep inside, everyone wants to be modern" (2007:156–57). As the hegemonic force of modernity continues to spread, the a-modern is segregated into the past, either as primitive and to be modernized, or else as the Noble Savage to be emulated. In this way, modernity is naturalized as reality in the present.

From within this naturalized modernity we have been witnessing the slow and unfinished attempts to include other human ethnicities in political representation, and a certain Christian mea culpa regarding colonial subjection has become common. Yet relations with nonhuman beings, such as elephants, mountains, and rivers, have been excluded from the modern political sphere and relegated to science (which objectifies them) or to folklore, tourism, or ecology. In a "One-World World" (Law 2011), we perpetuate existing power relations by subordinating the truths of other worlds to our own. On the ground, this means that a-moderns are always forced into a modern framework of nation-state legal jurisdiction that does violence to their ontological realities.

By pressuring their governments to take their ontologies seriously as more than folklore, indigenous communities have been struggling for political representation and gaining ground. But such representation presents two conundrums. The first problem lies in forcing indigenous populations to adopt the legal and political framework of modernity in order to protect their ecosystems, though this framework contradicts their own ontology. Thus for example, many indigenous peoples fight for property rights to own their natural environments, even if, as anthropologist Mario Blaser has pointed out, rather than owning the land, they are owned by it (2009:891).

When, on the other hand, animist ontologies are taken seriously, and are legally represented, we are faced with the opposite problem: that of needing to accept that the earth beings of other worlds are as real to their inhabitants as Hurricane Katrina is for the inhabitants of New Orleans (Blaser 2012:4). This second problem requires that moderns sacrifice their one-world ontology in order to generalize personhood to entities that exist in indigenous ontologies that they do not acknowledge. This problem came to a head when indigenous populations in South America demanded that the earth-being Pachamama be represented as a person. Blaser explains: "Comfortable on the assumption that the subaltern cannot speak, we surrender any effort to hear about 'things' that our categories cannot grasp; we cannot bear ourselves to treat seriously the claim that pachamama is an active and sentient being" (Blaser 2013a:4).

Yet national governments in Ecuador and Bolivia granted legal personhood to Pachamama and her protection is now included in their national constitutions. Ecuador decided to recognize the intrinsic value of Pachamama

158 | Grounding God

legally in its constitution in 2008, establishing in article 255 the principles of "harmony with nature, defense of biodiversity and the prohibition of private appropriation for use and exclusive exploitation of plants, animals, microorganisms, and any living matter" (cited in Idelbar:2013:270). Bolivia then similarly passed the Ley de Derechos de la Madre Tierra (Law of the Rights of Mother Earth) in 2010. In securing rights for Pachamama, Ecuador and Bolivia overthrew the one-world world of modernity, showing that what is true and real for certain peoples cannot be understood and known by means of the cultural categories of modernity. At stake is a transformation of politics from existing in a one-world ontology to a cosmopolitics of diplomacy between worlds, where we must accept the reality of beings who do not exist in our own ontology. By overflowing the stable categorizations of modern dichotomies, like human/more-than-human and nature–culture, we enter into a realm of cosmopolitics where we are forced to accept and work with ontological differences that cannot be sublated, and learn the art of diplomacy in order to respond to a multiplicity of worlds. Blaser notes: "Ontological conflicts fall into the domain of cosmopolitics, the terrain where multiple and diverging worlds encounter each other and the possibility (without guarantees) of composing mutually enlivening rather than destructive relations" (2013a:21).

Such a cosmopolitics is currently underway, as we witness indigenous communities engage in Pachakuta, the social revolution taking place in the Andean world against the hegemony of modernity and its many coercions. At stake is much more than ownership of resources. At stake is the right to defend the truth of an ontology and the many beings it protects. As noted in chapter 5, such work has been taken up in the field of the law in "Indigenous Governance Systems" as well as "Earth Jurisprudence" and "Wild Law" (Cormac Cullinan), which adhere to laws where "the Earth itself is the source of law" (Hosken 2011:25–26, cited in Alberts 2015:136). Such a nonanthropocentric legal basis has enabled animist communities to give legal personhood to nonhuman entities such as rivers and mountains. The Whanganui River in New Zealand, the Ganges and Yamuni Rivers in India, the Vilcabamba River in Ecuador, and the Atrato and Amazon Rivers in Colombia were all allowed to defend themselves in court, with the help of "negotiators" or "legal guardians" who were in all cases interlocutors and not Western scientists. The Whanganui River demanded, in the voice of its advocate Gerrard Albert, to be treated "as an indivisible whole" rather than "from a perspective of ownership and management" (cited in Roy 2017). Similarly, the Vilcabamba River won a legal suit as plaintiff, calling for its own right to "exist" and to "maintain itself" over and against the Loja government, which wanted to build a highway that would interfere with the river's flow. The a-moderns who are fighting to extend legal representation to the more-than-human world reject García Linera's claim that "everyone wants to be modern," and prefer the motto of sociologist Boaventura Santos that there can be "no modern solutions for modern problems" (Santos 2002:13, cited in Blaser 2009:892).[7]

One could argue that the modern bias lies in assuming that there is one single reality to begin with, and then taking for granted that different cultures and different peoples interpret that reality in different ways, some of these ways being closer to the truth than others. Indeed, moderns have now had several centuries to take for granted a one-world ontology that attributes to different peoples different cultural perspectives on a single reality. Yet even though the modern ontology is becoming ever less plausible, we are ill-adapted to grapple with the epistemological questions raised by the pluriverse. Either we uphold better or worse standards of access to a common reality, and are accused of cultural hegemony, or we admit multiple worlds, and thereby imprison ourselves in incompatible and often contradictory realities. And this choice becomes even more problematic when we look at examples of foreign cultures that contradict universal human rights. African and Indonesian tribes are free to perform clitoridectomy on young girls. Afghans are free to marry off their daughters at the age of eight. In certain Islamic lands, women can be stoned to death for infidelity or for running away from abusive husbands. Though we may feel moral outrage when we contemplate the rampant patriarchy that limits the freedom of so many women in so many countries, we are quickly reminded that we cannot judge a foreign worldview from our own Western, modern perspective. Because some of these practices contradict universal human rights, some of us feel justified in judging such actions as wrong for universally valid reasons. Yet doing so takes for granted that the Western scientific view has access to objective truth or reality, while the foreign view is merely a particular cultural perspective.

The two sides of this debate are clearly exemplified in the classic disagreement between anthropologists E. E. Evans-Pritchard and Peter Winch. Winch contests Evans-Pritchard's approach to anthropology because the latter takes sides between two different value conceptions of reality. Rather than noting that the Zande believer in magic has a different view of reality than the Western believer in modern science, Evans-Pritchard claims that one of these conceptions, that of Western science, correlates to objective reality

160 | Grounding God

while the other does not. Science, after all, is objectively verifiable—anywhere, by anyone. The probability rates of science are the same in Papua New Guinea as in London, because the laws of reality are the same for all. And though psychosomatic illnesses may be caused by witchcraft, witchcraft cannot control the rain. Yet Winch asserts:

> Evans-Pritchard is right in a great deal of what he says here, but wrong, and crucially wrong, in his attempt to characterize the scientific in terms of that which is "in accord with objective reality." . . . Although he emphasizes that a member of scientific culture has a different conception of reality from that of a Zande believer in magic, he wants to go beyond merely registering this fact and making the differences explicit, and to say, finally, that the scientific conception agrees with what reality actually is like, whereas the magical conception does not. (1964:308)

Reminiscent of Latour's deconstruction of the objective validity of science in the name of its social constructedness, and hence his focus on the social practices by means of which science holds authority, Winch as well is undermining the possibility of humans using science to gain access to the noumenal world as-it-is-in-itself, an objective reality that could arbitrate between competing and contradicting worldviews, since each worldview constructs reality in a different way. So for the Zande, the cause of rainfall, and the cause of disease, lie in the magical power of witches, whereas for Evans-Pritchard, the rain is caused by sea evaporation that creates cumulonimbus clouds, and illnesses are caused by viruses or bacteria or pathogens infiltrating the immune systems of living organisms.

Anthropologist David Graeber has recently come to the defense of Evans-Pritchard, after being singled out by anthropologist Eduardo Viveiros de Castro for similarly dismissing the belief that a particular Ravololona charm can impede hail. Viveiros de Castro argues that Graeber is clinging

> to the old habits of breezily dismissing what used to be called "apparently irrational beliefs"—in this case, that a charm called Ravololona can stop hailstorms from falling on farmers' crops—as untrue in the literal sense, and therefore, having to be explained as a projection of social relations of some sort. Such an approach, he suggests, has really not advanced in any fundamental way

since Evans-Pritchard (1937) argued that Zande ideas about witchcraft cannot be literally true, and that rather than simply compile apparently contradictory statements and try to imagine what these people would have to think in order for all these statements to be consistent, the real task of the ethnographer is to understand how society is organized in such a way that no one ever notices the statements are contradictory in the first place. (2015:2)

Graeber defends himself and Evans-Pritchard by explaining the parallels between the Zande people and Western moderns, both of whom believe in radically absurd claims without seeming to realize the contradictions between their beliefs and the everyday reality that surrounds them. Being a sociologist or an anthropologist means cultivating the skills to detect such incongruences, whether those of the Zande or of Parisians or Parsis. Evans-Pritchard had pointed out that the Zande invariably claimed that witches were "a small collective of self-consciously evil agents" (Graeber 2015:2) while at the same time admitting that there are no witch lineages and that unconscious witchcraft is widespread. Just as the Zande are not sociologists and thus do not seek to generalize individual events to explain society as a whole, neither do Western moderns, who similarly contradict themselves. Graeber comments: "But is it not exactly the same in our own society, where it's commonplace to make equally absurd generalizations ('anyone who's sufficiently determined and genuinely believes in themselves can become successful')—despite the obvious day-to-day reality that, even if every single person in the country woke up one morning determined to become the next Sir Richard Branson, society is so arranged that there would still have to be bus drivers, janitors, nurses, and cashiers?" (3).

If, according to anthropologist Christian Kordt Højbjerg, different worldviews form a "mosaic of incommensurable units" (2012, cited in Gad, Winthereik, and Jensen, 2015), then each person is locked inside a particular culture, with no access to other cultures and no access to a shared common world. Neither the Zande nor the anthropologist can tell us anything about human beings in general. As Graeber puts it, "We must all leave the world, as Wittgenstein once said, precisely as we found it" (2015:7–8). From a one-world perspective, the pluriverse would lead to a loss of meaning, since there would be no common reality by means of which to interpret these different worlds. If there were no means of communication between worlds,

162 | Grounding God

such a fracti-verse would entail a form of essentialism, since only local subjects could speak for themselves and these worlds could not be analyzed or understood from outside. Since we cannot judge them from our own ontology, they can only be proved wrong from their own presuppositions, which are often formulated to justify them in the first place.

Yet, according to Viveiros de Castro, this was precisely Graeber's error: the assumption that his Western scientific view could somehow stand above the fray of culturally particular perspectives, thereby giving him the God's-eye view to claim that the "Ravololona cannot really prevent hail from falling on anyone's crops" (Viveiros de Castro 2015:8). In the presence of different cultures, with different presuppositions concerning reality, we should not impose the dualist ontology that grants objective knowledge of reality to the natural sciences and subjective, cultural knowledge to the human sciences. Since such foreign peoples "literally inhabit different worlds, we must accept the existence of 'multiple ontologies'" (18).

For this reason, many anthropologists have been claiming that it is precisely the view that there is one world and many different cultural interpretations of this single world that is the foundation of Western hegemony, and thus that a postcolonial solution must replace the uni-verse with a pluri-verse (de la Cadena) or a fracti-verse (Law). If such a pluriverse improves upon the unity that hid the hegemonic sublation of difference in colonialism, it is not without its own problems, and in particular, its own contradictions. If we were to accept a pluriverse where multiple worlds coexist with different ontologies, we would lose our capacity for judgment. In such a pluriverse, cultures are not relative because they do not share the ontological presuppositions that would allow for comparison. Instead of comparison, we can move between worlds by means of translation, which is always imperfect and contingent. Though the ambiguity of such "controlled equivocations" will frustrate our contemporary infatuation with algorithmic certainty, it nonetheless should be considered superior to the coercion involved in "single-reality" doctrines. Indeed, both the reduction of reality to beliefs about the world and the reduction of many worlds to a single one are typically Western. According to sociologist John Law, such "single-reality" doctrines are "one, worked up in the North; two, embedded in Northern practices; three, reproduced and re-enacted in those practices; and then, four, were transported to the South and imposed on reluctant First Nations" (2015:128). Along with many postcolonial scholars, Law asks if it does not make more sense to think of the earth as the home of multiple realities, which cannot be accumulated to create the universal totality so dear to Western moderns. Accepting multiple realities would entail leaving behind an epistemological multiculturalism and replacing it with an ontological multinaturalism. Law calls such an alternative a "fractiverse," which would entail that each world has its own truths, and that these truths cannot be "purified," "essentialized," or "extracted" from their environment and judged according to the criteria of another world.

Similarly, anthropologist Marisol de la Cadena calls these multiple worlds a "pluriverse," a concept she uses to deconstruct the modern interpretation of politics as "power disputes within a singular world," in order to find ways of giving voice to the indigenous peoples and allow for "the possibility of adversarial relations among worlds: a pluriversal politics" that would enable us "to undo, or more accurately, unlearn, the single ontology of politics" (2010:360–61). In a pluriverse, communication becomes cosmopolitics, requiring diplomacy and accepting "controlled equivocations" instead of truth in the singular. In such a multiverse, politics becomes "an international intrigue, a diplomatic negotiation, or a war operation that must be undertaken with maximum circumspection: cosmopolitics" (Danowski and Viveiros de Castro 2017:70–71). Once such objective truth has been sacrificed, it can be replaced with a planetary ethics that privileges planetary consequences instead of single-world truths.

Such a "pluriversal politics" is required to repair and celebrate the many worlds that populate our earth, and to engage with the moral exigencies of these worlds so that we can honor the many beings living in our many worlds and learn to defend their right to flourish. In his book *The Wake of Crows: Living and Dying in Shared Worlds*, Thom van Dooren maintains that to live and die in shared worlds, we must master the art of diplomacy, even when such diplomacy is fraught, and killing or disregarding represent easier solutions. Living with crows, for example, would require that we recognize them as "centers of needs and striving . . . and resistance and opacity." He notes:

> Diplomacy is the subtle art of working with and against another to produce mutually livable worlds. As such, it is a practice that demands more of both ravens and people than killing does: "Poisoning is easy but nurturing is a craft" (Stengers 2008:38). As previously noted, beyond simple questions of dead or alive, of population numbers and their impacts, these diplomatic projects demand that attention be paid to ravens as subjects, to their processes of learning and communication, to shifting understandings and sensitivities, to modes of becoming-otherwise. (Van Dooren 2019:157)

164 | Grounding God

Facing the Consequences

If worlds consist of the beings that inhabit them, as Viveiros de Castro and Watsuji Tetsuro both claim, then their perspectives *are* their worlds. And if this is the case, then seeking objective truth misses the point altogether. Because the different worlds of the pluriverse make contradictory truth claims, moderns seek scientific justifications to show that their truths are universally more valid than the truths of other worlds. Rain is not caused by witchcraft, the Ausangate mountain is just dead rock, and Pachamama does not exist. But if we cannot separate the truths from the people adhering to them, the perspective from the world perceived, then the modern view ends up condemning people themselves as wrong, as inferior, as dispensable. And this contradicts the human rights at the very heart of modern anthropocentrism, which holds all people to be of equal worth. If people cannot be separated from their worlds, and from these worlds' truths, then perhaps we need to understand truths as expressions of a given world, rather than as objective universal criteria. Viveiros de Castro explains: "The real world is the abstract space of divergence between species as points of view. Because there are no points of view onto things, things and beings are the points of view themselves. . . . The question for Indians, therefore, is not one of knowing 'how monkeys see the world' (Cheney and Seyfarth 1990), but what world is expressed through monkeys, of what world they are the point of view. I believe this is a lesson from which our own anthropology can learn" (Viveiros de Castro 2004b:11). If this argument is convincing, then perhaps focusing on truth is misguided. I would like to conclude this book by proposing consequences as an alternative (Viveiros de Castro 2019), in the hope that we might use such consequences to found a grounded anthropological philosophy that might replace truth and the tolerance founded in relativism with a tolerance of multiple worlds, each with its own truths. Adopting a pragmatic consequentialism can avoid the setbacks of adhering to the truth, and may be incremental in helping us move beyond theory toward ethical practice. Such a cosmopolitics can be a powerful tool in decolonizing not only anthropology but also the natural sciences.

Instead of asking ourselves if a statement is true, we would need to ask instead what the consequences would be for the earth if it were considered true. "What world," Viveiros de Castro asks, "would such a proposition give to be seen?" (2019). The examples he considers include indigenous peoples of the Andes claiming that their mountains are sacred, and that therefore, emptying them and blowing them up to find gold is wrong. In this case, he

Ecosophy | 165

claims, it is more true to agree that the mountains are sacred than that they are merely a pile of rocks with gold inside, since claiming the latter leads to the destruction of the environment and the impossibility for indigenous peoples to live there. Viveiros de Castro writes:

> So if a certain way of thinking of a river as a living being, or a spirit, or as having personality, blocks the construction of a dam that will kill the river, in the literal sense that the river has fish and people who depend upon the life in the river, then saying that the river is alive, is a person, is more true, from a pragmatic point of view, than to say that it is simply a (dead) body of water. . . . It is not about whether the river *is* sacred or not, but because it is *considered* sacred, the rights of the Maori must be respected, not the rights of the river. Trees don't have rights, people have rights in relation to trees. In my opinion, the ontological status of the river or the tree is not as important as the ethical consequences, and when the consequences are considered, we must choose the metaphysical position with the least bad consequences. (2019)

It is therefore the discipline of anthropology that can help us move beyond truth. For the anthropologist the truth regarding whether a pile of rocks is sacred, of whether a river is alive, is not a geological question, just as it is not a limnological question. As an anthropological question, it can be answered only by studying a particular world, inhabited by human and nonhuman agents, all of whom have intentionality. For the anthropologist, stating that stones don't think, or that the Ravololona spell cannot bring rain, "has the same value as stating that people don't think" (Viveiros de Castro 2019), since the anthropologist is not interested in neurology any more than she is interested in geology. The mountain or the river is sacred *for someone*, and what matters to the anthropologist is the truth *for someone*, not the truth abstracted from person and place. If the truth of anthropology is neither neurological nor geological, it is not philosophical either. Or rather, from an anthropological perspective, perhaps it is time to give back to ontology its skin, its soil, its temperature, and its temperament (*fudo*). If the phenomenological *epoché* allowed for a pure experience of the present, without past and future projection, an anthropological *epoché* would require the suspension of all truth claims in order to encounter the real. If there are as many philosophical ontologies as there are lifeworlds

166 | Grounding God

(*Umwelten*), as biologist Jakob von Uexküll pointed out long ago in his study of tick ontology, then abstracting Being from beings can be considered the anthropological version of the banality of evil. Such an anthropological suspension of truth in order to privilege the relational nature of the real was adopted by phenomenologist David Abram in his formulation of an ecological phenomenology:

> Ecologically considered, it is not primarily our verbal statements that are "true" or "false," but rather the kind of relations that we sustain with the rest of nature. A human community that lives in a mutually beneficial relation with the surrounding earth is a community, we might say, that lives in truth. The ways of speaking common to that community—the claims and beliefs that enable such reciprocity to perpetuate itself—are, in this important sense, *true*. They are in accord with a right relation between these people and their world. Statements and beliefs, meanwhile, that foster violence toward the land, ways of speaking that enable the impairment or ruination of the surrounding field of beings, can be described as *false* ways of speaking—ways that encourage an unsustainable relation with the encompassing earth. A civilization that relentlessly destroys the living land it inhabits is not well acquainted with *truth*, regardless of how many supposed facts it has amassed regarding the calculable properties of its world. (1997:264)

If we have been witnessing the slow and unfinished attempts to include other human genders and ethnicities in political representation, relations with nonhuman beings have been excluded from the political sphere and treated as objects to be commodified rather than subjects in a shared cosmopolitics. By shifting the focus away from the scientific truth about whether Pachamama *really* exists, or whether the stones of the Ausangate mountain are *truly* sentient, and toward the pragmatic concern that giving personhood to Pachamama and sacrality to the mountain is a way of protecting the mountain and the cultures it enables, the truth loses its objectivity and becomes a secondary attribute of justice and flourishing. So the question becomes that of ascertaining the pragmatic consequences of each position, so as to determine whether a position diminishes or enriches the world. And as Viveiros de Castro rightly points out, it is not a question of relativism at all. Rather, it is a question of politics. What kind of a world do we want to live in? Can we promote values instead of truths and can we promote our values without denying those of others?

Such a consequentialism would seek to avoid the injustices of majority rule, since it is easy to imagine examples where a tiny indigenous community could be destroyed by cutting down the forests upon which they depend, if such cutting would benefit a greater number of human beings elsewhere. In line with Guattari's call, we will need to resist the "tyranny of the majority" and become minoritarians (1995:120). By protecting all minorities, and respecting each ontology equally regardless of numbers, minoritarians resist majority rule and the homogenization that such rule ensures. Each world has the right to exist and flourish, and no one world any more than any other. Such values would need to be extended to nonhuman worlds as well, such as the world of the jaguar and the world of the elephant. The tragedy of watching unique species go extinct every day is insurmountable. So good consequences are those that privilege the flourishing of lifeworlds, and bad consequences are those that destroy lifeworlds, whether in the name of monetary profit or human overpopulation. Humans have lived without destroying the ecosystemic equilibrium of the earth for millions of years. Such a consequential ethic would allow the human species to privilege the flourishing of lifeworlds once more, and to enlarge moral consideration beyond intrinsic values to encompass the relationalities that allow all worlds to flourish.

If someone were to claim that only human values and only human worlds matter, and thus that killing elephants for ivory, or using bear bile to boost libido is justified, we would need to remind these humanists of the problems related to anthropocentrism discussed throughout this book, as well as teach them the nature of the real, which is absolutely interdependent. Humans cannot survive alone, and the havoc caused when a mere frog goes extinct creates an endless cycle of ecosystem disequilibria, beginning with an overpopulation of mosquitoes and ending with outbreaks of Zika virus, West Nile virus, dengue, and malaria. Frogs matter. This is something that all indigenous cultures understand, and safeguard. We might thus surmise, even after hundreds of years of cultivating callousness and indifference, that Western moderns as well can learn a consequentialist ethic that engages both human and more-than-human worlds.

For such a consequentialist approach to replace truth judgments, ecosophy must integrate anthropology, philosophy, and religion into a transversal discipline. The discipline of anthropology can teach philosophy and religion that intrinsic to universal truth claims is the violence of abstraction,

168 | Grounding God

of deworlding worlds, erasing feeling bodies and places that matter, and replacing the unique with unicity. We cannot reduce realities on the ground to judgments about the world, separating them from the very lifeworlds in which they are embedded, and where they find their sustenance and meaning. Truths have homes, on the ground and in bodies, on mountains and along rivers, where they actually matter. Focusing on consequences will allow us to protect these homes for all those who live there, so that their truths can continue to flourish.

Notes

Introduction

1. He writes:

The pending planetary catastrophe has raised anew the questions of whether there are alternatives to the kinds of economy, politics, science, and religion by which it was engendered as well as to the entire modern variation of thought that they constitute and cohere in, and thus too of whether it is in and through such nonmodern variations of thought that one might discover those specific alternatives. The anthropologists and philosophers contending with the crucial role played in the crisis by modern technics are asking whether and in what way other variations of thought might contain other technics—not just other arts of doing things but altogether distinct approaches to all arts—that render humans cohesive among themselves and with other beings, rather than working at all of their expense. (Skafish 2020:135)

2. Claude Lévi Strauss, *Totemism* (London: Merlin, 1964); Sharon Merz, *Totemism and Human-Animal Relations in West Africa* (London: Routledge, 2021); Deborah Bird Rose, *Dingo Makes Us Human: Life and Land in an Aboriginal Culture* (Cambridge: Cambridge University Press, 1992).

3. www.ecomodernism.org, April 2015.

4. Although nuclear energy makes up only 2 percent of world energy whereas renewables are close to 15 percent, the only solution the ecomodernists see to our growing energy consumption is nuclear, though they decline to mention the risks and the tremendous waste that such a solution would entail. Not only is building nuclear plants extremely capital intensive, but most countries do not possess uranium, which is a finite resource that could be depleted as early as 2080. Nuclear waste is radioactive and impossible to store long-term, since it takes thousands of years to lose its radioactivity, and power plants make enormous amounts of toxic waste.

170 | Notes to Chapter 1

Power plants are also prone to catastrophic disasters, and nuclear power entails the ability to make nuclear weapons.

5. "A Call to Look Past *An Ecomodernist Manifesto*: A Degrowth Critique," Resilience.org, May 6, 2015; Juanita Sundberg, Jessica Dempsey, and Rosemary-Claire Collard, "The Moderns' Amnesia in Two Registers," *Environmental Humanities* 7 (2015): 227–32; Chris Smaje, "Dark Thoughts on Ecomodernism," *Dark Mountain Project*, August 12, 2015; George Monbiot, "Meet the Ecomodernists: Ignorant of History and Paradoxically Old-Fashioned," *The Guardian*, September 24, 2015.

6. "Mais, au fond, quelque chose ne cesse de rebuter les Indiens dans ces deux discours sur la Nature, qui tient à leurs prémisses communes. Exploitation ou préservation renvoient en effet au même présupposé d'une Nature-objet, réifiée en instance coupée de l'humanité et soumise à ses desseins. Or, cette césure et cet anthropocentrisme sont on ne peut plus étrangers aux conceptions des sociétés amazoniennes, qui font du cosmos une totalité sociale régie par un complexe système d'échanges symboliques entre sujets humains et non humains, dont le chamanisme est la pierre de touche" (Albert 1993: 365).

Chapter 1

1. Elisabeth Povinelli gives a darker hue to such an event: "The Anthropocene marks the moment when human existence became the determinate form of planetary existence—and a malignant form at that—rather than merely the fact that humans affect their environment" (2016:9).

2. http://www.ipcc.ch/report/sr15/.

3. https://science2017.globalchange.gov/downloads/CSSR2017_FullReport.pdf.

4. https://www.un.org/press/en/2019/sgsm19757.doc.htm.

5. https://www.ecowatch.com/un-climate-actioncop27html?fbclid=IwAR0W9QKSkLAdR8nTLrAJzvp72NXNkrLN2HUdPTUv1FGEaXBq6A9xgZBdFOQ.

6. https://doi.org/10.3917/crieu.013.0088.

7. Florian was brought to my attention by philosopher Bernard Stiegler in his Summer School, 2015. Though Stiegler spoke of Florian as a real person, it appears that he was actually a fifteen-year-old character in the novel *L'Effondrement du temps* by the anonymous writer collective L'impansable (2006).

8. https://www.newscientist.com/article/2217418-greta-thunberg-you-have-stolen-my-childhood-with-your-empty-words/.

9. From the *Egyptian Streets* newspaper, April 1, 2017, https://egyptianstreets.com/2017/04/01/egypt-plans-to-build-first-city-on-mars/.

10. I use the term *habitus* to connote a way of life in relation to an environmental setting.

Notes to Chapter 1 | 171

11. https://www.bbc.com/future/article/20200513-the-bunker-builders-preparing-for-doomsday.

12. https://www.theguardian.com/cities/2019/dec/16/a-cinema-a-pool-a-bar-inside-the-post-apocalyptic-underground-future.

13. https://www.bbc.com/future/article/20200513-the-bunker-builders-preparing-for-doomsday.

14. https://www.businessinsider.com/billionaire-bunkers-shelter-wealthy-during-apocalypse-2019-6.

15. https://www.bbc.com/future/article/20200513-the-bunker-builders-preparing-for-doomsday.

16. https://www.loveproperty.com/gallerylist/78262/affordable-bunkers-to-survive-the-apocalypse.

17. https://dornob.com/world-ending-elite-apocalypse-proof-underground-homes/.

18. https://edition.cnn.com/style/article/doomsday-luxury-bunkers/index.html.

19. https://www.theguardian.com/cities/2019/dec/16/a-cinema-a-pool-a-bar-inside-the-post-apocalyptic-underground-future.

20. https://www.businessinsider.com/billionaire-bunkers-shelter-wealthy-during-apocalypse-2019-6.

21. https://www.bbc.com/future/article/20200513-the-bunker-builders-preparing-for-doomsday.

22. https://www.cnet.com/features/inside-the-survival-condo-nuclear-bunker-protecting-the-ultrarich-hacking-the-apocalypse/.

23. http://opentranscripts.org/transcript/anthropocene-capitalocene-chthulucene/.

24. "One of the most urgent tasks that we mortal critters have is making kin, not babies. This making kin, both with and among other humans and not humans, should happen in an enduring fashion that can sustain through generations. . . . I propose making kin nongenealogically, which will be an absolute need for the eleven-plus billion humans by the end of this century—and is already terribly important. I'm interested in taking care of the earth in a way that makes multispecies environmental justice the means and not just the goal. So I think of making kin as a way of being really, truly prochild—making babies rare and precious—as opposed to the crazy pronatalist but actually antichild world in which we live. It's making present the powers of mortal critters on earth in resistance to the anthropocene and capitalocene" (Donna Haraway, as told to Lauren O'Neill-Butler at Art Forum, http://www.artforum.com/words/id=63147).

25. https://www.ekah.admin.ch/inhalte/ekah-dateien/dokumentation/publikationen/e-Broschure-Wurde-Pflanze-2008.pdf.

26. Alberts points out that such an alliance has replaced the "noble savage" of yore with the "ecological Indian" in order to "articulate a critique of anthropocentric mastery of nature" (2015:132). The idealization of the "ecological Indian" is just as

172 | Notes to Chapter 2

problematic as that of the "noble savage" and continues a longstanding tradition of moderns speaking *for* the indigenous. But while indigenous scholar Deborah McGregor states that this "boils down to extracting knowledge from Aboriginal people" (2004:397), things are slowly changing, and the voices of indigenous shamans and scholars are being heard today.

Chapter 2

1. "In lui si riscontra fino a che punto sono inseparabili la preoccupazione per la natura, la giustizia verso i poveri, l'impegno nella società et la pace interiore" (34).

2. "Cercare solamente un rimedio tecnico per ogni problema ambientale che si presenta, significa isolare cose che nella realtà sono connesse, e nascondere i veri e più profondi problemi del sistema mondiale" (111–12).

3. "asfissiante rinchiudersi nell'immanenza" (117).

4. Metropolitan John of Pergamon, "Towards an Environmental Ethic," http://www.rsesymposia.org/themedia/File/1151678281-Ethic.pdf (cited in Grim and Tucker 2014:105).

5. Spoken in November 1997, Saint Barbara's Church, Santa Barbara, California. Reported in Chryssavgis, "Cosmic Grace, Humble Prayer" (221) (cited in Grim and Tucker 2014:104).

6. John F. Haught, "Christianity and Ecology" (cited in Gottlieb 2004:232–47).

7. Common Declaration of John Paul II and the Ecumenical Patriarch His Holiness Bartholomew I, Monday, June 10, 2002 (cited in Grim and Tucker 2014: Appendix A, 185–86).

8. She adds on p. 96: "For then and now, the images of God's lordship that dominate religious imagination are those of a divine governor exercising imperial power on earth through a male hierarchy. The image of God this projects is that of an omnipotent, invulnerable being who exercises absolute arbitrary authority over the lives and deaths of all other beings. Such images implicitly and explicitly condone and indeed legitimat violence against other members of the community of life on earth."

9. Wallace seems to have misunderstood the meaning of animism in his attempt to salvage an immanent Christianity. Whereas in the Christian tradition God takes on human form in the figure of Christ, or bird form, according to his analysis, in the figure of the Holy Spirit, in animism, each person is ontologically itself, not an incarnation of a transcendent deity that remains ontologically other.

10. "What if God and gods are our invention, our homes for our deepest spiritual nature? Is the Old Testament any less sacred if it is our invention, our language, our discourse? Is the King James Bible any the less miraculous if it is the writing of humans, not the transcription of God's words? Are the Shinto shrines surrounding Kyoto any less sacred if they are a fully human invention?" (2010:287).

11. Dave Foreman, author interview, Tucson, Arizona, February 23, 1993.

Notes to Chapter 3 | 173

Chapter 3

1. Most notable in this regard is the work of biologist Lynn Margulis (1998) on evolutionary symbiosis. See also Jablonka and Lamb (2005), Richerson and Boyd (2005), and Capra and Luisi (2014).

2. "We are persuaded that Asian traditions of thought can help the West reconstruct its world view in the ways suggested in the introduction to this volume. Firstly, they can help along the process of Western self-criticism by providing an alternative place to stand, an outsider's point of view, from which the West can more clearly discern the deeper substrata of its inherited intellectual biases and assumptions. And secondly, if, as some scholars have suggested, the historical dialectic of Western thought is being impelled in what until now been a predominantly Oriental direction, Eastern traditions, rich in metaphor, simile, and symbol, can help the West articulate, in ways that are culturally assimilable, the very untraditional abstract ideas forthcoming from contemporary theoretical studies of the nature of nature" (Callicott and Ames 1989b:288).

3. There are, or course, many different schools of Buddhism, and Buddhism is practiced in myriad ways across the world. In this introduction I will be presenting a form of Mahayana Buddhism that is inflected by Buddhist modernism; in other words, by the academic study of Buddhism. This is the form of Buddhism adopted by Watsuji himself, and thus consonant with his environmental project.

4. The Noble Eightfold Path:

> Right understanding (*Samma ditthi*)
> Right thought (*Samma sankappa*)
> Right speech (*Samma vaca*)
> Right action (*Samma kammanta*)
> Right livelihood (*Samma ajiva*)
> Right effort (*Samma vayama*)
> Right mindfulness (*Samma sati*)
> Right concentration (*Samma samadhi*)

5. In the Theravada tradition, the cycle of interdependent origination is used to explain the origin of suffering in ignorance (*avidya*) rather than the relational nature of the real.

6. However ecologically sound these views are, and in seeming agreement with Earth System Science, there are of course ways of interpreting Buddhism in a more problematic light. Some scholars have noted that Buddhism can be interpreted in terms of cosmological dualism, pointing to the distinction between samsara (the world of illusion) and nirvana. Is seeking nirvana, as an escape from the earthly realm of illusion, similar in this sense to the role that heaven plays in Christianity? Is nirvana an existence in a dimension not of this earth? As Buddhist scholar Joel Krueger points out, such a dualistic interpretation is supported by the Four Stages

174 | Notes to Chapter 3

of Enlightenment of the Theravada tradition. He asks: "If the nonreturner continues to practice after death, where does he or she reside while doing so? If nibbana is a place or a state that transcends this world, it is a version of cosmological dualism" (2011:52). Yet as Krueger himself points out, such an interpretation is contradicted in the Mahayana tradition, and in particular in the *Mūlamadhyamakakārikā* written by Nagarjuna (200 CE). In this text, he famously stated that "there is not the slightest difference between nirvana and samsara" (cited in Garfield 1995:75). There is thus a single reality that can phenomenologically be perceived differently depending upon one's level of understanding. Nirvana is samsara without illusions. There may therefore be aspects of dualism in the Theravada tradition that were later resolved in the Mahayana tradition.

Another risk that is particularly apparent in Western New Age interpretations of Buddhism is what Buddhist teacher and scholar Joanna Macy calls a "spiritual trap," by which she means the trend to think that reality is solely constituted by the mind, and thus that "thinking positively" is all one needs to do to reach individual happiness and set the world straight. If the power of our mind influences the world we perceive, this is often interpreted to mean that thinking positive thoughts is enough to transform the world, and thus no struggles to defend the vulnerable and to improve ecological and political standards are necessary. As Macy notes: "We feel then so peaceful that the world will become peaceful without our need to act" (1991:55). Though it is true that samsara is conditioned by ignorance as a mental state, this in no way implies that our actions and their results are immaterial. The ethical rules the Buddha set down, such as vegetarianism and sexual abstinence, would make no sense otherwise.

7. Such a theory is similar to those such as Gilbert Simondon's theory of individuation, that seek to focus on the social processes of individuation, and the semiotic modes of communication between individual and group (see Simondon 1995 and 2005).

8. Bein points out: "Nevertheless, Buddhism is not simply *śūnyatā*, and so while it is certain that Watsuji and his Buddhist contemporaries largely agree on the *importance* of this principle, they do not necessarily agree on the *nature* of the principle, and they certainly do not agree on its religious significance (or lack thereof). If Watsuji's philosophy takes emptiness as its cohering principle, it is in the end a Watsujian emptiness, not necessarily a Buddhist one" (2017:223).

9. Sevilla notes: "This consistency across Watsuji's readings of Hīnayāna and Mahāyāna Buddhisms demonstrates that his view of Buddhism is not necessarily faithful to the doctrine or the historical practices of various forms of Buddhism. Rather, it is best seen as a form of modern Buddhism, deeply inspired by phenomenology and dialectics, and largely peculiar to Watsuji himself" (2017:268).

10. This book on Japanese temples was followed immediately by another book titled *Nihon kodai bunka* (*Ancient Japanese Culture*). Lafleur attributes this turn back to Japanese traditions to the death of Watsuji's favorite novelist, Natsume

Soseki (Lafleur 1978:240), and in 1918 Watsuji indeed published a book reminiscing about both Soseki and Buddhism, *Guzo Saiko* (*Resurrecting Idols*). In 1926 he wrote his *Shamon Dōgen* (*Dōgen the Monk*), a widely read book on Soto Zen monk Dōgen, followed in 1929 by an edited translation of Dōgen's *Shōbōgenzō*, which brought Dōgen back from oblivion and to the center of Japanese Buddhist research. As Lafleur points out, "Were it not for this book, it is entirely possible that no one outside of the Sōtō sect would be reading Dōgen today" (1978:213). In 1927 Watsuji wrote his most cogent treatise on Buddhism, *Genshi Bukkyō no jissen tetsugaku* (*The Practical Philosophy of Primitive Buddhism*), followed in 1935 by a book about the reception of Buddhism in Japan, *Zoku Nihon seishinshi kenkyū* (*Further Studies on the History of Japanese Spirit*). The last book he published—in 1963, after publishing his masterpieces *Fudo* (*Climate and Culture*) in 1935 and *Rinrigaku* (his three-volume *Ethics*) in 1937, 1942, and 1949—was also devoted to Buddhism, his *Bukkyô tetsugaku no saisho no tenkai* (*The Early Development of Buddhist Philosophy*).

11. In his book *Fudo*, only the first chapter actually deals with *fudo* and *fudosei*, the following four chapters being devoted to *kokumin jikaku*, or national character. This shift to nationalism during World War II tarnished his reputation, and the book gained little recognition. Indeed, for this reason in addition to his celebration elsewhere of the emperor, Watsuji was criticized as being conservative.

12. Drawing deeply on Buddhist, Chinese, and Japanese sources, Watsuji's work helps us advance toward an understanding of the relationality of human being that Western philosophy has only begun to fathom. While Continental, feminist, and environmental philosophies have struggled to find ways of thinking about selfhood, body and nature in ways that avoid the pitfalls of dualism and essentialism, they have not been fully successful as these ideas are so well entrenched in most of Western philosophy. Watsuji's philosophy provides us with ways of thinking through who we are and how we inhabit our world in ways that are nondualistic and yet still allow for difference (McCarthy 2017:519).

13. If Heidegger's influence on Watsuji is explicit, Reinhard May and Graham Parkes have suggested that Heidegger as well may very well have been influenced by the Japanese thinkers in his milieu to integrate the concept of emptiness into *Being and Time*, which he developed into his central idea of *das Nicht*. Indeed, in his text "A Dialogue on Language between a Japanese and an Inquirer" in his book *On the Way to Language*, Heidegger notes the correspondence between emptiness and *das Nicht* (D. W. Johnson 2019:6), particularly in its relation to death, which is of course central to Buddhist thought and Japanese philosophy (May 1996).

14. *Fudo* has been variously translated into English as *climate and culture*, *climate*, and *milieu*. The problem with the term *climate* is that it does not register the connection to human life and culture that is intimated in the term *fudo*. . . . The phrase *climate and culture*, which was used to translate the title of Watsuji's book into English, has the virtue of indicating the way *fudo* extends beyond the mere

176 | Notes to Chapter 3

physicality of nature, but this pair is too cumbersome to use in translating every instance of the occurrence of the term *fudo*. In addition, the use of a pair of terms to translate a single concept also gives the mistaken impression that *fudo* consists of, or can be divided into, two distinct and separate entities. The geographer and theorist Augustin Berque—who is also the French translator of Watsuji's *Fudo*—has made a case for translating *fudo* as *milieu* in both French and English. This usage has certain advantages, especially in terms of moving the reader away from the idea of an objective "natural environment." On the other hand, in English *milieu* primarily connotes a social environment, and it does not really convey the vital and all-important sense of nature as the ground of *fudo* (D. W. Johnson 2019:24).

15. Watsuji's nondualistic concepts of self and *milieu* stand in sharp contrast to dominant Western notions of self (and ethics), which are dualistic. A view is dualistic if it conceives of the self, and consequently the world, in terms of the dichotomies of mind and body, self and other, and so on. Dualists typically locate the self in some subset of the elements of human being (such as reason, individual consciousness, the brain, or an individual soul) and view these core elements as more authentically human than the others and thereby worthy of more weight, authority, or value (McCarthy 2017:511).

16. Watsuji, "The Study of Human Being" (cited in Lafleur 1978:219). Watsuji repeats this concept in his *Rinrigaku*: "What I have described as a human being's existence as betweenness is that which renders individuals and societies capable of occurring in their reciprocal negations" (101–2, cited in Mochizuki 2006:49).

17. Sevilla claims that "Watsuji gives two separate models" (2014:112), hesitating between an endless cycle, and a dialectic with absolute totality figuring as the final synthesis. Yet Sevilla himself points out that in the *Rinrigaku* absolute totality is always dependent upon individual contingent traditions to give it form, and thus that the dialectic is codependent and cannot be sublated.

18. See, for instance, Odin (1992), Bernier (2006), and Shuttleworth (2019).

19. Mochizuki explains:

The reason why totality is fundamental lies in the fact that the essence of human existence (ningen's sonzai), which means nothing but a "mutual relationship" (or "betweenness"), consists in its "emptiness." Because the movement of negation doesn't begin with a finite being such as an individual or the whole, but with an infinite "emptiness" (which is not a "nothingness," for it really exists as a movement of negation), therefore the restoration of this "emptiness" (which is another name for the "absolute totality," lacking the selfness as such in itself), should be proclaimed (2006:51).

20. Watsuji seemed to have regretted his understanding of Japanese exclusivity after the end of the war. Indeed, he made significant changes in the third and last volume of the *Rinrigaku*, removing those statements that had earlier defended the

sacrifice of the individual for the state. In this third volume, Watsuji introduced the concept of humankind as a dialectical value able to limit the power and authority of the nation-state as "national *sonzai*." In order to allow for the dialectical play between humankind and nation, he also advocated an open-boundary politics for Japan, and blamed the closed-country policy for Japan's failure during the war (Sevilla 2014).

Chapter 4

1. "asfissiante rinchiudersi nell'immanenza" (2015:117).
2. https://plato.stanford.edu/entries/pantheism/.

Chapter 5

1. Now that mosquitoes are DEET resistant, and the heavens punctured by an ozone hole, there is no nature that is not cultural. This is indeed the view of the inventor of the term Anthropocene, climate scientist Crutzen, when he tells us, with journalist Schwägerl, to "remember, in this new era, nature is us" (2011: http://e360. yale.edu/features/living_in_the_anthropocene_toward_a_new_global_ethos). Similarly, Ulrich Beck notes: "At the end of the twentieth century nature *is* society and society is also '*nature.*' Anyone who continues to speak of nature as non-society is speaking in terms from a different century, which no longer capture our reality" (1992:81). Political scientist Elmar Altvater points out: "The separation of nature and society that characterizes modern thought since Descartes has no basis in reality—only a basis in the European rationality of world domination" (2016:149).

2. Ethnologist Charles Stepanoff comments: "If, for ethnologists, animism is an ontology linked to particular cultural contexts, from a psychological point of view, it is a fundamental psychological disposition of our species. It is only under the effects of a long training that we are able, in modern societies, to repress, blunt and finally forget it" (2019:49, my translation).

3. I follow Juanita Sundberg, who herself follows Shaw, Herman, and Dobbs, in defining the term *indigenous* "to refer to groups with ancestral ties/claims to particular lands prior to colonization by outside powers and 'whose nations remain submerged within the states created by those powers' " (2014:34).

4. This idea of a "philosophical animism" was inspired by philosopher Val Plumwood: "Val Plumwood was, at the time of her death, working to articulate just such an account of human and nonhuman sentient life that would be defensible philosophically and that could engage dialogically with Indigenous peoples' animism. The term she used was 'philosophical animism,' and in her words, this project 'opens the door to a world in which we can begin to negotiate life membership of an ecological community of kindred beings' " (cited in Bird Rose 2015:131).

178 | Notes to Chapter 6

5. Though Viveiros de Castro's research has met with wide approval within the field of anthropology, his research focus is the Amazon basin, and other anthropologists have pointed to other animist cultures that do not always humanize all other beings. For several examples of other ontological taxonomies, see the articles by anthropologists Mathias Lewy and Laura Rival in volume 29 (2012) of the journal *Indiana*.

6. "The mode of participation makes it impossible to conceive of beings and things in isolation. It makes unthinkable the conception of identity as the selfsame, just as it does the strict division of an 'inside' and an 'outside.' . . . Knowledge, therefore, is inherently dialogic, not monologic. Knowledge is never knowledge *about*, but always knowledge *with*, a *process* constituting both knower and known" (Franke 2012b:171).

7. However promising such an engagement between philosophy and cognitive science may be, the naturalization of consciousness should not be adopted too readily. It is important to not reify the brain as some cognitive scientists tend to do, essentializing it (as was done with the "selfish gene") outside of its symbiotic relationality to the entire organism and its environment. Furthermore, experience should not be reduced to brain function, as has become typical of much reductionist science. Reducing experience to behavior entails a significant loss of reality as it is actually lived.

8. "Only an ethico-political articulation which I call ecosophy between the three ecological registers (the environment, social relations and human subjectivity) would be likely to clarify these questions" (Guattari 2000:28).

9. Deleuze and Guattari write: "But what we are saying is that the idea of assemblage can replace the idea of behaviour, and thus with respect to the idea of assemblage, the nature-culture distinction no longer matters" (2013:179).

10. Guattari comments: "I am more inclined to propose a model of the unconscious akin to that of a Mexican Cuandero or of a Bororo, starting with the idea that spirits populate things, landscapes, groups, and that there are all sorts of becomings, of haecceities everywhere and thus, a sort of objective subjectivity, if I may, which finds itself bundled together, broken apart, and shuffled at the whims of assemblages. The best unveiling among them would be found, obviously, in archaic thought" (cited in Melitopoulos and Lazzarato 2012b:240).

Chapter 6

1. "The religious attitude can thus be understood as including the belief that mentality is eternal" (Clarke 2003:147).

2. "It is by drawing a boundary between the world of objects and the world of meanings that the modern project has emerged. By, as it were, distilling Nature into its material properties alone, uncontaminated by symbolic meanings or social relations, modernists have been freed to manipulate it in ways unthinkable

Notes to Chapter 6 | 179

in pre-modern contexts. Objectivism thus suggests a kind of moral or emotional dissociation from that part of reality classified as object" (Hornborg 2014a:246).

3. Biologist Wilfred Agar similarly claims that "we must ascribe consciousness to every living agent, such as a plant cell or bacterium, and even (if the continuity of nature is not to be broken) to an electron" (cited in Skrbina 2017:247). Likewise, Daniel Dombrowski notes: "In the amoeba there is a center of activity, exploration, and planning; and primitive choice can even be found in bacteria" (1988:38). Similarly, neuroscientist Francisco Varela points out: "The behavior of a bacterium or amoeba is one of avoiding some things and seeking others, much like the behavior of clearly sentient beings like cats and humans. . . . The amoeba intrinsically manifests a differentiation between what it likes and what it doesn't like. In that sense, there is sentience. . . . This is why, as a scientist, I can say that the behavior of the bacterium is cognitive behavior in that it makes discriminations through this form of sensory-motor correlations I have described. The mechanism is the same as, say, in cats. I know psychologists shudder when I say this, but I'm talking as a neuroscientist" (1992:67–68).

4. "Definition: idealist panpsychism is the doctrine that the universe is composed of hierarchies of experiential entities, and of nothing else. These experiential entities can both perceive one another and be perceived" (Ells 2011:83).

5. She comments: "When we say, 'let's fix the world up—let's pull down these slummy old tenement blocks and build a brand new permacultural-urban-ecovillage in their stead'—we are just as much in the grip of the old ethos of domination and control as the city fathers were. We are rejecting the given in favour of an abstract or imagined alternative of our own—we are refusing to let things be—and it is this hubristic mentality which is the motor of modern civilization and the source of the environmental crisis" (2005:37).

6. Such a trend is typical of posthumanism and of Object-Oriented Ontology. See, for instance, Verbeek (2009, 2014) and Bryant (2014).

7. Such a position is quite common among transhumanists like Nick Bostrom (2005) and those seeking a future on the unliving star Mars. It is also fairly common among philosophers of technology like Lucas Introna (2009), who see no difference between stones and dogs, and maintain that it is ontologically unfair to discriminate against the stone.

8. Cited in 2010b:99. In a 2010 interview with Peter Gratton, she defends anthropomorphizing the inorganic: "The human body is itself a composite of many different it-bodies, including bacteria, viruses, metals, etc. and . . . when we recognize a resemblance between a human form and a nonhuman one, sometimes the connecting link is a shared *inorganicism*. I think that anthropomorphizing can be a valuable technique for building an ecological sensibility in oneself, but of course it is insufficient to the task" (100). Cited in *Speculations* 1, no. 1 (2010): 84–134.

9. It should be noted that animism is the rule, not the exception, in anthropological studies of indigenous peoples; see Descola (1993, 2005, 2011) and Viveiros

de Castro (2009, 2015). What is original in Eduardo Kohn's research is his fruitful integration of indigenous anthropology and Peircean semiotics. Such an integration could go far in pointing to the ways that animistic worldviews contribute to a politics of nature with important repercussions for the Anthropocene.

10. Viveiros de Castro is repeating a phrase that philosophers Bruno Latour and Emilie Hache had themselves repeated from Michel Serres (Hache and Latour 2010:319).

Chapter 7

1. Félix Guattari, "Vers une nouvelle démocratie écologique," 1992, https://www.multitudes.net/Vers-une-nouvelle-democratie/.

2. These quotes are translated by myself from the French edition.

3. http://fcmconference.org/img/CambridgeDeclarationOnConsciousness.pdf.

4. This study was requested by the European Food Safety Authority (EFSA): https://efsa.onlinelibrary.wiley.com/doi/epdf/10.2903/sp.efsa.2017.EN-1196.

5. It was this dichotomy that allowed Kant to propound transcendent reason over and against our "inclinations" in order to reach the universal good, which could be lived only over and against our bodies and their unpredictable desires. Since not all people have good inclinations, Kant famously stated that we could not trust our biological natures and thus that we had to use our reason to seek the universal right beyond our subjective natural inclinations. Such a distrust of our natures was taken much further by the founder of psychoanalysis Sigmund Freud, who famously repeated the adage *homo homini lupus*, "man is wolf to man," to characterize our natural state as that of each person seeking to take advantage of others. Freud therefore celebrated human civilization and legal systems as absolutely necessary to stop our "beastly" nature from expressing itself.

6. Though Whitehead retains the intrinsic value of the real as event, since nature itself, and therefore existence, has intrinsic value simply by occurring, such intrinsic value does not inhere in selves as enclosed substances, which simply do not exist in Whitehead's theory. In this way, our perception is not something enclosed inside a soul, but is directly in contact with the events that cause the sensual organization of the world. By generalizing experience to all of matter, Whitehead is able to move beyond the divide between mind and matter, as well as that between subject and object, and thereby show how subjective experience cannot be limited to the notion of substance.

7. This is of course a reiteration of Einstein's famous maxim that "we can't solve problems by using the same kind of thinking we used when we created them."

Bibliography

Abram, David. 1997. *The Spell of the Sensuous: Language and Perception in a More-Than-Human World*. New York: Vintage Books.

———. 2007. "Earth in Eclipse." In *Merleau-Ponty and Environmental Philosophy: Dwelling on the Landscapes of Thought*, edited by Suzanne L. Cataldi and William S. Hamrick, 149–76. Albany: State University of New York Press.

———. 2011a. *Becoming Animal: An Earthly Cosmology*. New York: Vintage Books.

———. 2011b. "In the Depths of a Breathing Planet: Gaia and Transformation." In *Panpsychism: The Philosophy of the Sensuous Cosmos*, edited by Peter Ells, 221–42. Alresford, UK: O-Books.

———. 2014. "The Invisibles: Toward a Phenomenology of the Spirits." In *The Handbook of Contemporary Animism*, edited by Graham Harvey, 124–32. London: Routledge.

———. 2017. "In the Depths of a Breathing Planet: Gaia and Transformation." In *Panpsychism*, edited by Godehard Brüntrup and Ludwig Jaskolla, 221–42. London: Oxford University Press.

Abrams, Nancy Ellen. 2015. *A God That Could Be Real: Spirituality, Science, and the Future of Our Planet*. Boston: Beacon.

Albert, Bruce. 1993. "L'or cannibale et la chute du ciel: Une critique chamanique de l'économie politique de la nature." *L'Homme* 33, no. 126–128 (April–December): 349–78.

Alberts, Thomas Karl. 2015. *Shamanism, Discourse, Modernity*. London: Routledge.

Alliez, Eric, and Andrew Goffey, eds. 2011. *The Guattari Effect*. London: Continuum.

Altvater, Elmar. 2016. "The Capitalocene, or, Geoengineering against Capitalism's Planetary Boundaries." In *Anthropocene or Capitalocene? Nature, History, and the Crisis of Capitalism*, edited by Jason W. Moore, 138–152. Oakland, CA: PM Press.

Amsterdamska, Olga. 1990. "Surely You're Joking Monsieur Latour." *Science, Technology, & Human Values* 15, no. 4 (Autumn): 495–504.

Anders, Günther. 2007. *Le temps de la fin*. Paris: Lherne.

182 | Bibliography

Angus, Ian. 2016. *Facing the Anthropocene: Fossil Capitalism and the Crisis of the Earth System*. New York: Monthly Review Press.

Arendt, Hannah. 1977/2006. "Truth and Politics." In *Between Past and Future*. New York: Penguin Books.

Arhem, Kaj. 1996. "The Cosmic Food-Web: Human-Nature Relatedness in the Northwest Amazon." In *Nature and Society: Anthropological Perspectives*, edited by Philippe Descola and Gisli Palsson, 185–204. London: Routledge.

Arias-Maldonado, Manuel. 2015. *Environment and Society: Socionatural Relations in the Anthropocene*. New York: Springer.

Armstrong-Buck, Susan. 1986. "Whitehead's Metaphysical System as a Foundation for Environmental Ethics." *Environmental Ethics* 8, no. 3 (Fall): 241–59.

Augendre, Marie, Jean-Pierre Llored, and Yann Nussaume. 2018. *La mésologie, un autre paradigme pour l'anthropocène? Autour et en présence d'Augustin Berque*. Paris: Hermann Editeurs.

Badiner, Allan Hunt, ed. 1990. *Dharma Gaia: A Harvest of Essays in Buddhism and Ecology*. Berkeley, CA: Parallax.

Baek, Jin. 2010. "Climate, Sustainability and the Space of Ethics." *Architectural Theory Review* 15, no. 3: 377–95.

Barad, Karen. 2007. *Meeting the Universe Halfway: Quantum Physics and the Entanglement of Matter and Meaning*. Durham, NC: Duke University Press.

Barbieri, Marcello. 2008. "The Code Model of Semiosis: First Steps toward a Scientific Biosemiotics." *American Journal of Semiotics* 24, no. 1–3: 23–37.

Barner-Barry, C. 2005. *Contemporary Paganism: Minority Religions in a Majoritarian America*. New York: Palgrave Macmillan.

Barry, Andrew, and Georgina Born, eds. 2013. *Interdisciplinarity: Reconfigurations of the Social and Natural Sciences*. London: Routledge.

Basile, Pierfrancesco. 2009. "Galen Strawson and the Rediscovery of Panpsychism." In *Mind That Abides: Panpsychism in the New Millennium*, edited by David Skrbina, 179–99. Amsterdam: John Benjamins.

Bateson, Gregory. 1972. *Steps to an Ecology of Mind*. New York: Random House.

Bauman, Whitney A. 2014. *Religion and Ecology: Developing a Planetary Ethic*. New York: Columbia University Press.

Beck, Ulrich. 1992. *Risk Society: Toward a New Modernity*. London: Sage.

Bein, Steve. 2017. "Watsuji Tetsuro: Accidental Buddhist?" In *The Bloomsbury Research Handbook of Contemporary Japanese Philosophy*, edited by Michiko Yusa, 207–30. London: Bloomsbury Academic.

Bekoff, Marc, Colin Allen, and Gordon Burghardt, eds. 2002. *The Cognitive Animal: Empirical and Theoretical Perspectives on Animal Cognition*. Cambridge, MA: MIT Press.

Benjamin, Walter. 1968. "Theses on History." In *Illuminations*. New York: Schocken Books.

Bibliography | 183

Bennett, Jane. 2010a. "Thing Power." In *Political Matter: Technoscience, Democracy, and Public Life*, edited by Bruce Braun and Sarah Whatmore, 35–62. Minneapolis: University of Minnesota Press.

———. 2010b. *Vibrant Matter: A Political Ecology of Things*. Durham, NC: Duke University Press.

———. 2010c. "A Vitalist Stopover on the Way to a New Materialism." In *New Materialisms: Ontology, Agency, and Politics*, edited by Samantha Frost and Diana Coole, 47–69. Durham, NC: Duke University Press.

———. 2015. "Systems and Things: On Vital Materialism and Object-Oriented Philosophy." In *The Nonhuman Turn*, edited by Richard Grusin, 223–40. Minneapolis: University of Minnesota Press.

Berardi, Francesco. 2017. *Futurability: The Age of Impotence and the Horizon of Possibility*. London: Verso Books.

Berger, John. 2001. *The Shape of a Pocket*. New York: Vintage Books.

Bergmann, Sigurd. 2009. "Climate Change Changes Religion: Space, Spirit, Ritual, Technology through a Theological Lens." *Studia Theologica*, no. 63: 98–118.

———. 2010. "Dangerous Environmental Change and Religion: How Climate Discourse Changes the Perception of Our Environment, the Spiritual Fabrication of Its Meaning and the Interaction of Science and Religion." In *Religion and Dangerous Environmental Change: Transdisciplinary Perspectives on the Ethics of Climate and Sustainability*, edited by Sigurd Bergmann and Dieter Gerten, 13–37. Berlin: Lit Verlag/New Brunswick, NJ: Transaction.

———. 2017. "Religion at Work within Climate Change: Eight Perceptions about Its Where and How." In *Religion in the Anthropocene*, edited by Celia Deane-Drummond, Sigurd Bergmann, and Markus Vogt, 67–84. Eugene, OR: Cascade Books.

Bergmann, Sigurd, and Dieter Gerten, eds. 2010a. *Religion and Dangerous Environmental Change: Transdisciplinary Perspectives on the Ethics of Climate and Sustainability*. Berlin: Lit Verlag/New Brunswick, NJ: Transaction.

Bergmann, Sigurd, and Dieter Gerten. 2010b. "Religion in Climate and Environmental Change: Towards a Symphony of Voices, Memories and Visions in a New Polycentric Field." In *Religion and Dangerous Environmental Change: Transdisciplinary Perspectives on the Ethics of Climate and Sustainability*, edited by Sigurd Bergmann and Dieter Gerten, 1–12. Berlin: Lit Verlag/New Brunswick, NJ: Transaction.

Berman, Morris. 1989. *The Reenchantment of the World*. New York: Bantam Books.

Bernier, Bernard. 2006. "National Communion: Watsuji Tetsuro's Conception of Ethics, Power, and the Japanese Imperial State." *Philosophy East and West* 56, no. 1: 84–105.

Berque, Augustin. 1987/2015. *Ecoumène: Introduction à l'étude des milieux humains*. Paris: Belin.

184 | Bibliography

———. 1996(a). *Etre humain sur la terre*. Paris: Gallimard.

———. 1996(b). "The Question of Space from Heidegger to Watsuji." *Ecumene* 3, no. 4 (October 1): 373–83.

———. 2001. "Overcoming Modernity, Yesterday and Today." *European Journal of East Asian Studies*, no. 1: 89–102.

———. 2004a. "Ce qui fonde l'éthique environnementale." *Diogène* 3, no. 207: 3–14.

———. 2004b. "Milieu et identité humaine/Milieu and human identity." *Annales de Géographie* 113e Année, no. 638–639 (July–October): 385–99.

———. 2004c. "Offspring of Watsuji's Theory of Milieu (Fûdo)." *GeoJournal* 60, no. 4: 389–96.

———. 2010. "La théorie de la médiance de Watsuji Tetsurō et son actualité." In *Philosophes japonais contemporain*, edited by Jacynthe Tremblay, 229–40. Montreal: Presses de l'Université de Montréal.

Bhaskar, Roy, Cheryl Frank, Karl George Høyer, Petter Naess, and Jenneth Parker, eds. 2010. *Interdisciplinarity and Climate Change: Transforming Knowledge and Practice for Our Global Future*. New York: Routledge.

Biermann, Frank, and Oran Young. 2014. *Earth System Governance: World Politics in the Anthropocene*. Cambridge, MA: MIT Press.

Bird Rose, Deborah. 2013. "Val Plumwood's Philosophical Animism: Attentive Interactions in the Sentient World." *Environmental Humanities*, no. 3: 93–109.

———. 2015. "Dialogue." In *Manifesto for Living in the Anthropocene*, edited by Katherine Gibson, Deborah Bird Rose, and Ruth Fincher, 127–31. Brooklyn, NY: Punctum.

Blamauer, Michael, ed. 2011. *The Mental as Fundamental: New Perspectives on Panpsychism*. Heusenstamm, Germany: Ontos Verlag.

Blaser, Mario. 2009. "Political Ontology." *Cultural Studies* 23, no. 5–6: 873–96.

———. 2012. "Ontology and Indigeneity: On the Political Ontology of Heterogeneous Assemblages." *Cultural Geographies* 21, no. 1 (December): 49–58.

———. 2013a. "Notes towards a Political Ontology of 'Environmental' Conflicts." In *Contested Ecologies: Dialogues in the South on Nature and Knowledge*, edited by Lesley Green, 13–27. Cape Town: HSRC Press.

———. 2013b. "Ontological Conflicts and the Stories of Peoples in Spite of Europe: Toward a Conversation on Political Ontology." *Current Anthropology* 54, no. 5 (October): 547–68.

Bloch, Maurice. 2013. *In and Out of Each Other's Bodies: Theory of Mind, Evolution, Truth and the Nature of the Social*. London: Paradigm.

Bodley, John H. 2014. *Victims of Progress*. Lanham, MD: Rowman & Littlefield.

Bohm, David. 1986. "A New Theory of the Relationship of Mind and Matter." *Journal of the American Society for Psychical Research* 80, no. 2–3: 113–35.

Bohm, David, and B. J. Hiley. 1995. *The Undivided Universe*. London: Routledge.

Bonneuil, Christophe. 2015. "The Geological Turn: Narratives of the Anthropocene." In *The Anthropocene and the Global Environmental Crisis*, edited by Clive Hamilton, François

Bibliography | 185

Bonneuil, Christophe, and Jean-Baptiste Fressoz. 2013. *L'événement Anthropocène: La Terre, l'histoire et nous*. Paris: Le Seuil. Gemenne, and Christophe Bonneuil, 17–31. London: Routledge.

Borgès, Jorge Luis. 2000a. *Fictions*. London: Penguin Classics.

———. 2000b. *Labyrinths*. London: Penguin Classics.

Bostrom, Nick. 2005. "A History of Transhumanist Thought." *Journal of Evolution and Technology* 14, no. 1: 1–25.Bracken, J. A. 1995. "Substance—Society—Natural System: A Creative Rethinking of Whitehead's Cosmology." *International Philosophical Quarterly*, no. 25: 3–13.

Breithaupt, Fritz. 2009. *Kulturen der Empathie*. Frankfurt: Suhrkamp.

Brey, Philip. 2014. "From Moral Agents to Moral Factors: The Structural Ethics Approach." In *The Moral Status of Technical Artefacts*, edited by Peter Kroes and Peter-Paul Verbeek, 125–42. Dordrecht, Netherlands: Springer.

Brocchi, Davide. 2010. "The Cultural Dimension of Un/Sustainability: Delicate Distinctions between Societal Survival and Collapse." In *Religion and Dangerous Environmental Change: Transdisciplinary Perspectives on the Ethics of Climate and Sustainability*, edited by Sigurd Bergmann and Dieter Gerten, 145–76. Berlin: Lit Verlag/New Brunswick, NJ: Transaction.

Brüntrup, Godehard, and Ludwig Jaskolla, eds. 2017. *Panpsychism*. London: Oxford University Press.

Bryant, Levi. 2014. *Onto-Cartography: An Anthology of Machines and Media*. Edinburgh: Edinburgh University Press.

Bunge, Mario. 1979. *Causality and Modern Science*. Cambridge, MA: Harvard University Press.

Cabanac, Michel, Arnaud Cabanac, and André Parent. 2009. "The Emergence of Consciousness in Phylogeny." *Behavioural Brain Research* 198, no. 2 (March): 30–80.

Cahoone, L. 2008. "Reduction, Emergence, and Ordinal Physicalism." *Transactions of the Charles S. Peirce Society* 44, no. 1 (Winter): 40–62.

Cajete, Gregory. 2000. *Native Science: Natural Laws of Interdependence*. Santa Fe, NM: Clear Light.

Callicott, J. Baird. 1999. *Beyond the Land Ethic: More Essays in Environmental Philosophy*. Albany: State University of New York Press.

Callicott, J. Baird, and Roger T. Ames. 1989a. "Epilogue: On the Relation of Idea and Action." In *Nature in Asian Traditions of Thought: Essays in Environmental Philosophy*, edited by J. Baird Callicott and Roger T. Ames, 279–89. Albany: State University of New York Press.

———. 1989b. "Introduction: The Asian Traditions as a Conceptual Resource for Environmental Philosophy." In *Nature in Asian Traditions of Thought: Essays in Environmental Philosophy*, edited by J. Baird Callicott and Roger T. Ames, 1–21. Albany: State University of New York Press.

Callon, Michel, and John Law. 1997. "After the Individual in Society: Lessons on Collectivity from Science, Technology and Society." *Canadian Journal of Sociology/Cahiers canadiens de sociologie* 22, no. 2 (Spring): 165–82.

186 | Bibliography

Capra, Fritjof, and Pier Luigi Luisi. 2014. *The Systems View of Life: A Unifying Vision*. Cambridge: Cambridge University Press.

Carlson, Carey R. 2009. "Finite Eventism." In *Mind That Abides: Panpsychism in the New Millennium*, edited by David Skrbina, 231–50. Amsterdam: John Benjamins.

Cataldi, Suzanne L., and William S. Hamrick, eds. 2007. *Merleau-Ponty and Environmental Philosophy: Dwelling on the Landscapes of Thought*. Albany: State University of New York Press.

Chabot, Pascal. 2013. *The Philosophy of Simondon: Between Technology and Individuation*. London: Bloomsbury.

Chakrabarty, Dipesh. 2009. "The Climate of History: Four Theses." *Critical Inquiry* 35, no. 2 (Winter): 197–222.

———. 2015. "The Anthropocene and the Convergence of Histories." In *The Anthropocene and the Global Environmental Crisis*, edited by Clive Hamilton, François Gemenne, and Christophe Bonneuil, 44–56. London: Routledge.

———. 2016. "Humanities in the Anthropocene: The Crisis of an Enduring Kantian Fable." *New Literary History* 47, no. 2–3 (Spring and Summer): 377–97.

———. 2018. "Anthropocene Time." *History and Theory* 57, no. 1 (March 2018): 5–32.

Charbonnier, Pierre. 2019. "Splendeurs et misères de la collapsologie: Les impensés du survivalisme de gauche." *Revue du Crieur* 13, no. 2: 88–95.

Charbonnier, Pierre, Gildas Salmon, and Peter Skafish, eds. 2017. *Comparative Metaphysics: Ontology after Anthropology*. London: Rowman & Littlefield.

Christ, Carol P., and Judith Plaskow. 2016. *Goddess and God in the World: Conversations in Embodied Theology*. 1517 Media, Fortress Press.

Clammer, John. 2004. "The Politics of Animism." In *Figured Worlds: Ontological Obstacles in Intercultural Relations*, edited by John Clammer, Sylvie Poirier, and Eric Schwimmer, 83–109. Toronto: University of Toronto Press.

Clark, Nigel. 2010. *Inhuman Nature: Sociable Life on a Dynamic Planet*. London: Sage.

———. 2012. "Rock, Life and Fire: Speculative Geophysics and the Anthropocene." *Oxford Literary Review* 34, no. 2 (December): 259–76.

Clark, Nigel, and Bronislaw Szerszynsk. 2020. *Planetary Social Thought: The Anthropocene Challenge to the Social Sciences*. London: Polity.

Clark, Timothy. 2015. *Ecocriticism on the Edge: The Anthropocene as a Threshold Concept*. London: Bloomsbury.

Clarke, D. S. 2003. *Panpsychism and the Religious Attitude*. Albany: State University of New York Press.

Clayton, Philip. 2004. "Panentheism in Metaphysical and Scientific Perspective." In *In Whom We Live and Move and Have Our Being*, edited by Philip Clayton and Arthur Peacocke, 73–91. Cambridge, UK: William B. Eerdmans.

Clayton, Philip, and Arthur Peacocke, eds. 2004. *In Whom We Live and Move and Have Our Being*. Cambridge, UK: William B. Eerdmans.

Clayton, Philip, and Elizabeth Singleton. 2017. "Agents Matter and Matter Agents: Interpretation and Value from Cells to Gaia." In *Entangled Worlds: Religion, Science, and New Materialisms*, edited by Catherine Keller and Mary-Jane Rubinstein, 136–53. New York: Fordham University Press.

Clifton, Chas. S. 2006. *Her Hidden Children: The Rise of Wicca and Paganism in America.* Lanham, MD: Altamira.

Cobb Jr., John B. 2004a. "Protestant Theology and Deep Ecology." In *This Sacred Earth: Religion, Nature, Environment*, edited by Roger S. Gottlieb, 248–61. New York: Routledge.

———. 2004b. "Thinking with Whitehead about Nature." In *Whitehead's Philosophy*, edited by Janusz A. Polanowski and Donald W. Sheerburne, 175–96. Albany: State University of New York Press.

Coccia, Emanuele. 2018. *The Life of Plants: A Metaphysics of Mixture.* London: Polity.

Coetzee, J. M. 1999. *The Lives of Animals.* Princeton, NJ: Princeton University Press.

Coleman, Sam. 2009. "Mind under Matter." In *Mind That Abides: Panpsychism in the New Millennium*, edited by David Skrbina, 83–107. Amsterdam: John Benjamins.

Collins, Harry. 2010. "Humans not Instruments." *Spontaneous Generations: A Journal for the History and Philosophy of Science* 4, no. 1: 138–47.

Collins, Harry, and Stephen Yearley. 2010. "Epistemological Chicken." In *Science as Practice and Culture*, edited by Andrew Pickering, 301–26. Chicago: University of Chicago Press.

Connolly, William E. 2013 "The 'New Materialism' and the Frailty of Things." *Millennium: Journal of International Studies* 41, no. 3: 399–412.

———. 2017. *Facing the Planetary: Entangled Humanism and the Politics of Swarming.* Durham, NC: Duke University Press.

Conty, Arianne. 2013. "Techno-Phenomenology: Martin Heidegger and Bruno Latour on How Phenomena Come to Presence." *South African Journal of Philosophy* 32, no. 4: 311–26.

———. 2016ba. "The Evil Berger in the Good Berger's Habit: Heidegger, Sloterdijk and the Apocalyptic Playground of Post-Humanism." In "Antropocene: Fine, medium o sintomo dell'uomo?," edited by Sarah Baranzoni, Antonio Lucci, and Paolo Vignola, special issue, *Lo Sguardo: Rivista di filosofia* 22, no. 3: 95–107.

———. 2016b. "Who Is to Interpret the Anthropocene? Nature and Culture in the Academy." In "GeoPower: A Strato-Analysis of the Anthropocene," edited by Benoît Dillet, special issue, *La Deleuziana* 4 (April): 19–44.

———. 2017. "How to Differentiate a Macintosh from a Mongoose: Technological and Political Agency in the Age of the Anthropocene." Special issue, edited by Zwier, Lemmons, Blok, and Winner, *Techné: Research in Philosophy and Technology* (October): 1–24.

188 | Bibliography

————. 2018. "The Politics of Nature: New Materialist Responses to the Anthropocene." *Theory, Culture & Society* 35, no. 7–8 (October 11): 73–96.

————. 2021a. "Animism in the Anthropocene." *Theory, Culture & Society* 39, no. 5 (September 30): 1–27.

————. 2021b. "Panpsychism: A Response to the Anthropocene Age." *Journal of Speculative Philosophy* 35, no. 1: 27–49.

————. 2021c. "Religion in the Anthropocene." *Environmental Values* 30, no. 2 (January 4): 215–34.

Couteau, Pauline. 2006. "Watsuji Tetsuro's Ethics of Milieu." In *Essays in Japanese Philosophy*, edited by James W. Heisig, 269–90. Nagoya, Japan: Nanzan Institute for Religion and Culture.

Cowan, Douglas E., and David G. Bromley. 2015. *Cults and New Religions: A Brief History*. 2nd ed. Hoboken, NJ: John Wiley & Sons.

Crary, Jonathan. 2013. *24/7: Late Capitalism and the Ends of Sleep*. New York: Verso.

Crist, Eileen. 2015. "The Reaches of Freedom: A Response to an Ecomodernist Manifesto." *Environmental Humanities* 7, no. 1 (January): 245–54

Crist, Eileen, and H. Bruce Rinker, eds. 2010. *Gaia in Turmoil: Climate Change, Biodepletion, and Earth Ethics in an Age of Crisis*. Cambridge, MA: MIT Press.

Crosby, Donald A. 2013. *The Thou of Nature: Religious Naturalism and Reverence for Sentient Life*. Albany: State University of New York Press.

Crutzen, Paul, and Christian Schwägerl. 2011. "Living in the Anthropocene: Toward a New Global Ethos." *Yale Environment* 360, January 24, https://e360.yale.edu/features/living_in_the_anthropocene_toward_a_new_global_ethos.

Crutzen, Paul, and Will Steffen. 2003. "How Long Have We Been in the Anthropocene Era? An Editorial Comment." *Climatic Change* 61, no. 3: 251–57.

Crutzen, Paul, and Eugene Stoermer. 2000. *IGBP Newsletter*, no. 41.

Dalai Lama, 2017. *A Call for Revolution.* London: Penguin Books.

Dalbotten, Diana. 2014. *Future Earth: Advancing Civic Understanding of the Anthropocene*. Washington, DC: American Geophysical Union.

Dalby, Simon. 2016. "Framing the Anthropocene: The Good, the Bad and the Ugly." *Anthropocene Review* 3, no. 1: 33–51.

D'Allens, Gaspar, and Lucile Leclair. 2016. *Les néo-paysans*. Paris: Seuil.

Danowski, Déborah, and Eduardo Viveiros de Castro. 2017. *The Ends of the World*. Cambridge, UK: Polity.

Daston, Lorraine. 2000 "The Coming into Being of Scientific Objects." In *Biographies of Scientific Objects*, edited by Lorraine Daston, 1–14. Chicago: University of Chicago Press.

Dawkins, Richard. 1976. *The Selfish Gene*. Oxford: Oxford University Press.

Deacon, Terrence. W. 2012. *Incomplete Nature: How Mind Emerged from Matter*. New York: Norton.

Deane-Drummond, Celia, Sigurd Bergmann, and Markus Vogt, eds. 2017. *Religion in the Anthropocene*. Eugene, OR: Cascade Books.

de la Cadena, Marisol. 2010. "Indigenous Cosmopolitics in the Andes: Conceptual Reflections Beyond Politics." *Cultural Anthropology* 25, no. 2 (April): 334–70.

———. 2015. *Earth Beings: Ecologies of Practice across Andean Worlds.* Durham, NC: Duke University Press.

de la Cadena, Marisol, and Orin Starn. 2007. "Introduction." In *Indigenous Experience Today,* edited by Marisol de la Cadena and Orin Starn, 1–30. Oxford: Berg.

Delaughrey, Elizabeth, Jill Didur, and Anthony Carrigan. 2015. *Global Ecologies and the Environmental Humanities: Postcolonial Approaches.* New York: Routledge.

Deleuze, Gilles, and Félix Guattari. 1980. *Mille plateaux: Capitalisme et schizophrénie.* Paris: Editions de Minuit.

———. 2013. *A Thousand Plateaus.* London: Bloomsbury Academic.

de Quincey, Christian. 2002. *Radical Nature: The Soul of Matter.* Rochester, NY: Park Street.

Derrida, Jacques. 1978. "Structure, Sign and Play in the Human Sciences." In *Writing and Difference,* translated by Alan Bass. London: Routledge.

Descola, Philippe. 1993. *Les lances du crepuscule.* Paris: Plon.

———. 1996. "Constructing Natures: Symbolic Ecology and Social Practice." In *Nature and Society: Anthropological Perspectives,* edited by Philippe Descola and Gisli Palsson, 82–102. London: Routledge.

———. 2005. *Par delà nature et culture.* Paris: Gallimard.

———. 2011. *L'écologie des autres.* Versailles: Editions Quae.

———. 2014. "Beyond Nature and Culture." In *The Handbook of Contemporary Animism,* edited by Graham Harvey, 77–91. London: Routledge.

Descola, Philippe, and Gisli Palsson, eds. 1996. *Nature and Society: Anthropological Perspectives.* London: Routledge.

De Waal. 2019. *The Age of Empathy: Nature's Lessons for a Kinder Society.* London: Souvenir.

Dilworth, David. 1974. "Watsuji Tetsurô (1889–1960): Cultural Phenomenologist and Ethician." *Philosoph East and West* 24, no. 1: 3–22.

Dolphijn, Rick, and Iris van der Tuin. 2012. *New Materialism: Interviews & Cartographies.* London: Open Humanities Press.

Dombrowski, David., 1988. "Panpsychism." *The Wordsworth Circle* 19, no. 1 (Winter): 38–45.

Dumanoski, Dianne. 2009. *The End of the Long Summer: Why We Must Remake Our Civilization to Survive on a Volatile Earth.* New York: Crown.

Dutreuil, Sébastien. 2020. "Gaia Is Alive." In *Critical Zones: The Science and Politics of Landing on Earth,* edited by Bruno Latour and Peter Weibel, 180–83. Karlsruhe: ZKM.

Dwivedi, O. P. 2004. "Satyaraha for Conservation: Awakening the Spirit of Hinduism." In *This Sacred Earth: Religion, Nature, Environment,* edited by Roger S. Gottlieb, 145–57. New York: Routledge.

190 | Bibliography

Edelglass, William, and Jay Garfield, eds. 2009. *Buddhist Philosophy: Essential Readings.* Oxford: Oxford University Press.

Edelman, David, Bernard Baars, and Anil Seth. 2005. "Identifying Hallmarks of Consciousness in Non-Mammalian Species." ---I---Consciousness and Cognition %%%I%%%14, no. 1 (March): 169–87.

Edelman, David, and Anil Seth. 2009. "Animal Consciousness: A Synthetic Approach." *Trends in Neurosciences* 32, no. 9: 476–84.

Ellis, Erle. 2011. "Anthropogenic Transformation of the Terrestrial Biosphere." *Philosophical Transactions of the Royal Society A: Mathematical, Physical and Engineering Sciences* 369, no. 1938 (March): 1010–35, http://doi.org/10.1098/rsta.2010.0331

Ells, Peter. 2011. *Panpsychism: The Philosophy of the Sensuous Cosmos.* Alresford, UK: O-Books.

Emmett, Robert, and Thomas Lekan, eds. 2016. "Whose Anthropocene? Revisiting Dipesh

Chakrabarty's 'Four Theses.'" *RCC Perspectives: Transformations in Environment and Society,* no. 2. Munich: Rachel Carson Center.

Ernwein, Marion, Franklin Ginn, and James Palmer. 2021. *The Work That Plants Do.* Bielefeld, Germany: Transcript Verlag.

Escobar, Arturo. 2016. "Thinking-Feeling with the Earth: Territorial Struggles and the Ontological Dimension of the Epistemologies of the South." *Revista de Antropología Iberoamericana* 11, no. 1 (January–April): 11–32.

Evernden, Neil. 1999. *The Natural Alien: Humankind and Environment.* Toronto: Toronto University Press.

Farrar, Janet, and Stewart Farrar. 1984. *A Witch's Bible.* London: Magickal Childe.

Ferrara, Alessandro. 2008. *La forza del esempio.* Milan: Feltrinelli.

———. 2019. "Debating Exemplarity: The 'Communis' in Sensus Communis." *Philosophy and Social Criticism* 45, no. 2: 146–58.

Ferré, Frederick. 1996a. *Being and Value: Toward a Constructive Postmodern Metaphysics.* Albany: State University of New York Press.

———. 1996b. "Persons in Nature: Toward an Applicable and Unified Environmental Ethics." *Ethics and the Environment* 1, no. 1 (Spring): 15–25.

Folie, Sabine, and Franke Anselm, eds. 2012a. *Animism: Modernity through the Looking Glass.* Cologne: Verlag der Buchhandlung Walther Konig.

———. 2012b. "Introduction and Acknowledgments." In *Animism: Modernity through the Looking Glass,* edited by Sabine Folie and Franke Anselm, 14–17. Cologne: Verlag der Buchhandlung Walther Konig.

Foucault, Michel. 1977. *Discipline and Punish: The Birth of the Prison.* New York: Pantheon.

———. 2001. *The Order of Things: An Archaeology of the Human Sciences.* London: Routledge. Online version, 1994: https://foucault.info/documents/foucault.orderOfThings.en/.

Fox, Matthew. 1991. *Creation Spirituality: Liberating Gifts for the Peoples of the Earth.* New York: HarperCollins.

Franke, Anselm. 2012a. "Animism: Notes on an Exhibition." *E-flux journal,* no. 36 (July): 1–22.

———. 2012b. "Beyond the Return of the Repressed" In *Animism: Modernity through the Looking Glass,* edited by Sabine Folie and Franke Anselm, 167–82. Cologne: Verlag der Buchhandlung Walther Konig.

Frost, Samantha. 2016. *Biocultural Creatures: Toward a New Theory of the Human.* Durham, NC: Duke University Press.

Fuentes, Agustin. 2017. "Becoming Human in the Anthropocene." In *Religion in the Anthropocene,* edited by Celia Deane-Drummond, Sigurd Bergmann, and Markus Vogt, 103–18. Eugene, OR: Cascade Books.

Gad, Christopher, Brit Ross Winthereik, and Casper Bruun Jensen. 2015. "Practical Ontology: Worlds in STS and Anthropology." *NatureCulture,* no. 3 (October): 67–86.

Galloway, Alexander. 2013."The Poverty of Philosophy: Realism and Post-Fordism." *Critical Inquiry* 39, no. 2 (Winter): 347–66.

Garfield, Jay. 1995. *The Fundamental Wisdom of the Middle Way: Nagarjuna's Mulamadhyamakarika.* Oxford: Oxford University Press.

———. 2015. *Engaging Buddhism: Why It Matters to Philosophy.* Oxford: Oxford University Press.

Gemenne, François. 2015. "The Anthropocene and Its Victims." In *The Anthropocene and the Global Environmental Crisis.* London: Routledge.

Gibson-Graham, J. K., and Ethan Miller. 2015. "Economy as Ecological Livelihood." In *Manifesto for Living in the Anthropocene,* edited by Katherine Gibson, Deborah Bird Rose, and Ruth Fincher, 7–15. Brooklyn, NY: Punctum.

Gilbert, Scott F., Jan Sapp, and Alfred I. Tauber. 2012. "A Symbiotic View of Life: We Have Never Been Individuals." *Quarterly Review of Biology* 87, no. 4 (December): 325–41.

Glikson, Andrew, and Colin Groves. 2016, *Climate, Fire and Human Evolution.* Cham, Switzerland: Springer.

Goff, Philip. 2017. "The Phenomenal Bonding Solution to the Combination Problem." In *Panpsychism,* edited by Godehard Brüntrup and Ludwig Jaskolla, 283–302. Oxford: Oxford University Press.

Goodenough, Ursula. 1998. *The Sacred Depths of Nature.* New York: Oxford University Press.

Gottlieb, Roger S., ed. 2004. *This Sacred Earth: Religion, Nature, Environment.* New York: Routledge.

Graeber, David. 2015. "Radical Alterity Is Just Another Way of Saying 'Reality': A Reply to Eduardo Viveiros de Castro." *Journal of Ethnographic Theory* 5, no. 2 (October): 1–41.

192 | Bibliography

———. 2018. *Bullshit Jobs: A Theory.* New York: Simon & Shuster.

Gratton, Peter. 2014. *Speculative Realism: Problems and Prospects.* London: Continuum.

Greer, John Michael. 2012. *Mystery Teachings from the Living Earth.* San Francisco: Weiser Books.

Griffin, David Ray. 1998. *Unsnarling the World-Knot: Consciousness, Freedom, and the Mind-Body Problem.* Berkeley: University of California Press.

———. 2007. *Whitehead's Radically Different Postmodern Philosophy: An Argument for Its Contemporary Relevance.* Albany: State University of New York Press.

Grim, John A., ed. 2001. *Indigenous Traditions and Ecology.* Cambridge, MA: Harvard University Press.

Grim, John, and Mary Evelyn Tucker. 2014. *Ecology and Religion.* Washington, DC: Island.

Grimes, Ronald. 2014. "Performance Is Currency in the Deep World's Gift Economy: An Incantatory Riff for a Global Medicine Show." In *The Handbook of Contemporary Animism,* edited by Graham Harvey, 501–12. London: Routledge.

Guattari, Félix. 1992a. *Chaosmose.* Paris: Broché.

———. 1992b. "Vers une nouvelle démocratie écologique," https://www.multitudes.net/Vers-une-nouvelle-democratie/.

———. 1995. *Chaosmosis: An Ethico-Aesthetic Paradigm.* Paris: Broché.

———. 2000. *The Three Ecologies.* London: Athlone.

———. 2012. *Schizoanalytic Cartographies.* London: Continuum.

———. 2018. *Qu'est-ce que l'écosophie.* Paris: Broché.

Habermas, Jürgen. 1988. *The Theory of Communicative Action.* Vol. 2. Boston: Beacon.

Haila, Yrjö. 2000. "Beyond the Nature-Culture Dualism." *Biology and Philosophy* 15, no. 2: 155–75.

Halbmayer, Ernst. 2012. "Debating Animism, Perspectivism and the Construction of Ontologies." *Indiana,* no. 29: 9–23.

———, ed. 2018a. *Indigenous Modernities in South America.* Herefordshire, UK: Sean Kingston.

———. 2018b. "Introduction." In *Indigenous Modernities in South America,* edited by Ernst Halbmayer, 1–24. Herefordshire, UK: Sean Kingston.

———. 2018c. "Yukpa Modernity as Joint Becoming." In *Indigenous Modernities in South America,* edited by Ernst Halbmayer, 55–79. Herefordshire, UK: Sean Kingston.

Hall, Matthew. 2011. *Plants as Persons: A Philosophical Botany.* Albany: State University of New York Press.

Hamilton, Clive. 2013. *Earthmasters: The Dawn of the Age of Climate Engineering.* New Haven, CT: Yale University Press.

———. 2014a. "The Delusion of the Good Anthropocene." June 17. Available at: http://clivehamilton.com/the-delusion-of-the-good-anthropocene-reply-to-andrew-revkin/.

———. 2014b. "The New Environmentalism Will Lead Us to Disaster." *Scientific American*, June 19. Available at: http://www.scientificamerican.com/article/the-new-environmentalism-will-lead-us-to-disaster/.

———. 2015. "The Technofix Is In: A Critique of the Ecomodernist Manifesto." *Earth Island Journal*, April 21.

Hamilton, Clive, Claude Bonneuil, and François Gemenne. 2015. "Thinking the Anthropocene." In *The Anthropocene and Global Environmental Crisis: Rethinking Modernity in a New Epoch*, edited by Clive Hamilton, Claude Bonneuil, and François Gemenne, 1–13. London: Routledge.

Hamilton, Clive, and Jacques Grinevald. 2015. "Was the Anthropocene Anticipated?" *The Anthropocene Review* 2, no. 1: 59–72.

Hanh, Thich Nhat. 1988. *The Heart of Understanding: Commentary on the Prajnaparamita Heart Sutra*. Berkeley, CA: Parallax.

Haraway, Donna. 1998. "Deanimations: Maps and Portraits of Life Itself." In *Picturing Science Producing Art*, edited by Peter Galison and Caroline A. Jones, 181–207. New York: Routledge.

———. 2014. "Chthulucene, Capitalocene, Anthropocene," http://opentranscripts.org/transcript/anthropocene-capitalocene-chthulucene/.

———. 2015. "Anthropologists Are Talking—About the Anthropocene." *Ethnos* 81, no. 3 (November): 1–30.

———. 2016a. As told to Lauren O'Neill-Butler at Art Forum, http://www.artforum.com/words/id=63147.

———. 2016b. *Staying with the Trouble: Making Kin in the Cthulucene*. Durham, NC: Duke University Press.

———. 2017. "Symbiogenesis, Sympoiesis, and Art Science Activism for Staying with the Trouble." In *Arts of Living on a Damaged Planet*, edited by Anna Tsing, Heather Swanson, Elaine Gan, and Nils Bubandt, 25–50. Minneapolis: University of Minnesota Press.

Harding, Sandra. 2008. *Sciences from Below: Feminisms, Postcolonialities, and Modernities*. Durham, NC: Duke University Press.

Harding, Stephen. 2009. *Animate Earth: Science, Intuition and Gaia*. Cambridge, UK: Green Books.

Harman, Graham. 2014. *Bruno Latour: Reassembling the Political*. London: Pluto.

Harrison, Paul. 2013. *Elements of Pantheism: A Spirituality of Nature and the Universe*. Shaftesbury, UK: Element Books.

Hartley, Daniel. 2016. "Anthropocene, Capitalocene, and the Problem of Culture." In *Anthropocene or Capitalocene: Nature, History and the Crisis of Capitalism*, edited by Jason Moore, 154–65. Oakland, CA: PM Press.

Harvey, David. 1990. *The Condition of Postmodernity*. Oxford: Blackwell.

Harvey, Graham. 1994. "The Roots of Pagan Ecology." *Religion Today* 9, no. 3: 38–41.

———. ed. 2003. *Shamanism: A Reader*. New York: Routledge.

194 | Bibliography

———. 2005. *Animism: Respecting the Living World.* London: Hurst.

———. 2006. "Animals, Animists and Academics." Zygon 41, no. 1 (March): 9–20.

———. 2007. *What Do Pagans Believe?* London: Granta Books.

———. 2011. *Contemporary Paganism: Religions of the Earth from Druids and Witches to Heathens and Ecofeminists.* New York: New York University Press.

———. ed. 2014. *The Handbook of Contemporary Animism.* London: Routledge.

———. ed. 2020. *Indigenizing Movements in Europe.* Sheffield, UK: Equinox.

Haught, John F. 2004. "Christianity and Ecology." In *This Sacred Earth: Religion, Nature, Environment*, edited by Roger S. Gottlieb, 232–47. New York: Routledge.

———. 2006. *Is Nature Enough? Meaning and Truth in the Age of Science.* Cambridge: Cambridge University Press.

Hawken, Paul. 2007. *Blessed Unrest: How the Largest Movement in the World Came into Being, and Why No One Saw It Coming.* New York: Viking.

Henning, Brian G. 2005. *The Ethics of Creativity: Beauty, Morality, and Nature in a Processive Cosmos.* Pittsburgh: University of Pittsburgh Press.

Herrmann, Robert L. 2004. "Emergence of Humans and the Neurobiology of Consciousness." In *In Whom We Live and Move and Have Our Being*, edited by Philip Clayton and Arthur Peacocke, 121–30. Cambridge, UK: William B. Eerdmans.

Hickmann, Thomas, Lena Partzsch, Philipp Pattberg, and Sabine Weiland, eds. 2018. *The Anthropocene Debate and Political Science.* London: Routledge.

Hird, Myra J. 2009. *The Origins of Sociable Life: Evolution after Science Studies.* New York: Palgrave Macmillan.

———. 2010. "Indifferent Globality: Gaia, 'Other Worldliness,' and Symbiosis." *Theory, Culture & Society* 27, no. 2–3 (May): 54–72.

Hodder, Ian. 2012. *Entangled: An Archaeology of the Relationships between Humans and Things.* Malden, MA: Wiley-Blackwell.

Hoffman, Andrew. 2015. *How Culture Shapes the Climate Debate.* Stanford, CA: Stanford University Press.

Hoffmeyer, Jesper. 2008. *Biosemiotics: An Examination into the Signs of Life and the Life of Signs.* Scranton, PA: University of Scranton Press.

Hojbjerg, Christian Kordt. 2012. "Den 'ontologiske vendings' utilstrækkelighed." *Tidsskriftet Antropologi*, no. 67: 29–35.

Holmes, Rolston, III. 1987. "Can the East Help the West to Value Nature?" *Philosophy East and West* 37, no. 2: 172–90.

Horn, Eva, and Hannes Bergthaller. 2019. *The Anthropocene: Key Issues for the Humanities.* Abingdon, UK: Taylor & Francis.

Hornborg, Alf. 1998. "Ecological Embeddedness and Personhood: Have We Always Been Capitalists?" *Anthropology Today* 14, no. 2 (April): 3–5.

———. 2013. *Global Ecology and Unequal Exchange: Fetishism in a Zero-Sum World.* London: Routledge.

———. 2014a. "Submitting to Objects: Animism, Fetishism, and the Cultural Foundations of Capitalism." In *The Handbook of Contemporary Animism*, edited by Harvey Graham, 244–59. London: Routledge.

———. 2014b. "Technology as Fetish: Marx, Latour and the Cultural Foundations of Capitalism." *Theory, Culture & Society* 31, no. 4 (July): 119–40.

———. 2015. *The Political Ecology of the Technocene*. Oxford: Routledge.

Hulme, Mike. 2014. *Can Science Fix Climate Change? A Case against Climate Engineering*. Cambridge: Polity.

Huntington, C. W. Jr. 1989. *The Emptiness of Emptiness: An Introduction to Early Indian Madhyamika*. Honolulu: University of Hawaii Press.

Idelbar, Avelar. 2013. "Amerindian Perspectivism and Nonhuman Rights." *Ciencia y Cultura*, no. 31: 255–75.

Imanishi, Kinji. 2015. *La liberté dans l'évolution.* Marseille: Editions Wildproject.

Ingold, Tim. 2006. "Rethinking the Animate, Re-Animating Thought." *Ethnos* 71, no. 1 (March): 9–20.

———. 2008. "Globes and Spheres: The Topology of Environmentalism." In *Environmental Anthropology: A Historical Reader*, edited by Michael R. Dove and Carol Carpenter, 462–69. Oxford: Blackwell.

———. 2011. *Being Alive: Essays on Movement, Knowledge and Description*. New York: Routledge.

———. 2014. "Being Alive to a World without Objects." In *The Handbook of Contemporary Animism*, edited by Harvey Graham, 213–25. London: Routledge.

Introna, Lucas. 2009. "Ethics and the Speaking of Things." *Theory, Culture & Society* 26, no. 4 (January): 398–419. Isamu, Nagami. 1981. "The Ontological Foundation in Tetsurô Watsuji's Philosophy: Kû and Human Existence." *Philosophy East and West* 31, no. 3: 279–96.

Jablonka, Eva, and Marion J. Lamb. 2005. ~~~I~~~*Evolution in Four Dimensions: Genetic, Epigenetic,* Behavioral, and Symbolic Variation in the History of Life. %%%I%%%Cambridge, MA: MIT Press.

Janz, Bruce B. 2011. "Watsuji Tetsuro, Fudo, and Climate Change." *Journal of Global Ethics* 7, no. 2 (August): 173–84.

Johnson, David W. 2019. *Watsuji on Nature: Japanese Philosophy in the Wake of Heidegger*. Evanston, IL: Northwestern University Press.

Johnson, John (Bruno Latour). 1988. "Mixing Humans and Nonhumans Together: The Sociology of a Door-Closer." *Social Problems* 35, no. 3 (June): 298–310.

Jonas, Hans. 1996. *Mortality and Morality: A Search for the Good after Auschwitz*, edited by Lawrence Vogel. Evanston, IL: Northwestern University Press.

Jorion, Paul. 2017. *Le dernier qui s'en va éteint la lumière*. Paris: Fayard/Pluriel.

Jullien, François. 2002. "Do Philosophers Have to Become Fixated on Truth?" *Critical Inquiry* 28, 4 (Summer): 803–24.

Kapfhammer, Wolfgang, and Luiza Garnelo. 2018. "'We Bought a Television Set from Lidia': Social Programs and Indigenous Agency among the Sateré-Mawé

196 | Bibliography

of the Brazilian Lower Amazon." In *Indigenous Modernities in South America*, edited by Ernst Halbmayer, 131–62. Herefordshire, UK: Sean Kingston.

Karner, Dietrich. 2012. "Preface." In *Animism: Modernity through the Looking Glass*, 9–10. Cologne: Verlag der Buchhandlung Walther Konig.

Kauffman, Stuart A. 2010. *Reinventing the Sacred.* New York: Basic Books.

———. 2016. *Humanity in a Creative Universe.* Oxford: Oxford University Press.

Kekoff, Marc. 2014. *Rewilding Our Hearts.* Novato, CA: New World Library.

Keller, Catherine. 2017. "Tingles of Matter, Tangles of Theology." In *Entangled Worlds: Religion, Science, and New Materialisms,* edited by Catherine Keller and Mary-Jane Rubinstein, 111–35. New York: Fordham University Press.

Keller, Catherine, and Mary-Jane Rubenstein, eds. 2017. *Entangled Worlds: Religion, Science, and New Materialisms.* New York: Fordham University Press.

Khong, Lynette. 2003. "Actants and Enframing: Heidegger and Latour on Technology." *Studies in History and Philosophy of Science,* part A, 34, no. 4 (December): 693–704.

Kim, Grace Ji-Sun, and Hilda Koster, eds. 2017. *Planetary Solidarity: Global Women's Voices on Christian Doctrine and Climate Justice.* Minneapolis: Fortress.

Kinji, Imanishi. 2015. *La liberté dans l'évolution.* Marseille: Editions Wildproject.

Kohak, Erazim. 1984. *The Embers and the Stars: A Philosophical Inquiry into the Moral Sense of Nature.* Chicago: University of Chicago Press.

Kohn, Eduardo. 2013. *How Forests Think: Toward an Anthropology beyond the Human.* Berkeley: University of California Press.

———. 2015. "Anthropology of Ontologies." *Annual Review of Anthropology,* no. 44: 1–35.

———. 2017. "Thinking with Thinking Forests." In *Comparative Metaphysics: Ontology after Anthropology,* edited by Pierre Charbonnier, Gildas Salmon, and Peter Skafish, 181–99. London: Rowman & Littlefield.

Krueger, Joel W. 2011. "The Who and the How of Experience." In *Self, No Self? Perspectives from Analytical, Phenomenological, and Indian Traditions,* edited by Mark Siderits, Evan Thompson, and Dan Zahavi, 27–55. Oxford: Oxford University Press.

Kull, Kalevi, Claus Emmeche, and Jesper Hoffmeyer. 2011. "Why Biosemiotics? An Introduction to Our View on the Biology of Life Itself." In *Towards a Semiotic Biology: Life Is the Action of Signs,* edited by Claus Emmeche and Kalevi Kull, 1–21. London: Imperial College Press.

Laclau, Ernesto, and Chantal Mouffe. 1985. *Hegemony and Socialist Strategy: Toward a Radical Democratic Politics,* translated by Winston Moore and Paul Cammack. London: Verso.

Lafleur, William R. 1978. "Buddhist Emptiness in the Ethics and Aesthetics of Watsuji Tetsurō." *Religious Studies* 14, no. 2 (June): 237–50.

Larson, Gerald James. 1989. " 'Conceptual Resources' in South Asia for 'Environmental Ethics.' " In *Nature in Asian Traditions of Thought: Essays in Environmental*

Philosophy, edited by J. Baird Callicott and Roger T. Ames, 267–77. Albany: State University of New York Press.

Latour, Bruno. 1991. *Nous n'avons jamais été modernes*. Paris: La Découverte.

———. 1993. *We Have Never Been Modern*, translated by Catherine Porter. Cambridge, MA: Harvard University Press.

———. 1994. "Pragmatogonies: A Mythical Account of How Humans and Nonhumans Swap Properties." *American Behavioral Scientist* 37, no. 6 (May): 791–808.

———. 1996. "Pursuing the Discussion of Interobjectivity with a Few Friends." *Mind, Culture, and Activity* 3, no. 4: 266–69.

———. 1998. "How to Be Iconophilic in Art, Science and Religion?" In *Picturing Science Producing Art*, edited by Peter Galison and Caroline A. Jones, 418–40. New York: Routledge.

———. 1999. *Politiques de la nature: Comment faire entrer les sciences en démocratie*. Paris: La Découverte.

———. 2002. "Morality and Technology: The End of the Means." *Theory, Culture & Society* 19, no. 5–6 (December): 247–60.

———. 2003. "What if We *Talked* Politics a Little?" *Contemporary Political Theory* 2, no. 2 (January): 143–64.

———. 2004a. *Politics of Nature: How to Bring the Sciences into Democracy*. Cambridge, MA: Harvard University Press.

———. 2004b. "Whose Cosmos, Which Cosmopolitics?" *Common Knowledge* 10, no. 3 (October): 450–62.

———. 2004c. "Why Has Critique Run Out of Steam? From Matters of Fact to Matters of Concern." *Critical Inquiry* 30, no. 2 (Winter): 225–48.

———. 2005. "What Is Given in Experience?" *Boundary* 2, 32, no. 1 (Spring): 22–237.

———. 2007. *Reassembling the Social: An Introduction to Actor-Network Theory*. Oxford: Oxford University Press.

———. 2008. "Ecologie et démocratie: Pour une politique de la nature." Agora Conference, January 18.

———. 2011. "Waiting for Gaia." Available at: http://www.bruno-latour.fr/sites/default/files/124-GAIA-LONDON-SPEAP_0.pdf.

———. 2012. *Enquête sur les modes d'existence: Une anthropologie des modernes*. Paris: La Découverte.

———. 2013a. "Biography of an Inquiry: On a Book about Modes of Existence." *Social Studies of Science* 43, no. 2 (April): 287–301.

———. 2013b. *Facing Gaia*. Cambridge, UK: Polity. Available at: http://www.bruno-latour.fr/node/487.

———. 2014. "Agency at the Time of the Anthropocene." *New Literary History* 45, no. 1 (December): 1–18.

———. 2015a. *Face à Gaïa: Huit conferences sur le nouveau régime climatique*. Paris: La Découverte.

198 | Bibliography

———. 2015b. "Fifty Shades of Green." Available at: http://www.bruno-latour.fr/node/701.

———. 2015c. "Make It Work/Theatre of Negotiations." Available at: https://nanterre-amandiers.com/en/evenement/le-theatre-des-negociations/

———. 2017. "A Dialogue about a New Meaning of Symmetric Anthropology." In *Comparative Metaphysics: Ontology after Anthropology*, edited by Pierre Charbonnier, Gildas Salmon, and Peter Skafish, 327–45. London: Rowman & Littlefield.

Latour, Bruno. "GAIA Global Circus." N.d. Available at: http://www.bruno-latour.fr/fr/node/359.

Latour, Bruno, and Timothy Lenton. 2019. "Extending the Domain of Freedom, or Why Gaia Is So Hard to Understand." *Critical Inquiry* 45, no. 3 (Spring): 659–80.

Latour, Bruno, and Vincent Antonin Lépinay. 2008. *L'économie: Science des interest passionnés*. Paris: La Découverte.

Latour, Bruno, and Isabelle Stengers, Anna Tsing, and Nils Bubandt. 2018, "Anthropologists Are Talking—About Capitalism, Ecology, and Apocalypse." *Ethnos* 83, no. 3 (June): 587–606.

Law, John. 1999."After ANT: Complexity, Naming and Topology." In *Actor Network Theory and After*, edited by John Law and John Hassard, 1–14. Oxford: Blackwell.

———. 2011. "Collateral Realities." In *The Politics of Knowledge*, edited by Fernando Dominguez Rubio and Patrick Baert, 156–78. London: Routledge.

———. 2015. "What's Wrong with a One-World World?" *Distinktion: Scandinavian Journal of Social Theory* 16, no. 1: 126–39.

Lenton, Timothy, and Sébastien Dutreuil. 2020. "Distinguishing Gaia from the Earth System(s)." In *Critical Zones: The Science and Politics of Landing on Earth*, edited by Bruno Latour and Peter Weibel, 176–79. Karlsruhe: ZKM.

Levine, Michael P. 1994. *Pantheism: A Non-Theistic Concept of Divinity*. London: Routledge.

Lewis, Ioan M. 2003. "Possession and Public Morality." In *Shamanism: A Reader*, edited by Graham Harvey, 69–91. New York: Routledge.

Lewis, Simon, and Mark Maslin. 2015a. "Defining the Anthropocene." *Nature*, no. 519 (March): 171–80.

———. 2015b. "A Transparent Framework for Defining the Anthropocene Epoch." *The Anthropocene Review* 2, no. 2 (June): 128–46.

Linden, Eugene. 2011. "Gaia Going Forward." In *Panpsychism: The Philosophy of the Sensuous Cosmos*, edited by Peter Ells, 337–42. Alresford, UK: O-Books.

Linera, García. 2007. "Neoliberalism and the New Socialism." A speech published in *Political Affairs,* January 15, http://www.politicalaffairs.net/neo-liberalism-and-the-new-socialism-speech-by-alvaro-garcia-linera.

Livingstone, Glenys. 2016. "A PaGaian Perspective." In *Godless Paganism: Voices of Non-Theistic Pagans*, edited by John Halstead, 128–35. Morrisville, NC: Lulu.

Lordon, Frédéric. 2016. *Les affects de la politique*. Paris: Editions du Seuil.

Lövbrand, Eva, and Silke Beck, Jason Chilvers, Tim Forsysth, Johan Hedrén, Mike Hulme, Rolf Lidskog, and Eleftheria Vasileiadou. 2015. "Who Speaks for the Future of the Earth? How Critical Social Science Can Extend the Future of the Anthropocene." *Global Environmental Change*, no. 32: 211–18.

Lovelock, James. 1972. "Gaia as Seen through the Atmosphere." *Atmospheric Environment* 6, no. 8: 15–25.

———. 2000. *Homage to Gaia: The Life of an Independent Scientist*. Oxford: Oxford University Press.

———. 2006. *The Revenge of Gaia: Earth's Climate Crisis and the Fate of Humanity*. New York: Basic Books.

———. 2016. *Gaia: A New Look at Life on Earth*. Oxford: Oxford University Press.

Lovelock, James, and Lynne Margulis. 1974. "Atmospheric Homeostasis by and for the Biosphere: The Gaia Hypothesis." *Tellus* 26, no. 1–2: 2–10.

Lowenthal, David. 2016. "Origins of Anthropocene Awareness." *The Anthropocene Review* 3, no. 1: 52–63.

Loy, David R. 2015. *A New Buddhist Path: Enlightenment, Evolution, and Ethics in the Modern World*. Somerville, MA: Wisdom.

Luke, Timothy. 2015a. "On the Politics of the Anthropocene." *Telos*, no. 172 (Fall): 139–62.

———. 2015b. "Political Critiques of the Anthropocene." *Telos*, no. 172 (Fall): 3–14.

Lyotard, Jean-François, 1979. *The Postmodern Condition: A Report on Knowledge*. Manchester: Manchester University Press.

Macdonald, B. J., and W. E. Connolly. 2015. "Confronting the Anthropocene and Contesting Neoliberalism." *New Political Science* 37, no. 2: 259–75.

Macfarlane, Robert. 2016. "Generation Anthropocene." *The Guardian*, April 1.

Macy, Joanna. 1991. *The Dharma of Natural Systems: Mutual Causality in Buddhism and General Systems Theory*. Albany: State University of New York Press.

Madden, Kristin, ed. 2005. *Exploring the Pagan Path: Wisdom from the Elders*. Franklin Lakes, NJ: New Page Books.

Malm, Andreas. 2016. *Fossil Capital: The Rise of Steam Power and the Roots of Global Warming*. London: Verso.

Maniglier, Patrice. 2017. "Anthropological Meditations: Discourse on Comparative Method." In *Comparative Metaphysics: Ontology after Anthropology*, edited by Pierre Charbonnier, Gildas Salmon, and Peter Skafish, 109–31. London: Rowman & Littlefield.

Margulis, Lynn. 1999. *Symbiotic Planet: A New Look at Evolution*. New York: Basic Books.

Margulis, Lynn, and James Lovelock. 1974. "Biological Modulation of the Earth's Atmosphere." *Icarus* 21, no. 4: 471–89.

Margulis, Lynn, and Oona West. 1997. "Gaia and the Colonization of Mars." In *Slanted Truths: Essays on Gaia, Symbiosis, and Evolution*, edited by Lynn Margulis and Dorian Sagan, 221–34. New York: Copernicus.

Maslin, Mark A., and Simon L. Lewis. 2015. "Anthropocene: Earth System, Geological, Philosophical and Political Paradigm Shifts." *The Anthropocene Review* 2, no. 2: 108–16.

Massumi, Brian. 2014. *What Animals Teach Us about Politics*. Durham, NC: Duke University Press.

Mathews, Freya. 1991. *The Ecological Self*. London: Routledge.

———. 2005. *Reinhabiting Reality: Toward a Recovery of Culture*. Albany: State University of New York Press.

———. 2010. "A Contemporary Metaphysical Controversy." *Sophia* 49, no. 2 (June): 231–36.

———. 2011. "Panpsychism as Paradigm." In *The Mental as Fundamental: New Perspectives on Panpsychism*, edited by Michael Blamauer, 141–55. Heusenstamm, Germany: Ontos Verlag.

———. 2015. "Earth as Ethic." In *Manifesto for Living in the Anthropocene*, edited by Katherine Gibson, Deborah Bird Rose, and Ruth Fincher, 91–95. Brooklyn, NY: Punctum.

Maxwell, Nicholas. 2007. *From Knowledge to Wisdom: A Revolution for Science and the Humanities*. London: Pentire.

May, Reinhardt. 1996. *Heidegger's Hidden Sources: East Asian Influences on His Work*. Translated by Graham Parkes. London: Routledge.

Mazzochi, Fulvio. 2020. "A Deeper Meaning of Sustainability: Insights from Indigenous Knowledge." *The Anthropocene Review* 7, no. 1: 77–93.

Mbembe, Achille. 2017. "Rethinking Democracy beyond the Human." Lecture presented at the European Graduate School, Valetta, Malta, October 16. Available at: http://www.egs.edu.

McAfee, Kathleen. 2016. "The Politics of Nature in the Anthropocene." In "Whose Anthropocene? Revisiting Dipesh Chakrabarty's 'Four Theses,'" edited by Robert Emmett and Thomas Lekan, 65–72. *RCC Perspectives: Transformations in Environment and Society*, no. 2.

McBrian, Justin. 2016. "Accumulating Extinction: Planetary Catastrophism in the Necrocene." In *Anthropocene or Capitalocene? Nature, History, and the Crisis of Capitalism*, edited by Jason W. Moore, 116–137. Oakland, CA: PM Press.

McCarthy, Erin. 2017. "Watsuji Tetsurō: The Mutuality of Climate and Culture and an Ethics of Betweenness." In *The Oxford Handbook of Japanese Philosophy*, edited by Bret W. Davis. Oxford: Oxford University Press.

McGregor, Deborah. 2004. "Coming Full Circle: Indigenous Knowledge, Environment, and Our Future." Special issue: "The Recovery of Indigenous Knowledge," *American Indian Quarterly* 28, no. 3–4 (Summer–Autumn): 385–410.

McLaughlin, Brian P. 2017. "Mind Dust, Magic, or a Conceptual Gap Only?" In *Panpsychism*, edited by Godehard Brüntrup and Ludwig Jaskolla, 305–33. London: Oxford University Press.

Melitopoulos, Angela, and Mauritio Lazzarato. 2012a. "Assemblages." In *Animism: Modernity through the Looking Glass*, edited by Sabine Folie and Franke Anselm, 136–45. Cologne: Verlag der Buchhandlung Walther Konig.

———. 2012b. "Machinic Animism." *Deleuze Studies* 6, no. 2: 240–49.

Mendieta, Eduardo. 2015. "Globalization, Cosmopolitics, Decoloniality: Politics for/ of the Anthropocene." In *The Bloomsbury Companion to Political Philosophy*, edited by Andrew Fiala, 213–22. London: Bloomsbury.

Merchant, Carolyn. *The Death of Nature: Women, Ecology, and the Scientific Revolution*. New York: HarperOne.

Merchant, Carolyn. 2020. *The Anthropocene and the Humanities: From Climate Change to a New Age of Sustainability*. New Haven, CT: Yale University Press.

Merker, Bjorn. 2005. "The Liabilities of Mobility: A Selection Pressure for the Transition to Consciousness in Animal Evolution." *Consciousness and Cognition* 14, no. 1 (April): 89–114.

Metzinger, Thomas. 2009. *The Ego Tunnel: The Science of the Mind and the Myth of the Self*. New York: Basic Books.

Michon, Perrine. 2018. "Les bien communs: Une figure d'actualisation du paradigme mésologique?" In *La mésologie: Un autre paradigme pour l'anthropocène*, edited by Marie Augendre, Jean-Pierre Llored, and Yann Nussaume, 209–16. Paris: Hermann Editeurs.

Midgley, Mary. 2010. *The Solitary Self: Darwin and the Selfish Gene*. London: Routledge.

Milton, Kay. 1996. *Environmentalism and Cultural Theory*. Abingdon, UK: Taylor & Francis.

Mitchell A. 2015. "Decolonizing the Anthropocene." *Worldly IR*, blog, March 17. Available at: https://worldlyir.wordpress.com/2015/03/17/decolonising-the-anthropocene/.

Mochizuki, Taro. 2006. "Climate and Ethics: Ethical Implications of Watsuji Tetsuro's Concepts: 'Climate' and 'Climaticity.'" *Philosophia Osaka*, no. 1: 43–55.

Monbiot, George. 2014. *Feral: Rewilding the Land, Sea and Human Life*. London: Penguin Books.

Moore, Jason. 2014. *The Capitalocene*, https://jasonwmoore.com/wp-content/uploads/2017/08/Moore-The-Capitalocene-Part-I-published-JPS-2017.pdf

———. 2015. Capitalism in the Web of Life. London: Verso.

———, ed. 2016a. *Anthropocene or Capitalocene? Nature, History, and the Crisis of Capitalism*. Oakland, CA: PM Press.

———. 2016b. "The Rise of Cheap Nature." in *Anthropocene or Capitalocene? Nature, History, and the Crisis of Capitalism*. Oakland, CA: PM Press.

Morowitz, Harold J. 1989. "Biology of a Cosmological Science." In *Nature in Asian Traditions of Thought: Essays in Environmental Philosophy*, edited by J. Baird Callicott and Roger T. Ames, 37–49. Albany: State University of New York Press.

Bibliography

Morris, Brian. 2014. *Anthropology, Ecology, and Anarchism: A Brian Morris Reader.* Oakland, CA: PM Press.

Morton, Timothy. 2010. "Interviews: Graham Harman, Jane Bennett, Tim Morton, Ian Bogost, Levi Bryant and Paul Ennis." *Speculations* 1, no. 1: 84–134.

Müller, Ralf. 2009. "Watsuji's Reading of Dōgen's Shōbōgenzō." *Frontiers of Japanese Philosophy*, no. 6: 174–91.

Nagel, Thomas. 1979. *Mortal Questions.* Cambridge: Cambridge University Press, 181–95.

Nancy, Jean-Luc. 1990. *Une pensée finie.* Paris: Galilée/

Naveh, Danny, and Nurit Bird-David. 2014a. "Animism, Conservation and Immediacy." In *The Handbook of Contemporary Animism*, edited by Graham Harvey, 27–37. London: Routledge.

———. 2014b. "How Persons Become Things: Economic and Epistemological Changes among Nayaka Hunter-Gatherers." *Journal of the Royal Anthropological Institute*, no. 20: 74–92.

Nicholson, Simon, and Sikina Jinnah, eds. 2016. *New Earth Politics: Essays from the Anthropocene.* Cambridge, MA: MIT Press.

Nobuo, Kioka. 2010. "La contribution mésologique de Watsuji Tetsurō." In *Philosophes japonais contemporain*, edited by Jacynthe Tremblay, 241–56. Montreal: Presses de l'Université de Montréal.

Northcott, Michael S. 2007. *A Moral Climate: The Ethics of Global Warming.* Maryknoll, NY: Orbis Books.

———. 2017. "On Going Gently into the Anthropocene." In *Religion in the Anthropocene*, edited by Celia Deane-Drummond, Sigurd Bergmann, and Markus Vogt, 19–34. Eugene, OR: Cascade Books.

Odin, Steve. 1992. "The Social Self in Japanese Philosophy and American Pragmatism: A Comparative Study of Watsuji Tetsurō and George Herbert Mead." *Philosophy East and West* 42, no. 3: 475–501.

Orr, Emma Restall. 2005. "The Ethics of Paganism." In *Pagan Visions for a Sustainable Future*, edited by Ly de Angeles, Emma Restall Orr, and Thom van Dooren, 1–38. Woodbury, MN: Llewellyn.

Palsson, Gisli. 1996. "Human-Environmental Relations: Orientalism, Paternalism, Communalism." In *Nature and Society: Anthropological Perspectives*, edited by Philippe Descola and Gisli Palsson, 63–81. London: Routledge.

Panksepp, Jaak. 2005. "Affective Consciousness: Core Emotional Feelings in Animals and Humans." *Consciousness and Cognition* 14, no. 1 (March): 30–80.

Parajuli, Pramod. 2001. "Learning from Ecological Ethnicities: Toward a Plural Political Ecology of Knowledge." In *Indigenous Traditions and Ecology*, edited by John A. Grim, 559–89. Cambridge, MA: Harvard University Press.

Parkes, Graham. 1997. "The Putative Fascism of the Kyoto School and the Political Correctness of the Modern Academy." *Philosophy East and West* 47, no. 3: 305–36.

Peirce, Charles Sanders. 1892. "Man's Glassy Essence." *The Monist* 3, no. 1 (October): 1–22. Reprinted in *The Essential Peirce*, vol. 1., edited by Nathan Houser and Christian J. W. Kloesel (Bloomington: Indiana University Press, 1999).

Pellizzoni, Luigi, and Ross Abbinnett. 2015. *Ontological Politics in a Disposable World: The New Mastery of Nature.* Abingdon, UK: Taylor & Francis.

Peterson, Anna. 2000. "In and of the World? Christian Theological Anthropology and Environmental Ethics." *Journal of Agricultural and Environmental Ethics* 12, no. 3 (January): 237–61.

Phillips, Stephen. 2009. *Yoga, Karma, and Rebirth.* New York: Columbia University Press.

Pierotti, Raymond, and Daniel Wildcat. 2000. "Traditional Ecological Knowledge: The Third Alternative." *Ecological Applications* 10, no. 5 (October): 1333–40.

Pignarre, Philippe, and Isabelle Stengers. 2003. *La sorcellerie capitaliste: Pratiques de désenvoûtement.* Paris: La Découverte.

Plumwood, Val, 2001. *Environmental Culture: The Ecological Crisis of Reason.* London: Routledge.

———. 2007. "A Review of Deborah Bird Rose's 'Reports from a Wild Country: Ethics for Decolonisation.'" *Australian Humanities Review*, no. 42: 1–4.

Pope Francis. 2015. *Laudato si': Enciclica sulla cura della casa commune.* Vatican City: Libreria Editrice Vaticana.

Povinelli, Elisabeth. 2016. *Geontologies: A Requiem to Late Liberalism.* Durham, NC: Duke University Press.

Povinelli, Elizabeth A., Mathew Coleman, and Kathryn Yusoff. 2017. "An Interview with Elizabeth Povinelli: Geontopower, Biopolitics and the Anthropocene." Special issue: "Geosocial Formations and the Anthropocene," *Theory, Culture & Society* 34, no. 1 (February): 0(0) 1–17. DOI:10.1177/0263276417689900.

Praet, Isvan. 2014. *Animism and the Question of Life.* London: Routledge.

Prigogine, Ilya. 2008. *Les lois du chaos.* Paris: Flammarion.

Primavesi, Anne. 2009. *Gaia and Climate Change: A Theology of Gift Events.* New York: Routledge.

———. 2010. "What's in a Name? Gaia and the Reality of Being Alive in a Relational World." In *Religion and Dangerous Environmental Change: Transdisciplinary Perspectives on the Ethics of Climate and Sustainability*, edited by Sigurd Bergmann and Dieter Gerten, 87–102. Berlin: Lit Verlag/New Brunswick, NJ: Transaction.

Puig della Bellacasa, Maria. 2017. *Matters of Care: Speculative Ethics in More than Human Worlds.* Minneapolis: University of Minnesota Press.

Raffnsoe, Sverre. 2016. *Philosophy of the Anthropocene: The Human Turn.* Hampshire, UK: Palgrave Macmillan.

Rambelli, Fabio. 2019. *Spirits and Animism in Contemporary Japan: The Invisible Empire.* London: Bloomsbury.

204 | Bibliography

Revkin, Andrew. 2014a. "A Darker View of the Age of Us—the Anthropocene." June 18. Available at: http://dotearth.blogs.nytimes.com/2014/06/18/a-darker-view-of-the-age-of-us-the-anthropocene/.

———. 2014b. "Exploring Academia's Role in Charting Paths to a 'Good' Anthropocene." June 16. Available at: http://dotearth.blogs.nytimes.com/2014/06/16/exploring-academias-role-in-charting-paths-to-a-good-anthropocene/?_r=0.

———. 2014c. "Seeking a 'Good' Anthropocene." Keynote lecture to the annual conference of the AESS, Pace University, June. Available at: https://www.youtube.com/watch?v=oIHeqLKGd3Q.

Richerson, Peter, and Robert Boyd. 2005. *Not By Genes Alone: How Culture Transformed Human Evolution.* Chicago: University of Chicago Press. Rizzolatti, Giacomo, and Corado Sinigaglia. 2008. *Les Neurones miroirs.* Paris: Odile Jacob.

Romm, Janet, 2014. "Words Matter when Talking about Global Warming: The Good Anthropocene Debate." *Climate Progress,* June 19. Available at: https://archive.thinkprogress.org/words-matter-when-talking-global-warming-the-good-anthropocene-debate-f5c8bdd78cc9.

Rosenfield, Leonora Cohen. 1941. *From Beast-Machine to Man-Machine: Animal Soul in French: Letters from Descartes to La Mettrie.* New York: Oxford University Press.

Rosengren, Dan. 2018. "The Fashion of Politics and the Politics of Fashion: On Indigenous Modernities and Matsigenka Struggles." In *Indigenous Modernities in South America,* edited by Ernst Halbmayer, 80–102. Herefordshire, UK: Sean Kingston.

Rountree, Kathryn. 2012. "Neo-Paganism, Animism, and Kinship with Nature." *Journal of Contemporary Religion* 27, 2: 305–20.

———. 2016. "'We Are the Weavers, We Are the Web': Cosmopolitan Entanglements in Modern Paganism." In *Cosmopolitanism, Nationalism, and Modern Paganism,* edited by Kathryn Rountree, 1–19. New York: Palgrave Macmillan.

Rowan, Rory. 2015. "Extinction as Usual? Geosocial Futures and Left Optimism." *e-flux journal.* Available at: http://supercommunity.e-flux.com/texts/extinction-as-usual-geo-social-futures-and-left-optimism/.

Roy, Eleanor Ainge. 2017. "New Zealand River Granted Same Legal Rights as Human Being." *The Guardian,* March 16.

Rubenstein, Mary-Jane. 2018. *Pantheologies: Gods, Worlds, Monsters.* New York: Columbia University Press.

Ruddiman, William F., Erle C. Ellis, Jed O. Kaplan, and Dorian Q. Fuller. 2015. "Defining the Epoch We Live In." *Science,* no. 348 (April): 38–39.

Rue, Loyal. 2011. *Nature Is Enough: Religious Naturalism and the Meaning of Life.* Albany: State University of New York Press.

Ruse, Michael. 2013. *The Gaia Hypothesis: Science on a Pagan Planet.* Chicago: University of Chicago Press.

Russell, Bertrand. 1927. *Why I Am Not a Christian.* London: Watts.

———. 1956. *Portraits from Memory and Other Essays*. London: George Allen & Unwin.

Sagan, Dorion. 2015. "Life on a Margulisian Planet: A Son's Philosophical Reflections." In *Earth, Life, and System: Evolution and Ecology on a Gaian Planet*, edited by Bruce Clarke, 13–38. New York: Fordham University Press.

Sagan, Dorion, Lynn Margulis, and Ricardo Guerrero. 1997. "Descartes, Dualism, and Beyond." In *Slanted Truths: Essays on Gaia, Symbiosis, and Evolution*, edited by Lynn Margulis and Dorion Sagan, 172–83. New York: Copernicus.

Saldanha, Arun, and Hannah Stark, eds. 2016. *Deleuze and Guattari in the Anthropocene*. Edinburgh: Edinburgh University Press.

Salmon, Enrique. 2000. "Kincentric Ecology: Indigenous Perceptions of the Human-Nature Relationship." *Ecological Applications* 10, no. 5 (October): 1327–32.

Salmon, Gildas, and Pierre Charbonnier. 2014. "The Two Ontological Pluralisms of French Anthropology." *Journal of the Royal Anthropological Institute* 20, no. 3: 567–73.

Santos, Boaventura. 2002. *Towards a New Legal Common Sense*. London: Butterworth.

———. 2007. *The Rise of the Global Left: The World Social Forum and Beyond*. London: Zed Books.

———. 2014. *Epistemologies of the South: Justice against Epistemicide*. Boulder, CO: Paradigm.

Sayes, Edwin. 2014. "Actor-Network Theory and Methodology: Just What Does It Mean to Say That Nonhumans Have Agency?" *Social Studies of Science* 44, no. 1 (January): 134–49.

Schmitz, Oswald. 2017. *The New Ecology: Rethinking a Science for the Anthropocene*. Princeton, NJ: Princeton University Press.

Scranton, Roy. 2016. *Learning to Die in the Anthropocene*. San Francisco: City Lights Bookstore.

Selin, Hélaine. 2003. *Nature across Cultures: Views of Nature and the Environment in Non-Western Cultures*. Dordrecht, Netherlands: Springer.

Seth, Anil, Bernard Baars, and David Edelman. 2005. "Criteria for Consciousness in Humans and Other Mammals." *Consciousness and Cognition* 14, no. 1 (March): 119–39.

Sevilla, Anton Luis. 2014. "Concretizing an Ethics of Emptiness: The Succeeding Volumes of Watsuji Tetsurô's Ethics." *Asian Philosophy* 24, no. 1: 82–101.

———. 2016. "The Buddhist Roots of Watsuji Tetsurō's Ethics of Emptiness." *Journal of Religious Ethics* 44, no. 4: 606–35.

———. 2017. *Watsuji Tetsuro's Global Ethics of Emptiness: A Contemporary Look at a Modern Japanese Philosopher*. Cham, Switzerland: Palgrave Macmillan.

Shapin, Stephen. 1988. "Following Scientists Around." *Social Studies of Science* 18, no. 3 (August): 533–50.

Sheets-Johnstone, Maxine. 2016. *Insides and Outsides: Interdisciplinary Perspectives on Animate Nature*. Exeter, UK: Imprint Academic.

206 | Bibliography

Shepard, Paul. 1996. *Coming Home to the Pleistocene*. Washington, DC: Island.

Shuttleworth, Kyle. 2019. "Watsuji Tetsurō's Concept of 'Authenticity.'" *Comparative and Continental Philosophy 11, no. 3: 235–50.*

Simondon, Gilbert. 1995. *L'Individu et sa genèse physico-biologique*. Grenoble, France: Million.

———. 2005. *L'individuation à la lumière des notions de forme et d'information*. Paris: Million.

Sister MacGillis, Miriam. 2016."The Work of Genesis Farm: Interview with Sister Miriam MacGillis." In *Spiritual Ecology: The Cry of the Earth*, edited by Llewellyn Vaughan-Lee, 69–82. Point Reyes Station, CA: Golden Sufi Center.

Skafish, Peter. 2020. "Equivocations of the Body and Cosmic Arts: An Experiment in Polyrealism." *Angelaki* 25, no. 4: 135–53.

Skrbina, David, 2011. "Mind Space: Toward a Solution to the Combination Problem." In *The Mental as Fundamental: New Perspectives on Panpsychism*, edited by Michael Blamauer, 117–29. Heusenstamm, Germany: Ontos Verlag.

———. 2013. "Ethics, Eco-Philosophy, and Universal Sympathy." *Dialogue and Universalism* 23, no. 4: 59–74.

———. 2017. *Panpsychism in the West*. Cambridge, MA: MIT Press.

———, ed. 2009. *Mind That Abides: Panpsychism in the New Millennium*. Amsterdam: John Benjamins.

Souder, William. 2000. *A Plague of Frogs*. Westport, CT: Hyperion.

Sovacool, Benjamin, and Bjorn-Ola Linner. 2016. *The Political Economy of Climate Change Adaptation*. London: Palgrave Macmillan.

Spät, Patrick. 2009. "Panpsychism, the Big-Bang-Argument, and the Dignity of Life." In *Mind That Abides: Panpsychism in the New Millennium*, edited by David Skrbina, 159–76. Amsterdam: John Benjamins.

Stanescu, James. 2013. "Beyond Biopolitics: Animal Studies, Factory Farms, and the Advent of Deading Life." *PhaenEx* 8, no. 2 (Fall–Winter): 135–60.

Stanley, John, David R. Loy, and Gyurme Dorje, eds. 2009. *A Buddhist Response to the Climate Emergency*. Somerville, MA: Wisdom Publications.

Starhawk. 1989. *Truth or Dare: Encounters with Power, Authority, and Mystery*. New York: HarperCollins.

———. 1999. *Spiral Dance: A Rebirth of the Ancient Religion of the Great Goddess*. New York: HarperOne.

Stiegler, Bernard. 2013.*What Makes Life Worth Living: On Pharmacology*. Cambridge, MA: Polity.

Steffen, Will et al. 2011. "The Anthropocene: From Global Change to Planetary Stewardship." *Ambio* 40, no. 7: 739–61.

Steffen, Will, and Katherine Richardson, Johan Rockström, and Sarah Elisabeth Cornell. 2015. "Planetary Boundaries: Guiding Human Development on a Changing Planet." *Science* 347, no. 6223. DOI:10.1126/science.1259855

Steffen, Will, and Angelina Sanderson, Johan Peter Tyson, Jill Jäger, Pamela Matson, Berrien Moore, Frank Oldfield, Katherine Richardson, H. John Schellnhuber, B. L. Turner, and Robert J. Wasson. 2005. *Global Change and the Earth System: A Planet under Pressure.* Heidelberg: Springer. .

Stengers, Isabelle. 2002. "Beyond Conversation: The Risks of Peace." In *Process and Difference: Between Cosmological and Poststructuralist Postmodernisms,* edited by Catherine Keller and Anne Daniell, 235–55. Albany: State University of New York Press.

———. 2009. *Au temps des catastrophes.* Paris: La Découverte.

———. 2012. "Reclaiming Animism." *e-flux journal,* no. 36 (July).

———. 2013. *L'invention des sciences modernes.* Paris: Flammarion.

Stepanoff, Charles. 2019. *Voyager dans l'invisible: Techniques chamaniques de l'imagination.* Paris: La Découverte.

Strawson, Galen. 2009. "Realistic Monism: Why Physicalism Entails Panpsychism." In *Mind That Abides: Panpsychism in a New Millennium,* edited by David Skrbina, 33–65. Amsterdam: John Benjamins.

———. 2017. "Mind and Being: The Primacy of Panpsychism." In *Panpsychism,* edited by Godehard Brüntrup and Ludwig Jaskolla, 75–112. Oxford: Oxford University Press.

Strick, James. 2015. "Exobiology at NASA: Incubator for the Gaia and Serial Endosymbiosis Theories." In *Earth, Life, and System: Evolution and Ecology on a Gaian Planet,* edited by Bruce Clarke, 80–104. New York: Fordham University Press.

Stuart, Simon, Michael Hoffmann, Janice Chanson, Neil Cox, Richard Berridge, Pavithra Ramani, and Bruce Young, eds. 2002. *Threatened Amphibians of the World.* Exeter, Devon, UK: Lynx Edicions.

Stuckey, Priscilla. 2010. "Being Known by a Birch Tree: Animist Refigurings of Western Epistemology." *Journal for the Study of Religion, Nature and Culture* 4, no. 3: 182–205.

———. 2014. "The Animal versus the Social: Rethinking Individual and Community in Western Cosmology." In *The Handbook of Contemporary Animism,* edited by Graham Harvey, 191–208. London: Routledge.

Sueki, Fumihiko. 2004. *"Watsuji Tetsurô no genshi Bukkyô ron" Kindai Nihon to Bukkyô: Kindai Nihon no shisô/saikô II.* Tokyo: Transview.

Sundberg, Juanita. 2014. "Decolonizing Posthumanist Geographies." *Cultural Geographies* 21, no. 1 (January): 33–47.

Sundberg, Juanita, Jessica Dempsey, and Rosemary-Claire Collard. 2015. "The Moderns' Amnesia in Two Registers." *Environmental Humanities,* no. 7: 227–32.

Suzuki, David, and Peter Knudtson. 1993. *Wisdom of the Elders: Sacred Native Stories of Nature.* New York: Bantam Books.

208 | Bibliography

Swyngedouw, Eric. 2010. "Apocalypse Forever? Post-Political Populism and the Spectre of Climate Change." *Theory, Culture & Society* 27, no. 2–3 (May): 213–32.

———. 2013. "The Non-Political Politics of Climate Change." *ACME* 12, no. 1 (January): 1–8.

———. 2014. "Anthropocenic Promises: The End of Nature, Climate Change and the Process of Post-Politicization." Lecture presented at the CERI, Sciences Po, Paris, June 2, 2014.

Szerszynski, Bronislaw. 2017. "From the Anthropocene Epoch to a New Axial Age." In *Religion in the Anthropocene*, edited by Celia Deane-Drummond, Sigurd Bergmann, and Markus Vogt, 35–52. Eugene, OR: Cascade Books.

Szerszynski, Bronislaw, Matthew Kearnes, Phil Macnaghten, Richard Owen, and Jack Stilgoe. 2013. "Why Solar Radiation Management Geoengineering and Democracy Won't Mix." *Environment and Planning A*, no. 45: 2809–16.

Tafjord, Bjorn Ola. 2020. "Modes of Indigenizing: Remarks on Indigenous Religion as a Method." In *Indigenizing Movements in Europe*, edited by Graham Harvey, 139–63. Sheffield, UK: Equinox.

Tanaka, Koji. 2014. "In Search of the Semantics of Emptiness." In *Nothingness in Asian Philosophy*, edited by JeeLoo Liu and Douglas Berger, 55–63. New York: Routledge.

Taussig, M. 2009. *What Color Is the Sacred?* Chicago: University of Chicago Press.

Taylor, Bron. 2010. *Dark Green Religion: Nature Spirituality and the Planetary Future.* Berkeley: University of California Press.

Taylor, Marcus. 2015. *The Political Ecology of Climate Change Adaptation.* London: Routledge.

Tesson, Sylvain. 2011. *Dans les forêts de Sibérie.* Paris: Gallimard.

Thomas, Julia Adeney. 2014. "History and Biology in the Anthropocene: Problems of Scale, Problems of Value." *American Historical Review* 119, no. 5 (December): 1587–1607.

Thomas, Lewis. 1974. *The Lives of a Cell: Notes of a Biology Watcher.* New York: Viking.

Thompson, Evan. 2007. *Mind in Life: Biology, Phenomenology, and the Sciences of Mind.* Cambridge, MA: Harvard University Press.

Toadvine, Ted. 2009. *Merleau-Ponty's Philosophy of Nature.* Evanston, IL: Northwestern University Press.

Todorov, Tzvetan. 1984. *The Conquest of America.* New York: Cambridge University Press.

Tomasello, Michael. 2019. *Becoming Human: A Theory of Ontogeny.* Cambridge, MA: Harvard University Press.

Tomlinson, Gary. "Toward the Anthropocene: Deep-Historical Models of Continuity and Change." *South Atlantic Quarterly* (forthcoming).

Tsing, Anna. 2012. "Unruly Edges: Mushrooms as Companion Species." *Environmental Humanities* 1, no. 1 (November): 141–54.

Bibliography | 209

Tsing, Anna Lowenhaupt, Heather Anne Swanson, Elaine Gan, and Nils Bubandt. 2017. "Haunted Landscapes of the Anthropocene." In *Arts of Living on a Damaged Planet*, edited by Anna Lowenhaupt Tsing, Heather Anne Swanson, Elaine Gan, and Nils Bubandt, 1–14. Minneapolis: University of Minnesota Press.

Turner, Terry. 2009. "The Crisis of Late Structuralism. Perspectivism and Animism: Rethinking Culture, Nature, Spirit, and Bodiliness." *Tipití: Journal of the Society for the Anthropology of Lowland South America* 7, no. 1 (June): 3–42. Available at: http://digitalcommons.trinity.edu/tipiti/vol7/iss1/1.

Tyrrell, Toby. 2013. *On Gaia: A Critical Investigation of the Relationship between Life and Earth*. Princeton, NJ: Princeton University Press.

Valladolid, Julio, and Frédérique Apffel-Marglin. 2001. "Andean Cosmovision and the Nurturing of Biodiversity." In *Indigenous Traditions and Ecology*, edited by John A. Grim, 639–70. Cambridge, MA: Harvard University Press.

Van Dooren, Thom. 2014. *Flight Ways: Life and Loss at the Edge of Extinction*. New York: Columbia University Press.

———. 2019. *The Wake of Crows: Living and Dying in Shared Worlds*. New York: Columbia University Press.

Varela, Francisco. 1992. *The Tree of Knowledge: The Biological Roots of Human Understanding*. Berkeley, CA: Shambhala.

Vaughan-Lee, Llewellyn, ed. 2016, *Spiritual Ecology: The Cry of the Earth*. Point Reyes Station, CA: Golden Sufi Center.

Veldman, Robin Globus, Andrew Szasz, and Randolph Haluza-Delay. 2012. "Climate Change and Religion: A Review of Existing Research." *Journal for the Study of Religion, Nature and Culture* 6, no. 3 (September): 255–75.

———. 2014a. "Climate Change and Religion as Global Phenomena." In *How the World's Religions Are Responding to Climate Change: Social Scientific Investigations*, edited by Robin Globus Veldman, Andrew Szasz, and Randolph Haluza-DeLay, 297–315. New York: Routledge.

———, eds. 2014b. *How the World's Religions Are Responding to Climate Change: Social Scientific Investigations*. New York: Routledge.

Velmans, Max. 2014. "Sentient Matter." In *The Handbook of Contemporary Animism*, edited by Graham Harvey, 363–72. London: Routledge.

Verbeek, Peter Paul. 2009. "Ambient Intelligence and Persuasive Technology: The Blurring Boundaries between Human and Technology." *Nanoethics* 3, no. 3: 231–42.

———, ed. 2014. *The Moral Status of Technical Artefacts*. Dordrecht, Netherlands: Springer.

Vetlesen, Arne Johan. 2019. *Cosmologies of the Anthropocene: Panpsychism, Animism, and the Limits of Posthumanism*. London: Routledge.

Vitebsky, Piers. 2003. "From Cosmology to Environmentalism: Shamanism as Local Knowledge in a Global Setting." In *Shamanism: A Reader*, edited by Graham Harvey, 276–98. New York: Routledge.

210 | Bibliography

Viveiros de Castro, Eduardo. 1998. "Cosmological Deixis and Amerindian Perspectivism." *Journal of the Royal Anthropological Institute* 4, no. 3 (September): 469–88.

———. 2004a. "Exchanging Perspectives: The Transformation of Objects into Subjects in Amerindian Ontologies." *Common Knowledge* 10, no. 3 (Fall): 463–84.

———. 2004b. "Perspectival Anthropology and the Method of Controlled Equivocation." *Tipití: Journal of the Society for the Anthropology of Lowland South America* 2, no. 1: 3–22.

———. 2009. *Métaphysiques Cannibales*. Paris: PUF.

———. 2013. "Economic Development and Cosmopolitical Re-Involvement: From Necessity to Sufficiency." In *Contested Ecologies: Dialogues in the South on Nature and Knowledge*, edited by Lesley Green, 28–41. Cape Town: HSRC Press.

———. 2015. *The Relative Native: Essays on Indigenous Conceptual Worlds*. Chicago: Hau Books.

———. 2017. "Metaphysics as Mythophysics: Or, Why I Have Always Been an Anthropologist." In *Comparative Metaphysics: Ontology after Anthropology*, edited by Pierre Charbonnier, Gildas Salmon, and Peter Skafish, 249–73. London: Rowman & Littlefield.

———. 2019. Interview with author. Paris, January 6–8.

Wallace, Mark I. 2018. *When God Was a Bird: Christianity, Animism, and the Re-Enchantment of the World*. New York: Fordham University Press.

Wallis, Robert J. 2003. *Shamans/Neo-Shamans: Ecstasies, Alternative Archaeologies and Contemporary Pagans*. London: Routledge.

Wapner, Paul 2010. *Living through the End of Nature*. Cambridge, MA: MIT Press.

———. 2014. "The Changing Nature of Nature: Environmental Politics in the Anthropocene." *Global Environmental Politics* 14, no. 4 (November): 36–54.

Waters, Marcus Woolombi. 2018. *Indigenous Knowledge Production: Navigating Humanity within a Western World*. New York: Routledge.

Watson, Paul. 2005. "A Call for Biocentric Religion." In *Encyclopedia of Religion and Nature*, edited by Bron Taylor. London: Continuum.

Watsuji, Tetsuro, 1961. *A Climate: A Philosophical Study*. Japanese Ministry of Education.

———. 1996. *Watsuji Tetsuro's Rinrigaku: Ethics in Japan*. Albany: State University of New York Press.

"Watsuji, Tetsuro." 2019. *Stanford Encyclopedia of Philosophy*, November 27, https://plato.stanford.edu/entries/watsuji-tetsuro/.

Weber, Andreas. 2019. *Enlivenment: Toward a Poetics for the Anthropocene*. Cambridge: MIT Press.

Weber, Max. 2004. *The Protestant Ethic and the Spirit of Capitalism*. London: Penguin Modern Classics.

White, Ethan. 2015. *Wicca: History, Belief, and Community in Modern Pagan Witchcraft*. Eastbourne, East Sussex, UK: Sussex Academic Press.

White Jr., Lynn. 1967. "The Historical Roots of Our Ecologic Crisis." *Science* 155, no. 3767 (March 10): 1203–07.

Whitehead, Alfred North. 1911. *Introduction to Mathematics.* London: Williams & Norgate.

———. 1929. *The Function of Reason.* Princeton, NJ: Princeton University Press.

———. 1967. *Science and the Modern World.* New York: Free Press.

———. 1968. *Modes of Thought.* New York: Free Press.

———. 1978. *Process and Reality.* New York: Free Press.

Wildman, Wesley J. 2014. "Religious Naturalism: What It Can Be, and What It Need Not Be." *Philosophy, Theology, and the Sciences* 1, no. 1: 36–58.

Wilson, Catherine. 2006. "Commentary on Galen Strawson." *Journal of Consciousness Studies* 13, no. 10–11: 177–83.

Winch, Peter. 1964. "Understanding a Primitive Society." *American Philosophical Quarterly* 1, no. 4 (October): 307–24.

Wohlleben, Peter. 2016. *The Hidden Life of Trees: What They Feel, How They Communicate—Discoveries from a Secret World.* Vancouver: Greystone Books.

Wolfe, David. 2002. *Tales from the Underground: A Natural History of Subterranean Life.* New York: Basic Books.

Wood, Jr., Harold. 1985. "Modern Pantheism as an Approach to Environmental Ethics." *Environmental Ethics* 7, no. 2: 151–63, at 157, 160–61.

Wright, Kate. 2014. "Becoming-With: Living Lexicon for the Environmental Humanities." *Environmental Humanities*, no. 5: 277–81.

Yandell, Keith E. 1998. "Pantheism." In *Routledge Encyclopedia of Philosophy*, edited by Edward Craig. New York: Routledge.

Yusoff, Kathryn. 2015. "Anthropogenesis: Origins and Endings in the Anthropocene." *Theory, Culture & Society* 33, no. 2 (April): 3–28.

Zalasiewicz, Jan, Mark Williams, Will Steffen, and Paul Crutzen. 2010. "The New World of the Anthropocene." *Environmental Science and Technology Viewpoint* 44, no. 7: 2228–31.

Zerilli, Linda. 2016. *A Democratic Theory of Judgment.* Chicago: University of Chicago Press.

Zerzan, John. 2012. *Future Primitive Revisited.* Port Townsend, WA: Feral House.

Index

Abram, David, 12, 112, 128, 166
Abrams, Nancy Ellen, 12, 49, 50, 51
Abreel, Ahmad, 27
Adivasa; Adivasis, 30, 31, 35, 37
Agency, 10, 34, 47, 52, 91, 92, 93,
 99, 100, 105, 106, 126, 130, 131,
 133, 134, 135, 136, 148; human
 agency, 7, 48, 129
Aidagara, 64, 66, 68, 69, 72
Albert, Bruce, 8
Albert, Gerrald, 116
Alberts, Thomas Karl, 36, 37, 115,
 158, 171
Analogism, 3
Anātman, 62
Anders, Günther, 23
Animism, 46, 47, 74, 78, 99–103,
 106, 109, 117, 123, 148, 172, 177,
 179; neoanimism (new animism),
 79, 102; machinic animism, 110,
 112; indigenous animism, 13, 14,
 53, 105, 113; pagan animism, 41,
 79
Anthropocene Age, 1, 3, 12, 14,
 15, 23, 47, 52, 58, 63, 71, 72,
 105, 111, 121, 129, 134, 143;
 Anthropocene, 2, 4, 5, 7, 9, 11,
 17, 18, 19, 20, 23, 25, 29, 30, 31,
 39, 41, 55, 71, 73, 99, 102, 106,
 113, 116, 117, 119, 121, 123, 134,

144, 146, 153, 154, 170, 177, 180;
 Good Anthropocenes, 5, 8
Anthropocentrism, 8–10, 12, 41, 42,
 46, 52, 58, 60, 101, 122, 128,
 129, 132, 146, 164, 167, 171;
 anthropocentric, 8, 12, 44, 52, 58,
 115, 145, 158, 171
Anthropos, 1, 17
Apocalypse, 21, 23, 25, 28–30, 37;
 apocalyptic, 1, 4, 11, 12, 19, 21,
 23, 28, 29; apocalypticism, 11, 21,
 24
Apologetic approach, 12, 43, 46, 52
Arendt, Hannah, 31, 114, 137
Armstrong-Buck, Susan, 138
Assemblages, 111, 145, 178

Baek, Jin, 68
Barner-Barry, Carol, 81, 84, 85
Basile, Pierfrancesco, 139
Benjamin, Walter, 1, 2, 3, 6
Bennett, Jane, 14, 131, 132, 133, 135,
 136
Berger, John, 74
Berman, Morris, 51
Berque, Augustin, 66–68, 71, 176
Biosemiotics, 56, 58, 114, 123, 133,
 135
Bird Rose, Deborah, 106, 169, 177
Block, Maurice, 109

214 | Index

Bodley, John, 37, 103
Bohm, David, 35, 125, 128
Bonneuil, Christophe and Fressoz, Jean-Baptiste, 3, 21
Bracken, Joseph, 137
Breithaupt, Fritz, 109, 116
Buddhism, 9, 12, 42, 53, 55, 59, 60, 61, 62, 64, 65, 77, 173–175
Buddhist modernism, 64, 173
Buen vivir, 33

Cahoone, Lawrence, 126–127
Callicot, J. Baird and Ames, 56, 173; Callicot, J. Baird, 56
Capitalism, 5, 18, 24, 26, 37, 83, 112, 145
Capitalocene, 30, 171
Carduño, Julio, 36
Cartesian *cogito,* 55, 146, 150, 151, 153; Cartesian dualism, 13, 80, 105, 141, 151
Chabot, Pascal, 154, 155
Chakrabarty, Dipesh, 113
Charbonnier, Pierre, 22–23
Christ, Carol and Plaskow, Judith, 76
Christianity, 41, 42, 44, 46, 47, 49, 55, 75–78, 81, 86, 112, 172, 173; Christian, 41–47, 55, 58, 63, 75, 77–79, 90, 81–84, 88, 124, 157, 161, 172
Chthulucene, 30, 31, 171
Clarke, D. S., 35, 136, 178
Clayton, Philip, and Elizabeth Singleton, 51, 153
Climate Change, 35–37, 113, 123, 130, 141
Cobb, Jr., John B., 52
Coetzee, J. M., 113
Cohen Rosefield, Leonora, 124
Collapsology, 22
Consciousness, 34, 47, 60, 62, 69, 84, 90, 92, 95, 106, 110, 124–128,

138, 139, 148–150, 176, 178–180; Self-consciousness, 34, 60, 139; ecological consciousness, 52, 78; altered states of consciousness, 85, 86; animal consciousness, 149
"Controlled equivocations," 162, 163
Conty, Arianne, 80, 102
Colonialism, 4, 29, 162, 148; postcolonialism, 148
Cosmopolitics, 14, 30, 108, 114, 115, 117, 142, 143, 146, 156, 158, 163, 164, 166
Cowan, Douglas, and Bromley, David, 76, 77, 78, 84, 86
Crist, Eileen, 5, 6
Crosby, Donald, 88
Crutzen, Paul, 17, 18, 71, 177
Cultural appropriation, 57

Dalai Lama, 60
Dawkins, Richard, 92, 151, 152
Deacon, Terrence, 127, 139
De Quincy, Christian, 124
Della Bellacasa, Maria Puig, 34
De la Cadena, Marisol, 100, 114, 117, 162, 163; de la Cadena and Starn, Orin, 100–101
Deleuze, Gilles, 110, 137, 178
Descola, Philippe, 3, 4, 99, 108, 179
Doolittle, Ford, 92
Doomsday bunkers; bunkers, 11, 27, 28, 171
Dual aspect monism, 126, 128

"Earth beings," v, 117, 157
Ecology, 5, 12, 15, 17, 31, 35, 51, 53, 58, 59, 63, 78, 80, 82, 102, 111, 114, 157, 172; kinship ecology, 79, 107; social ecology, 144, 145; religious ecology, 85, 89; indigenous ecology, 52, 83; relational ecology, 8
Ecomodernism, 4–8, 169, 170

Index | 215

Ecosophy, 11, 15, 110, 112, 143, 144, 146, 167, 178

Ecosphere, 1, 2, 18, 33, 105, 129

Ecosystem; ecosystems, 2, 11, 12, 14, 18–21, 26, 29, 32, 34, 35, 37, 45, 59, 67, 73, 79, 90, 92–96, 101, 107–109, 111, 116, 124, 129–135, 140, 141, 145–148, 157, 167

Egalitarianism, 15, 146, 147, 150

Empathy, 14, 109, 116, 117, 145, 149

Emptiness, 59, 61–65, 69–71, 73, 74, 174–176

Environment, 12, 13, 18, 23, 27, 29, 31, 37, 44, 45, 50, 56, 57, 64, 67, 68, 71, 72, 76, 84, 89, 93, 95, 96, 106, 145, 150, 151, 153, 154, 157, 125, 129, 130, 132, 133, 135, 138, 139, 141, 142, 144, 145, 150, 151, 153, 154, 157, 163, 165, 170, 173, 175, 176, 178, 179; environmental orientalism, 101; non-human environments, 2, 104; environmentalism/environmentalists, 7, 52, 129, 130; environmental justice, 171; environmental footprint, 51; environmental ethics, 58, 63, 65; environmental collapse/disaster/crisis, 11, 19–22, 32, 36, 43, 46, 55

Escobar, Arturo, 8, 19, 32

Ethical consequences, 14, 15, 129, 147, 165

Ethology, 34, 76, 109, 148, 149

Evans Pritchard, E. E., 159, 160, 161

Evernden, Neil, 150, 151

Evolution; evolutionary, 18, 24, 46–49, 51, 52, 55, 56, 60, 72, 77, 89, 93, 105, 122, 127, 130, 132, 135, 140, 152–154, 158, 173; evolutionary history, 124, 126; biological evolution, 116, 125; unconscious evolution, 50

Farrar, Janet and Farrar, Stewart, 84

Feminism, 82, 83, 148

Fenner, Frank, 24

Ferré, Frederick, 137, 138

Foreman, Dave, 51

Foucault, Michel, 146

Fox, Mathew, 12, 46, 47

Fractiverse, 163

Franke, Anselme, 101, 178

Fudo, 13, 55, 58, 63, 65–68, 70–74, 123, 145, 154, 165, 175, 176

Fuller, Steve, 24

Gaia, 13, 36, 44, 52, 75, 87 90–94, 96, 97, 102, 153, 154; Gaian, 51, 91, 97; Gaians, 76, 77, 91; Gaianism, 80, 90, 121

Garfield, Jay, 60, 62, 63, 174

Gibson-Graham, J. K., and Ethan Miller, 153

God, 9, 12, 13, 25, 44–51, 57, 63, 75, 76, 81, 84, 85, 87–89, 95, 97, 122, 172; gods, 48, 81, 121, 172

Goddess, 13, 76, 77, 81, 82, 84–86, 90, 91

Graeber, David, 35, 160–162

Griffin, David Ray, 122, 123, 127, 128

Guattari, Félix, 14, 15, 105, 110–112, 137, 143–146, 167, 178, 180

Gutteres, Antonio, 21

Hall, Mathew, 34, 149

Hamilton, Clive, 4, 5, 6, 7, 8, 20

Haraway, Donna, 5, 12, 30, 31, 153, 171

Harrison, Paul, 97

Harvey, Graham, 76–80, 87, 99, 105, 107, 109, 110, 116

Haught, John F., 43, 44, 46, 89, 90

Hawken, Paul, 36

Heidegger, Martin, 64–66, 175

216 | Index

Henning, Brian G., 137, 138, 141
Højbjerg, Christian Kordt, 161
Holmes III, Rolston, 58
Holobionts, 146, 150, 152, 153
Horn, Eva and Bergthaller, Hannes, 29
Hornborg, Alf, 104–105, 179
Human exceptionalism, 10, 14, 41, 43, 44, 55, 56, 59, 75, 100, 105, 122, 129
Hume, Lynne, 82

Idealistic monism, 126
Immanence, 12, 13, 43, 47, 75, 77, 83–85, 87, 88, 106
Indigenous, 37, 51, 83, 91, 107, 116, 131, 158, 167, 172, 180; indigenous traditions, 52, 79, 85; indigennous animism/animists, 13, 14, 53, 79, 105, 108, 110, 113; indigenous ontologies, 148, 150, 157; indigenous people(s)/populations/ tribes, 2, 3, 11, 14, 29, 33, 36, 80, 100, 102–106, 111, 115, 134, 147, 148, 157, 163–165, 177, 179
Infinite growth, 2, 5
Ingold, Tim, 14, 133, 134, 136
Inherent existence, 12, 57, 58, 61, 62, 70, 71
Interdependence, 12, 46, 56, 58–61, 72, 80, 146, 154; interdependent, 27, 36, 45–47, 56, 59, 60, 63, 71, 73, 92, 94, 105, 111, 134, 138, 146, 148, 153, 167, 173
Intrinsic essence, 13, 59, 61, 62, 70–72, 92, 94, 108, 111, 144

Janz, Bruce B., 67
Johnson, David W., 64, 66, 67, 71–73, 175, 176
Jonas, Hans, 17

Kauffman, Stuart, 35, 47–49, 89

Kin, 30, 31, 33, 97, 131, 171; kinship, 12, 14, 78, 79, 84, 85, 103, 105, 107, 110, 132
Kohn, Eduardo, 14, 106, 116, 133–136, 138, 139, 147, 180
Kopenawa, Davi, 37

Lafleur, William, 64, 65, 67–70, 174–176
Larson, Gerald James, 57
Latour, Bruno, 6, 7, 13, 30, 56, 73, 80, 99, 100, 102, 104, 105, 115, 131, 133, 160, 180
Law, John, 147, 157, 162, 163
Lawton, John, 92
Lenton, Timothy and Dutreuil, Sébastien, 95
Linera, Garcia, 156, 159
Livinstone, Glenys, 91
Lordon, Frédéric, 112
Lovelock, James, 36, 44, 90–96, 153

Macfarlane, Robert, 27
Macy, Joanna, 31, 33, 61, 174
Magic, 81, 82, 85–87, 159, 160; magician, 112, 114
Malm, Andreas, 6, 19, 21, 22
Margulis, Lynn, 35, 90, 91–93, 125, 146, 152, 173
Mars, 11, 22, 25–27, 30, 90, 93, 95, 96, 170, 179
Martinez-Alier, Joan, 5
Mathews, Freya, 14, 129, 130–134, 136, 141
McSherry, Lisa, 86
Mental emergentism, 126
Merchant, Carolyn, 8
Merleau-Ponty, Maurice, 137
Metropolitan John of Pergamon, 43
Midgley, Mary, 35, 152
Mirror neurons, 109

Modernity, 4, 15, 25, 30, 56, 78, 80, 99, 101, 105, 111, 125, 156–158; modernities, 8, 103; moderns, 18, 25, 27, 29, 34, 36, 37, 41, 100, 101, 110, 147, 148, 150, 156, 157, 159, 161, 163, 164, 167; a-modern, 156, 157, 159; Western modernity, 3, 8, 18, 55, 60, 61, 67, 70, 85, 104, 114, 123, 144; ideology of modernity, 19, 88; dichotomies of modernity, 104, 106

Monbiot, Georges, 34, 170

Monism, 14, 126, 127, 128, 140

Moore, Jason, 24, 102

Moral Perfectionism, 147, 148

Morowitz, Harold, 61

Musk, Elon, 26

Naess, Arne, 143

Nagarjuna, 62, 63, 174

Nagel, Thomas, 121, 128, 139

Nature, 42–44, 48, 50, 51, 55, 58, 59, 61, 66, 69, 76, 81–85, 87–90, 92, 100, 115, 116, 121, 124, 126, 128–130, 133, 143, 146, 151, 167, 170–172, 174–176; nature and culture; nature/cultures; nature-cultures, 3, 10, 12, 14, 19, 30, 47, 52, 56, 67, 71, 73, 75, 79, 80, 99, 101, 105, 106, 108, 111, 112, 122, 123, 147, 153, 158, 177, 178; stewards of nature, 97, 55; cheap nature, 18, 102; politics of nature, 30, 56, 111, 180; reenchantment of nature, 72; animal nature, 78; relational nature, 15, 56, 73, 155, 166, 173; human nature, 13, 72, 108, 140, 144, 152

Naveh, Danny and Bird-David, Nurit, 106

Net of Indra, 60

New Age, 3, 7, 11, 77, 78, 82, 83, 91, 174

Nhat Hanh, Thich, 60–61

"One-world world," 147, 157, 158; one-world, 8, 146, 157–159, 161, 162, 167

Ontological boundary crossing, 14, 78, 105, 112, 113, 116, 117

Ontology, 8, 52, 66, 80, 105, 121, 143, 144, 146, 156, 165–167, 179; ontologies, 2–4, 8, 14, 52, 154, 165; interspecies ontology, 60; analogical ontology, 12; one-world ontology, 157–159; naturalist ontology, 3, 32, 148; Western ontology, 4, 71; modern ontology, 3, 71, 159; dualist ontology, 15, 162; animist ontology, 13, 78, 100, 110, 177; relational ontology, 3, 108, 153

Otto, Rudolf, 80, 97

Pachamama, 36, 97, 148, 150, 157, 158, 164, 166

Paganism, 77, 80, 81, 91; Pagan, 41, 77–79, 81, 84, 87, 89, 91, 92, 96; Neopagan, 52, 77–81; Neopaganism, 53, 75–80, 87

Palsson, Gisli, 101; Palsson, Gisli and Descola, Philippe, 108

Panpsychism, 11, 14, 42, 90, 121–124, 128–132, 139, 140, 142, 143, 146, 179

Pantheism, 42, 51, 75, 87, 88, 90, 93, 121

Patriarch Bartholomew, 43, 44

Patriarchy, 76, 78, 81–83, 159

Peirce, Charles Sanders, 14, 123, 128, 134, 135, 180

Personhood, 34, 79, 105, 106, 108, 115, 147, 148, 150, 157, 158, 166; legal personhood, 115, 157, 158; person, 14, 105, 106, 108, 109, 110, 113, 116, 117, 147, 148, 157, 165

218 | Index

Peterson, Anna, 12, 44
Phenomenology, 34, 64, 66, 74, 148,
  165, 166, 174
Philosophy, 52, 57, 61, 66, 80, 87,
  100, 108, 112, 121, 122, 125, 134,
  136, 144–146, 151, 152, 154,
  155, 167, 174, 178; Buddhist
  philosophy, 63, 175; Watsuji's
  philosophy, 64, 65, 69–71, 74, 75;
  Environmental philosophy; ecological
  philosophy; philosophy of life, 15,
  55, 65, 143; Western philosophy,
  35, 137, 149, 175; Modern
  philosophy, 150; anthropological
  philosophy, 164
Planet, 2–4, 11, 17–19, 21, 23,
  25–27, 30, 31, 36, 45, 49, 50, 51,
  64, 67, 91–96, 102, 113, 125, 126,
  130, 131, 134, 143, 144, 147
Plants, 34, 35, 82, 95, 107, 116, 128,
  134, 148–150, 158, 169, 170
Plumwood, Val, 101, 177
Pluriverse, 15, 159, 161–164
Pope Francis, 42–44, 75, 90
Povinelli, Elisabeth, 131, 170
Pratītya samutpāda, 56, 60–62, 70;
  codependent origination, 64, 69, 70
Primavesi, Ane, 12, 45, 46
Progress, 1, 2, 4–8, 18, 19, 25, 27,
  30, 34, 37, 63, 78, 100, 101, 103,
  156

Rao, Desiraju, 36
Rawls, John, 114
Relationality, 47, 56–58, 60, 61, 66,
  68, 69, 72, 80, 93, 94, 105, 108,
  109, 125, 140, 144, 146, 155, 156,
  167, 175, 178; relational, 35, 56,
  68, 73, 108, 125, 131, 149, 153,
  154, 155, 166, 173
Religion, 9, 10, 15, 17, 42, 43, 46,
  48, 49, 51, 52, 64, 77, 78, 80, 82,

83, 85, 89, 90, 97, 122, 145, 167,
  169; religions, 42–44, 46, 48–52,
  64, 77, 78, 80, 82, 83, 85, 89, 90,
  97, 122, 145, 167, 169
Religious naturalism, 13, 80, 87–90,
  97, 121; Naturalism, 3, 4, 13, 15,
  80, 87–90, 97, 102, 121, 146, 148,
  153, 163
Res cogitans, 51, 141, 150
Res extensa, 141, 150
Rosengren, Dan, 100, 103–104
Roundtree, Kathryn, 79, 83, 77
Rubenstein, Mary-Jane, 5, 37, 75, 88,
  89, 91, 93, 94
Rue, Loyal, 88, 90
Russell, Bertrand, 135, 136, 139, 142

Sabbat, 13, 85, 86
Sacramental Approach, 12, 43, 46, 52
Saint Francis, 42, 43, 55
Salmon, Enrique, 107
Santiesteban, Gustavo Soto, 33
Santos, Boaventura, 159
Science, 42, 43, 46, 47–51, 53, 55,
  56, 58, 59, 63, 72, 74, 76, 80,
  87–92, 96, 99, 101, 108, 109,
  110, 113–115, 122, 124, 125, 144,
  147–150, 152, 156, 157, 159, 160,
  162, 164, 169, 173, 178
Schizoanalysis, 145
Second axial age, 51, 53
Second coming, 25, 26
Selfish gene, 56, 92, 146, 151, 152, 178
Sentience, 14, 91, 110, 115, 121–123,
  127–129, 131–133, 137, 139–141,
  149, 150, 179
Serres, Michel, 142, 180
Sevilla, Anton, 5, 64, 65, 70, 174, 176
Shamanism, 77; Shaman, 37, 77, 107,
  110, 112, 114, 145, 172
Simondon, Gilbert, 146, 154–156,
  174; Ontogenesis, 146, 154–156;

Individuation, 15, 146, 154–156, 174

Singularity, 111, 144, 145

Skrbina, David, 121, 125–129, 179

Smith, Adam, 152

Solidarity, 2, 12, 14, 26, 30, 35, 92, 110, 111, 117, 144, 145

Spät, Patrick, 129

Stanescu, James, 117

Starhawk, 81–86

Stengers, Isabelle, 108, 131, 137, 163

Stewardship, 2, 42, 44, 46, 52, 55

Strick, James, 92

Substance dualism, 31, 123, 126

Sueki, Fumihiko, 64

Sundberg, Juanita, Dempsey, Jessica and Collard, Rosemary-Claire, 5; Sundberg, Juanita, 35, 170, 177

śūnyatā, 58, 61, 62, 65, 70, 71, 174

Sustainability; sustainable, 5, 11, 13, 35, 37, 44, 49, 51, 94, 123, 132, 166

Symbiosis, 68, 92, 173

Szerszynski, Bronislaw, 52, 53

Taussig, Michael, 29

Taylor, Bron, 51

Technology, 42, 80, 99, 102, 110, 179

Thomas, Lewis, 154

Thunberg, Greta, 21, 24, 31

Totemism, 3, 169

Transition discourses, 33

Transversal, 15, 106, 110–112, 144, 167

Truth claims, 11, 146, 147, 164, 165, 167

Tsing, Anna, 108

Tyrrell, Toby, 91, 96

Van Dooren, Thom, 34, 163

Velmans, Max, 128

Vetlesen, Arne Johan, 9–10

Viveiros de Castro, Eduardo, 29, 102, 104–108, 110, 115, 142, 145, 160, 162–166, 178, 180; Danowski, Deborah and Viveiros de Castro, Eduardo, 29, 104, 108, 110, 163; perspectivism, 105

Von Uexküll, Jacob, 123, 135, 148, 166

Waal, Franz de, 34, 139, 152

Wallace, Mark, 12, 46, 47, 75, 172

Wallace-Wells, David, 21

Watson, Paul, 52

Watsuji, Tetsuro, 13, 58, 63–74, 123, 145, 164, 173–177

Weber, Max, 26

Welzer, Harald, 20

Western culture, 35, 36, 52, 99

Wicca, 13, 80, 81, 83, 87; Wiccan, 81, 83, 87

White Jr., Lynn, 8, 12, 34, 41, 42, 47, 55, 81–83

Whitehead, Alfred North, 14, 122, 127, 128, 135–141, 146, 154, 180; primary configurations of matter, 138; Nexus, 137, 138, 141; Prehension, 137, 138

Wildman, Wesley, 122

Winch, Peter, 159, 160

Witchcraft, 81–83, 85, 86, 160, 161, 164; witches, 76, 81–83, 85–87, 160, 161

Wright, Kate, 100

Zerzan, John, 109